AF361332

AND IN OUR HEARTS TAKE UP THY REST

The Trinitarian Pneumatology
of Frederick Crowe, SJ

And in Our Hearts Take Up Thy Rest

The Trinitarian Pneumatology of Frederick Crowe, SJ

MICHAEL EADES OF THE ORATORY

UNIVERSITY OF TORONTO PRESS
Toronto Buffalo London

© University of Toronto Press 2019
Toronto Buffalo London
utorontopress.com

ISBN 978-1-4875-0559-2

Lonergan Studies

Library and Archives Canada Cataloguing in Publication

Title: And in our hearts take up thy rest: the trinitarian pneumatology
   of Frederick Crowe, SJ / Michael Eades of the Oratory.
Names: Eades, Michael, 1981– author.
Series: Lonergan studies.
Description: Series statement: Lonergan studies | Includes bibliographical
   references and index.
Identifiers: Canadiana 20190099607 | ISBN 9781487505592 (hardcover)
Subjects: LCSH: Crowe, Frederick E. | LCSH: Holy Spirit. | LCSH:
   Trinitarians. | LCSH: Catholic Church – Doctrines.
Classification: LCC BT121.3 E23 2019 | DDC 231/.3—dc23

This book has been published with the help of a grant from the Federation
for the Humanities and Social Sciences, through the Awards to Scholarly
Publications Program, using funds provided by the Social Sciences and
Humanities Research Council of Canada.

University of Toronto Press acknowledges the financial assistance to its
publishing program of the Canada Council for the Arts and the Ontario Arts
Council, an agency of the Government of Ontario.

To Margaret Crowe and Margie Eades

Come, Holy Ghost, Creator Blest
And in our hearts take up Thy rest.
"Veni Creator Spiritus," *Liturgia Horarum*

Himself perchance in His mysterious nature,
is the Eternal Love whereby the Father and the Son have dwelt
    in each other,
as ancient writers have believed;
and what He is in heaven, that He is abundantly on earth.
He lives in the Christian's heart, as the never-failing fount
    of charity,
which is the very sweetness of the living waters.
John Henry Newman, "The Indwelling Spirit"

We are not engaged in proposing a theory in speculative theology.
We are giving an account of someone else's theories.... We ask
what he said, why he said it, and what he meant in saying it.[1]
Bernard Lonergan

Contents

Part II (1969–1984): Reversing the Relation of the Two Divine Missions

Part III (1985–2000): The Holy Spirit as the First Person in the Trinity

Illustrations

Tables

Preface

In Lent of 1853, John Henry Newman began work on a biography of
Saint Philip Neri (1515–1595). In its fourth chapter he mentions Philip
Neri's interest in the Roman catacombs and explains how Philip
"sought His God in the ancient hiding places and sepulchres of His
people, and had found Him. Especially he had addressed himself to the
third Person of the Blessed Trinity, and He had vouchsafed to him con-
solations more than ordinary."[1] In mentioning the Holy Spirit, the third
person of the Trinity, Newman was alluding to the famous visitation
that came to Philip when he was twenty-nine years old, during a long
stay in the catacomb of St Sebastian, shortly before the liturgical feast of
Pentecost on 1 June 1544. While he was praying for the gifts of the Holy
Ghost, he saw a ball of fire descend; it entered his mouth and lodged
in his breast. Immediately Philip began to experience those remarkable
flutterings of heart and tremors of body that attended him throughout
his life.[2]

Seven years later Philip Neri was ordained a Catholic priest. Gradually a group of followers gathered around him, drawn by "the attraction
with which the Divine Power had gifted him."[3] In 1575 Philip founded
the Congregation of the Oratory. The first priests and brothers of the
Oratory lived together without formal vows and dedicated themselves
to praying, administering the sacraments, and preaching.

St Philip wanted his Oratorians, bound together by charity, to be
"sons of the Holy Spirit."[4] With his own developed devotion to the
Holy Spirit, Newman found a patron in this saint.[5] When he went to
Rome to study for the Roman Catholic priesthood, he spent time with
the Oratorians and decided that the Oratory was the most congenial
environment for the pursuit of his vocation. After a brief novitiate
Newman brought the Oratorian way of life to England, beginning with
a house near Birmingham in 1848.

During my studies for the priesthood at the Oratory of St Philip in Toronto the problem of reconciling the thought of John Henry Newman with the philosophy and theology of Thomas Aquinas became real to me. Several years after ordination, when my community sent me to work on a doctorate in theology through Regis College at the University of Toronto, I was introduced to the writings of Bernard Lonergan, SJ (1904–1984). Lonergan repeatedly answered my questions about the compatibility of Newman and Aquinas. I was hooked.

Through Lonergan studies I encountered the writings of Frederick Crowe (1915–2012). My first direct encounter with Crowe's pneumatology was one of frustration, however. Crowe seemed to me to be in danger of separating the mission of the Holy Spirit from the mission of the incarnate Son. The frustration slowly gave way to a recognition that Crowe was on to something. My recognition grew into an admiration and an interest in understanding this theologian who wrote so earnestly about our communion with the Holy Spirit.

While he daily sought the companionship of the Holy Spirit, Philip Neri was also Christocentric. In his letter to Oratorians on the five-hundredth anniversary of the birth of St Philip, Pope Francis quoted a maxim of the saint: "He who wishes for anything but Christ, does not know what he wishes; he who asks for anything but Christ, does not know what he is asking."[6] Philip's spirituality was both Christological and pneumatological. There was no conflict for St Philip in his devotion to the Son and the Holy Spirit.

Through his union with the incarnate Son and in the Holy Spirit, Philip turned to the first person of the Trinity.[7] He savoured the words of the Lord's Prayer. When people asked him for help in learning to pray, he would sometimes teach them to meditate on the words of the Our Father.[8] Philip encouraged them to reflect on what it meant to have God as their Father and to continue dwelling on the prayer word by word.

Like the spirituality of Philip Neri, that of Frederick Crowe was Trinitarian. Crowe coined the neologism *Trinification*[9] to express the way in which human salvation involved a relationship with all three persons of the Trinity. But, like St Philip and Newman, Crowe was also especially interested in the role of the Holy Spirit in the Christian life. In his Trinitarian pneumatology he sought to explain the identity and role of the Holy Spirit in relation to the other two divine persons. In his appropriation of Thomas Aquinas's teaching on complacency, Crowe especially offers insights into the role of the Holy Spirit in our lives.

The main title of this book, *And in Our Hearts Take Up Thy Rest*, is taken from the hymn *Come, Holy Ghost*, a translation of the ancient *Veni,*

Creator Spiritus. The hymn's second line mentions *rest*. And rest is the central feature of Frederick Crowe's understanding of complacent love. Prior to love's role as a principle of desire, love is a restful acceptance of *what is.* Crowe has persuaded me that restful, complacent love provides an analogy for the Holy Spirit's eternal identity. What the Spirit eternally is, he brings into our hearts.

Acknowledgments

This book would not exist without all those who helped me and prayed for me during its writing, especially a Benedictine oblate. This book would also not exist without my professors and friends at the Toronto School of Theology and the Lonergan Research Institute at Regis College. Thank you, in particular, for opening the Crowe Archive to me.

In revisiting Crowe's account of complacency, I have become more deeply aware of how much I owe to the education and guidance that I received in Washington, DC, during my time in the Theodore Basselin program. I would like especially to express gratitude to my Catholic University of America professors, to my friends from Theological College, and to the priests at the Dominican House of Studies. In Washington I was given the novel *Brother Petroc's Return*, discovered my vocation to the Oratory, and began to learn the meaning of T.S. Eliot's line "the inner freedom from the practical desire."[10]

I am deeply grateful for the support and guidance of Stephen Shapiro and for the two anonymous readers of my manuscript during the initial phases of the editorial process. They provided criticisms, suggestions, and questions of the highest calibre. During the later phases of editing it has been a delight to work with Christine Robertson, Angela Wingfield, and the staff at the University of Toronto Press.

To the Fathers and Brothers of the Toronto Oratory, *sine quibus non*, thank you for your encouragement, prayers, and patience. I owe special thanks to my Superior, the Very Reverend Father Jonathan Robinson, as well as to Father Derek Cross, Father Juvenal Merriell, Father Philip Cleevely, and Father Daniel Utrecht for urging me to work on this publication, offering advice, and reviewing various drafts. I want to thank Brother Jason Flammini for making recommendations about using the image of the Trinity on the cover.

I am grateful to Anne Marie Mahoney, Emiko Koyama, Reid Locklin, Michael Vertin, Gilles Mongeau, SJ, and Jeremy Wilkins for their suggestions on how to revise my manuscript. I thank Michael Czesnik for producing illustrations, Leo Vincent Serroul for providing electronic copies of key resources, and William Hart McNichols for giving permission to use his striking artwork on the cover of this book.[11]

Crowe always considered himself a student of Aquinas. I am full of gratitude to the participants in the 2018 Aquinas Studium at Villanova University for their friendships and for helping me to revisit the questions on the Trinity in Aquinas's *Summa Theologiae*.

Inspired by the example of Aquinas, I submit this book to the judgment of the Church. May this work of *research* and *interpretation* be at the service of others who, like myself, are grappling with the possible contribution of Lonergan and Crowe to Trinitarian theology. I have tried in this book to interpret the Trinitarian pneumatology of Frederick Crowe as he himself understood it. I hope this work honours his memory, and the memory of his mother, Margaret Crowe. I am profoundly grateful to Fr Crowe's relatives and friends. In August 2015, they generously shared stories, pictures, and genealogy records with me when I travelled to his hometown in New Brunswick.

Besides Fr Crowe's family, I am indebted to my own family, especially my parents, Keith and Margie Eades, my brothers, John and David, and my sister-in-law, Amy Ellis Eades. They have supported me in many ways both known and unknown to them. In dedicating *Lonergan and the Level of Time* to his five brothers and sisters, Crowe quoted the very end of François Mauriac's novel *The Frontenac Mystery*: "Never would the Frontenac mystery know corruption, for it was one beam of the Eternal Love refracted through the prism of a race ... now made forever one."[12] Like the mother in the novel, Crowe wanted his own family, "one beam of the Eternal Love," to be "made forever one."

13 May 2019
The Toronto Oratory

AND IN OUR HEARTS TAKE UP THY REST

The Trinitarian Pneumatology of Frederick Crowe, SJ

Introduction

In his recent book on Bernard Lonergan, Louis Roy, OP, summarizes Frederick Crowe's basic interpretation of Lonergan's philosophical and theological project.[1] Crowe, Roy notes, understands Lonergan's writings "as an intellectual tool destined to be adopted by thinkers who wish to know thoroughly how their own conscious activities are structured and who wish to apply their talents in a sustained undertaking of understanding and scientific production."[2] This reading of Crowe's interpretation of Lonergan is correct. But Crowe also wanted to do something for Lonergan's thought, something that Lonergan did not think had been done for Aquinas's thought.

At the end of his March 1968 paper, "Belief: Today's Issue," Lonergan compared the science of modernity with the science of thirteenth-century Western Europe, insisting:

> One has to be creative. Modernity lacks roots. Its values lack balance and depth. Much of its science is destructive of man. Catholics in the twentieth century are faced with a problem similar to that met by Aquinas in the thirteenth century. Then Greek and Arabic culture were pouring into Western Europe and, if it was not to destroy Christendom, it had to be known, assimilated, transformed. Today, modern culture, in many ways more stupendous than any that ever existed, is surging around us. It too has to be known, assimilated, transformed. That is the contemporary issue.
>
> The contemporary issue, then, is a tremendous challenge. Nor should one opt out on the speciously modest plea that one is not another Aquinas. There could have been no Aquinas without the preceding development of Scholasticism. There would have been no Aquinas if there had not been the students to whom he lectured and for whom he wrote.
>
> Finally, there would have been a far more successful Aquinas, if human beings were less given to superficial opinions backed by passion, *for in*

*that case the work of Aquinas would not have been so promptly buried under the
avalanche* of the Augustinian-Aristotelian conflict that marked the close of
the thirteenth century.[3]

Frederick Crowe wanted to make sure that Lonergan's effort to
assimilate and to transform modern scientific methods for the service
of Catholic theology and faith would not be buried under an avalanche
at the end of the twentieth century.

Crowe thought that Lonergan was a new Aquinas for the twentieth
century. Crowe, a student and friend of Lonergan, tried to ensure that
his reception would be more successful than that of Aquinas. So in 1971
he set himself the task of continuing Lonergan's intellectual apostolate
by collecting primary and secondary materials, including record-
ings, in the Lonergan Center.[4] Crowe would go on to help establish
nine other centres throughout the world for the study of Lonergan's
thought.

What this book tries to make clear, however, is that Crowe was more
than the keeper of the Lonergan flame; he was also creative. Crowe was
a theologian in his own right. In particular, he explored and extended
Lonergan's pneumatology. Crowe advances three positions about the
Holy Spirit that build on Lonergan's work but go beyond Lonergan's
formulated theology of the Holy Spirit.

Frederick Crowe is not of the same stature as his teacher, Bernard
Lonergan, in terms of his philosophical and theological accomplishments. Hundreds of books have been written about Lonergan's thought,
and hundreds more could be written. But Frederick Crowe is unique in
his dedication to the thought of Bernard Lonergan. Until now, no book
has ever been written about Frederick Crowe.[5]

Methodology

This book argues that Crowe's pneumatology went through three
significant stages with two major transition points. In the first stage
(1953–1968) Crowe drew heavily on Thomas Aquinas and St Basil
to develop his own ideas about the Holy Spirit proceeding eternally
as complacent and concerned Love. In the second stage (1969–1984)
he argues that the Holy Spirit is the first divine person sent to us. In
the third stage (1985–2000) Crowe proposes two orderings of the divine
persons in the inner Trinitarian life and asks whether the Holy Spirit
can be thought of as the first person in the immanent Trinity.

In analysing these three stages, I use Crowe's own methodology
in his 1978 book, *Theology of the Christian Word: A Study in History.*[6]

Crowe's analysis of the history of Christian reflection on the word of God distinguishes seven stages based on the emergence of seven new and significant questions. *And in Our Hearts Take Up Thy Rest* applies Crowe's methodology to his own pneumatology.

In his analysis of the historical development of the theology of the word, Crowe argues that each stage comprises a movement from latent to explicit questions. Each new significant question and its answer have earlier "anticipations."[7] Gradually, from those pre-thematic reflections a question arises "as a separate concern."[8] Finally, the question itself is made thematic or brought into "the spotlight."[9] Like his analysis, this study of Crowe's development begins each stage with anticipations of his eventual focus of attention; it then looks at how that focus of attention emerged, and finally it studies the way in which Crowe concentrates on a particular, significant question. This historical methodology requires a certain amount of repetition as certain key texts from Lonergan and Crowe are analysed from different perspectives.

Overview

After an introduction to Crowe's life and Bernard Lonergan's influence upon it (chapter 1), the book divides into three parts. Part 1 (chapters 2 and 3) covers the first stage of Crowe's pneumatology (1953–68). Part 2 (chapters 4 and 5) corresponds to the second stage of Crowe's pneumatology (1969–84). Part 3 (chapters 6 and 7) examines the third stage of Crowe's theology of the Holy Spirit (1985–2000).

In the first stage the principal question driving Crowe's reflections was about the *proprium* or unique characteristic of the Holy Spirit. Crowe began stage one with a concern for the eternal personal property of the Spirit, but, under the influence of St Basil, he started to think more about the proper role of the Holy Spirit in the economy of salvation. Crowe's basic answer was that the Holy Spirit eternally and in time has the characteristic of proceeding complacent and concerned Love.

Crowe's second stage is marked by the subsequent question of the *relation* of the Spirit's mission to the Son's mission. In the first stage Crowe had consistently argued that the Spirit's mission was always to be understood in the context of the Son's mission.[10] But at the end of the second stage he argues that the Son's mission can also be understood within the context of the Spirit's. Crowe speaks of two steps in God's one plan of salvation: first, God gives his love in the sending of the Spirit; and, second, he discloses the fullness of his love in the mission of the Son.

How did Crowe arrive at this reversal of his normal way of relating the divine missions? First, he was trying to explain what Lonergan had taught concerning the relation of the divine missions. Second, Crowe was motivated by concerns about the state of the Catholic Church. His recognition of major shifts in Lonergan's thought and of a profound transition in the Catholic Church both occurred in 1969.

Crowe had been closely following Lonergan's thought throughout the 1960s. By the time of the 1970 International Lonergan Congress, however, he had begun to express his view that Lonergan had undergone a profound shift: "There is no doubt that Lonergan's thinking has undergone a profound reorientation in the last five years."[11] "What has happened," Crowe adds, "between 1964 and 1969, I would judge, is that a new understanding of values and their role has been added. This does not eliminate the role of truth; rather, it supplies it with a better dynamism, especially in the religious sphere."[12] In 1969, for example, Lonergan wrote, "[M]an exists authentically in the measure that he succeeds in self-transcendence, and I have found that self-transcendence has both its fulfilment and its enduring ground in holiness, in God's gift of his love to us."[13] In *Insight: A Study of Human Understanding*, the detached and disinterested desire to know, as that desire unfolds in questions, was the dynamic ground for self-transcendence. By the late 1960s Crowe thought that Lonergan had articulated another ground of cognitional development, the gift of religious love. It is precisely that gift of religious love that Crowe utilizes in his argument for the priority of the mission of the Holy Spirit.

In 1969 Crowe was dramatically affected by widespread dissent among Roman Catholics over Pope Paul VI's *Humanae vitae*. Writing in the summer of 1969, Crowe said, "To my mind we are in a new situation; we are not the Church we were a year ago; there is a new spirit at work."[14] The second stage of his pneumatology is the story of Crowe adapting himself to these perceived changes in both Lonergan's thought and the life of the Church. With Lonergan's death on 26 November 1984, this second stage of Crowe's development can be seen to come to a close. On that same day Crowe delivered the paper in which he most clearly set forward his thesis on the reversal of the missions.

Without his interaction with the method of the later Lonergan, Crowe would never have formulated his thesis on the missions in the way he did. Without the context of the crisis in authority within the Church, he would never have applied Lonergan's ideas on the mission of the Holy Spirit to the problems of his day. Part 2 follows this development in Crowe's understanding of the missions, while showing that Crowe never separated the mission of the Spirit from the mission of the Son.

In the third stage of his pneumatology Frederick Crowe asks a new question: Is the traditional ordering of the divine persons – Father, Son, Holy Spirit – the exclusive ordering of the Trinity? Or does the traditional "in the name of the Father and of the Son and of the Holy Spirit" also "admit, side by side with it, the formula 'In the name of the Spirit, and of the Son, and of the Father'?"[15] "This is really the fundamental question," Crowe says. "That is my question," he adds.[16]

The third part of this book attempts to shed light on what was behind Crowe's new question as set out in his 1995 essay "Rethinking the Trinity: Taking Seriously the *Homoousios*." Was Crowe rejecting Aquinas's and Lonergan's theology? Was he seriously thinking of another ordering of the divine persons that would begin with the Holy Spirit? Was there a deeper pedagogical reason for asking and answering his question in the way he did?

In his *Summa Theologiae* Thomas Aquinas says that among the three divine persons "there must be an order according to origin but without priority."[17] Commenting on this passage, Lonergan wrote: "But the order of the Son from the Father is by way of generation, the order of the Spirit from Father and Son is by way of spiration, and these two orders are ordered because the love that is spirated on the basis of holiness is from the Word that is generated on the basis of truth."[18] Since the generation of the Son and the spiration of the Spirit are eternal, Lonergan adds, "this order is not based on temporal succession."[19] He then distinguishes an order of cause and effect from a non-causal ordering. Since the order in God is not based on cause and effect, there is no priority among the persons. "Rather," Lonergan adds, "the order within God is based on origin and on the divine intellectual nature."[20] He is not saying that we believe that the Son is from the Father because we believe in God having an intellectual nature; we first believe that the Son is from the Father, and the Holy Spirit is from both, but then seek to understand how this is so. The psychological analogy, a comparative illustration of the Trinity based on ordered operations within the human soul (psyche), helps the theologian, according to Crowe, "to think out"[21] the order among the persons that faith accepts.

Crowe introduces his 1995 essay by asking his readers to perform an experiment. Are they willing to make the sign of the Cross while saying the words "In the name of the Spirit, and of the Son, and of the Father"?[22] Crowe suggests that, if we take seriously the perfect equality of the persons, then we should have no trouble saying this prayer while we make the sign of the Cross. But he is not simply asking us to name the Three in reverse order. He is asking us whether we can think of the "Three in such a way that just as the Father is first in the usual order, so the Spirit is first in the new formula."[23] Crowe is asking whether we will experiment with thinking of the order – Spirit, Son, Father – "as an order that reflects the Trinitarian relations themselves."[24] He admits that there is "a certain novelty"[25] in this approach, and he recounts hesitancy and resistance both within himself and among the limited number of people whom he asked to make the experiment. Thus he insists that this new line of thought "does not deny the traditional belief, nor is it a substitute for the traditional belief."[26]

Unlike the questions that distinguished the first and second stages of Crowe's development, the question of his third stage – whether the Holy Spirit could be first in the Trinitarian order – was not asked by Lonergan. In the third stage Crowe launches out into the deep. At the same time, however, he tries to give a Lonergan-inspired answer to the question. He uses categories derived from Lonergan to answer his question about a complementary ordering of the divine persons (Holy Spirit, Son, Father).

In the 1980s and 1990s Crowe wrote a series of six essays in which he tried to rethink certain answers to traditional theological questions in light of categories drawn from Lonergan's philosophy and theology. Two of these rethinking essays directly addressed questions about the mission and eternal identity of the Holy Spirit. In Crowe's 1989 essay, "Rethinking God-with-Us,"[27] the emergence of this new question on the Trinitarian order can be detected. In 1995, that question becomes thematized. Part 3 of this book tries to explain the pedagogical reasons behind Crowe's rethinking of the eternal ordering of the divine persons.

The conclusion of this book, chapter 8, argues for the unity of Crowe's development as a whole, provides an evaluation of each of the three stages, and suggests the lasting value of Crowe's trajectory, namely his confidence in using analogies (comparative illustrations) for under-standing the Trinity based on the activity of the human soul.

Crowe's Confidence in the Psychological Analogy

Where did Crowe acquire his confidence in the psychological analogy? Like Lonergan, he valued what the document *Dei Filius* of the First Vatican Council taught about the nature of theological understanding: "Reason illumined by faith, when it inquires diligently, reverently, and judiciously, with God's help attains some understanding of the mys-teries, and that a highly fruitful one, both from the analogy of what it naturally knows and from the interconnection of the mysteries with one another and with our last end."[28] The council distinguishes two ways to attain a fruitful, but imperfect, understanding of the mysteries of the Christian faith: analogy from something naturally known, and the interconnection of the mysteries.

Along these lines Anne Hunt distinguishes the Thomistic approach of Trinitarian theology, as found in the *Summa Theologiae*, and the approach of theologians like Hans Urs von Balthasar who try to understand the Trinity by means of the paschal mystery, namely the death, resurrection, and ascension of Christ. Hunt does not object *as such* to the Thomistic use of an analogy of human knowing and human loving to understand the eternal processions. "It is actually," Hunt writes, "the hegemony of the psychological image in the tradition that is being challenged in this approach, not its legitimacy and value."[29] In other words, there are two legitimate and valuable ways of gaining theological understanding of the Trinity. Basing itself on our knowledge of our interior acts of knowing and loving, the psychological analogy can be seen as one of the analogies for the Trinity that are derived from things known naturally. The paschal mystery, by contrast, sheds light on the Trinity as an example of the interconnection of the mysteries of faith. The two approaches can complement one another.

In a culture that does not think in terms of classical metaphysics the Trinity, looked at through paschal eyes, offers "a more experiential and existentially meaningful explication."[30] "The paschal method and approach," Hunt writes, "is justified to the degree which it prompts the conversion which the founding narrative prompted."[31] Far from rejecting classical metaphysics and theology, the paschal approach "renders traditional Trinitarian theology in more dynamic and relational terms."[32] If this approach does not repudiate Thomas's theology, what is left of value in such a Trinitarian theology? St Thomas's use of the psychological analogy provides answers and order to many of our questions about the Trinity.

What distinguishes the processions, the "interior coming forths,"[33] of the Son and the Spirit? Why is the Holy Spirit's procession not a generation? How can there be relations in God? We accept by faith that the Father is God, the Son is God, and the Holy Spirit is God. We confess that there are not three Gods, but one God. We believe that the Father, Son, and Holy Spirit are distinct persons. But "to *disclose* the faith to our minds," Gilles Emery writes, "it is precisely such an analogy that Thomas is looking for, so that we can grasp something of the content of the profession of faith, by putting it in the light of the knowledge of something whose object is proportioned to what we can know through our own human experience."[34] Aquinas uses something more known to us, our own acts of knowing and loving, to help us imperfectly, analogically, but fruitfully understand the Trinitarian mystery and to order our ideas about the Trinity.

In my experience of preparing adults for the sacraments of Christian initiation, using something we know by our own human experience continues to be of value in dispelling objections regarding the absurdness of the Christian faith in the Trinity. With such enquiring people we do not need to deploy the entirety of Thomas's Trinitarian theology, but the basic analogy of a proceeding word and a proceeding love remain fruitful in answering certain basic questions and giving some modest initial understanding of the Church's faith in the Trinity. There are other questions about the Trinity. And this is where one also finds the paschal mystery approach of great value in leading people deeper into the mystery and helping them grasp the relevance of the Trinity for their own conversion.

While Hunt acknowledges a qualified legitimacy and value to the psychological analogy, others, like David Coffey, strongly disagree. "The Thomist-Lonerganian system," Coffey writes, "to the extent that it rests on Augustine's psychological analogy, must be said to be a rather shaky edifice."[35] In other words, "lacking proper grounding in the Bible," the Thomistic approach of using a psychological analogy "should probably be characterized as philosophico-religious speculation rather than theology strictly so-called."[36]

Despite Coffey's objection, Crowe thought that the psychological analogy had a firmer grounding in the Scriptures than is often suspected. Following the long and profound final section in Lonergan's *De Deo Trino: Pars dogmatica*,[37] Crowe argues that there is a New Testament "basis for the procession of the eternal Word and eternal Love" based on "the psychological aspects of John's Son and Spirit."[38] Crowe does not argue that "the mode of the eternal processions was a question for John, not even vaguely,"[39] but he does argue that when the question arose of an analogy for the Son's procession based on the human mind, "it was largely on the basis of John's doctrine of the Logos that speculation proceeded."[40] Lonergan and Crowe are not justifying the psychological analogy simply by an appeal to how we are made "in the image of God" (Genesis 1:27);[41] they are looking for continuity between the Scriptures and later Trinitarian theology by appealing to the implicit presence of psychological elements in the texts of Scripture. The premises for the psychological analogy, Lonergan concludes, "are not found explicitly in the text, but are actively present in the mind of the author and expressed by him, not analytically or technically, but in both an ordinary and a symbolic way."[42]

Crowe also thought that there was solid evidence in many patristic writers before Augustine for speculating about the Son's eternal procession, by comparisons with the human mind. Crowe traces, for example, how Justin, Athenagoras, Theophilus of Antioch, Tertullian, Hippolytus, Origen, Dionysius of Alexandria, Athanasius, and Basil attempted "to explain the divine generation of the Son on the analogy of the human utterance of a word."[43] Nevertheless, it is in Augustine that Crowe most clearly finds analogies for the procession of the Son. According to Crowe, one of Augustine's problems in his *Trinity* was

> to find in the created universe some analogy that will endow this name, Word, with meaning for our human minds. His solution: we should go to the inner word of thought, the existence of which is not doubted, "for, although the words are not sounded, he who thinks utters (them) in his heart" (ch. 10, n. 17). But we are not to stop with the auditory image: "Whoever is able to get hold of a word ... not only before it is sounded, but even before the images of its sounds are revolved in fantasy (*cogitatione*) ... can see ... in this dim reflection some likeness of that Word of whom it is said: *In principio erat Verbum*" [in the beginning was the Word] (ch. 10, n. 19).[44]

While Augustine's speculations about the inner word had precursors in other patristic writers, Crowe thinks that Augustine's analogy for the Holy Spirit's procession was much more original.

Crowe mentions several patristic statements about the impenetrable nature of the Holy Spirit's procession. He quotes several passages from *The Trinity* that show Augustine almost despairing of finding an analogy to understand how the procession of the Spirit differs from the generation of the Son.[45] Referring to *The Trinity*, book 15, Crowe notes: "Yet it is Augustine who, in the very act of uttering these despairing cries, gives us the only analogy for the Holy Spirit that has made much headway in theology, namely, the analogy of proceeding love."[46] But Augustine did not give isolated analogies for the procession of the Son and the procession of the Spirit. He kept looking for interrelated triads within the human soul that corresponded to the unity and distinction of the Father, Son, and Holy Spirit.

In appropriating Augustine's analogy via Aquinas and Lonergan, Crowe was convinced that "what the human mind demands in the long run is an integral view."[47] By integral view Crowe means that we need more than an image to help us explain this or that aspect of the Trinity; we need some kind of holistic analogy. "Hence," he says, "the effort among theologians, reaching as far back as Tertullian, to think of the 'whole' Trinity in the light of one governing image or idea, and grasp it *per modum unius* [through the mode of one]."[48] Crowe then lists several of these attempts at making a picture of a whole Trinity. There are Tertullian's three different pictures of the Father, Son, and Holy Spirit: his *root, shoot, and fruit* image, his *spring, river, irrigation canal* image, and his *sun, ray, illumination* image. These examples provide a picture of two processions combined with a unity of three things. Crowe then adds other historical examples: "In the course of time catechetics has added many other such 'analogies': Basil's rainbow, Patrick's shamrock, Fr Heeg's three matches burning with a single flame, and that hardy perennial: the father, the mother, and their common child."[49] When looking for the best analogy for the Trinity, Crowe thinks seven questions have to be asked:

1. Does the analogy suffer from implications that are too material?
2. Does the analogy offer some reason for divine processions?
3. Does the analogy help us to understand why there are two and only two processions?
4. Does the analogy explain the difference between the first procession and the second?
5. Does the analogy show why the term of the procession is God and a distinct person?
6. Does the analogy explain why the processions do not destroy the unity of God?
7. Can the analogy, as a first requirement, be exposed coherently and intelligently?[50]

One value of the psychological analogy is the way in which it answers these questions. The psychological analogy provides a comparative illustration of how the Father, Son, and Holy Spirit are distinct from one another and yet so intelligibly related that the oneness of God is not violated. Crowe became convinced that Lonergan's version of the psychological analogy with its dynamic notion of rationality (discussed in chapter 1) answered these questions better than any other.[51]

Crowe's Writings

Beginning in 1953 Crowe taught at Regis College in Toronto for twenty-seven years with a special focus on Trinitarian theology. In 1980, at the age of sixty-five, he stopped teaching to make room for younger Jesuit professors. He then worked full-time at the Lonergan Center. In 1988, together with Robert Doran, SJ, Crowe began editing a projected twenty-five volume *Collected Works of Bernard Lonergan*.[52] Crowe's own list of publications includes nearly two hundred entries.[53]

Frederick Crowe's books consist mainly of four volumes of his collected essays, edited by Michael Vertin. In 1989, *Appropriating the Lonergan Idea* was published by the Catholic University of America Press.[54] It includes twenty-two essays as well as Crowe's homily for the funeral of Bernard Lonergan. In 2000, *Three Thomist Studies* appeared.[55] This volume contains Crowe's three long articles on Aquinas that were written between 1955 and 1961, as well as his most well-known article, "Complacency and Concern in the Thought of St Thomas."[56] In 2004 Michael Vertin brought out *Developing the Lonergan Legacy: Historical, Theoretical, and Existential Themes.*[57] This third volume contains twenty of Crowe's papers "that, like those of the first volume, explore and develop and employ various facets of Lonergan's work."[58] Finally, in 2010, a fourth volume of Crowe's writings was published: *Lonergan and the Level of Our Time.* This most recent volume "comprises twenty-eight papers that collectively span the period from 1961 to 2004."[59] Among these twenty-eight papers are five previously unpublished writings. "As in the first and third volumes," the editor notes, "the papers are divided into two groups, with the sequence in each group being roughly chronological."[60]

Besides these edited collections, Crowe published six books of his own. In 1968 a collection of his articles from the *Canadian Messenger of the Sacred Heart*[61] dealing with changes in the Catholic Church after the Second Vatican Council (1962–5) were reprinted together with some new material and published as *A Time of Change: Guidelines for the Perplexed Catholic.* In 1978 Crowe wrote *Theology of the Christian Word: A Study in History*, in an attempt to carry out one part of Lonergan's methodology. Two years later, in 1980, his third book appeared: *The Lonergan Enterprise.*[62] In 1985 he published, *Old Things and New: A Strategy for Education.*[63] In 1992, for the Outstanding Christian Thinkers Series, Crowe brought out his book *Lonergan.*[64] Finally, in 2005, when he was almost ninety, his book on the development of Lonergan's Christology was completed and published; *Christ and History: Bernard Lonergan's Christology (1932–1982)*[65] has recently been reprinted in conjunction with the publication of Lonergan's *The Incarnate Word*, volume 8 of *Collected Works of Bernard Lonergan.*

Last, but not least, are the course notes that Crowe published for his students at Regis College. These mimeographed notes can be found in the Lonergan Research Institute. Special mention must be made of his 1965–6 course notes, *The Doctrine of the Most Holy Trinity.* These notes, 280 pages in length, were reissued in a more permanent form in 1970 and will be discussed at great length in chapter 3. Over the years at least fifty people wrote to Crowe asking for copies of these notes. At various points efforts were made to find a major publisher for the work, but the book never appeared.[66]

Conclusion

Even if one wants to disagree with Crowe at various points, it is important to determine the questions that Crowe is really asking. It may be true that in the end his questions are more important than his answers, but Crowe's questions reach to the heart of the Trinitarian mystery. His pneumatology can be rightly called a "Trinitarian pneumatology."[67] Crowe always studied the Holy Spirit's eternal and temporal identity in relation to the Father and the Son.

As we will see in chapter 3, Frederick Crowe had a great love for St Basil of Caesarea. Matthew Levering has said that in terms of pneumatology "Basil's central goal is to combat the subordinationist views of the Spirit."[68] In a similar way we can say that Crowe's central goal in his Trinitarian pneumatology is to combat Sabellianism. In 1965 Crowe asked, "Would your theology be any different if Sabellius were right?"[69] "You may think my effort to discern the 'character' of each person in the world excessively formal," Crowe then added for his students, "but you have to ask of your own theology whether it would need revision if one and the same person had actually showed himself to the world as Father, Son, and Holy Spirit."[70]

Crowe's career of teaching Trinitarian theology spanned the years before and after the Second Vatican Council. Shaped by the Catholic Church's struggles after the council, Crowe's pneumatological development provides a glimpse into Catholic Trinitarian theology in the second half of the twentieth century. His writings on the Holy Spirit, moreover, still speak to us. In the words of Cardinal Newman, "*Cor ad cor loquitur*" (heart speaks to heart).[71]

1 Frederick Crowe, SJ

Dean of First Generation Lonergan Disciples

I remember well the years 1947–50 when he was our teacher and I would pester
him with questions.

Frederick Crowe on his teacher Bernard Lonergan in 2006,
Developing the Lonergan Legacy

In his book *Lonergan*, Crowe said that "it would be a mistake to start
our exposition of Lonergan's thought where his academic career
starts."[1] Instead, he began with Lonergan's family life in Buckingham,
Quebec, and "the dynamic mental and psychic background" in which
Lonergan grew up and from which his work emerged.[2] This chapter,
my introduction to Crowe, follows a similar path. It begins with the
"remote context"[3] of Crowe's Trinitarian pneumatology: the thirty
years before Crowe first took a theology class with Lonergan. The
second section of the chapter provides a basic background to Lonergan
and Crowe's interactions. The third section introduces the three main
texts in Lonergan's corpus that shaped Crowe's pneumatology: *Verbum*
(1946–9), *Insight* (1957), and *Method in Theology* (1972).

Early Years: New Brunswick and Jesuit Vocation

Frederick Ernest Crowe was the third of the six children of Jeremiah and
Margaret Crowe. Born on 15 July 1915, he was baptized in St Francis
Xavier Catholic Church in Sussex, New Brunswick, on 1 August. Crowe,
however, grew up fourteen kilometres outside Sussex in a tiny place
called Jeffries Corner. His parents ran a grocery store in a building attached to their home. According to Patricia Byrne, a first cousin of Crowe,
"the Crowes were always frugal."[4] Nevertheless, her aunt Margaret,
Frederick Crowe's mother, "always had candy for us. She made the best
crispy ginger snaps. She would give us chocolate bars at her store."[5]

In short, Crowe grew up within a rural Canadian Catholic family in the mid-1920s. "Imagine then an old-fashioned home," he writes:

> An ordinary number of ordinary children; ordinary parents for whom divorce is about as unreal as a trip to the moon; siblings who quarrel and fight as most siblings do, but are basically obedient and well enough behaved; a frugal home, where there is no cold or hunger, but no luxuries either; a home where the children are trained to help, each with chores to do; a home where there are games, especially in the long winter nights; where there is reading, if not much stimulating conversation; a religious home, where there are scenes of the Last Supper and the Crucifixion, where family prayers are said, the Rosary even, if you would be really old-fashioned.[6]

Like that of most ordinary Catholic families, Crowe's home life was not without its sorrows.[7] Nevertheless, we know that his childhood was filled with joys.[8] Many of these were based on his love of reading.

Across the street from the original Jeremiah Crowe property still stands the one-room schoolhouse where Frederick Crowe received his earliest formal schooling (the dilapidated building is now used as a storage shed). The basic curriculum was provided by a set of books called *New Brunswick Readers*.[9] His mother had been a teacher before marrying and instilled in him this love of reading. His principal teacher in those early years, however, was Irene Haugen.[10] In 2005 Crowe dedicated his book *Christ and History* to her with these words: "I dedicate this work to my cousin, Mrs. M. Irene Haugen. Seventy-eight years ago she prepared me for High School Entrance Examinations and taught me to prize scholastic excellence. For many years she has most generously supported my ventures in theological publications. Now she is an inspiration for a host of friends and relatives as she looks forward, alert and serene, to August 17, 2005, and the completion of her first hundred years. I join with them to wish her well as she starts year one hundred and one."[11] With the help of Haugen, twelve-year old Frederick enrolled in Sussex County High School in the fall of 1927, having completed the equivalent of two years of school work during each year of elementary school.

Three years later, just shy of his fifteenth birthday, Crowe graduated at the top of his high school class and won a Beaverbrook Scholarship to the University of New Brunswick. In 1934 he earned a bachelor of science degree in engineering. With the Great Depression being at one of its worst points, "there was not a single electrical engineering job in the whole of the Maritimes," his cousin Frank Cogger recalls.[12] As a result, Crowe took a job at his uncle and aunt's grocery store, Purtill's, in Norton, New Brunswick. During that time of working at the grocery store "he found himself again hearing a call that he had originally experienced in his early teens, a call to the religious life."[13]

On 6 September 1936 Frederick Crowe entered the novitiate for the Upper Canada (i.e., English-Canadian) Province of the Society of Jesus. The Jesuits are especially tied to the history of the Church in Canada.[14] With Crowe's academic abilities and family interest in teaching, the Jesuits must have seemed like a good fit for a young man who was hearing a call to the religious life.

Soon after their founding of the Society of Jesus in 1540, some of the first Jesuits were involved in missionary work. Others, including St Jean de Brebeuf, arrived in what is now Canada in 1611. Although difficulties forced them back to France, St Jean de Brebeuf and others returned to "New France" in 1625. The Jesuits were at work in Canada until they were suppressed worldwide in 1773 by Pope Clement XI. After being reinstituted in 1814 by Pope Pius VI, the Society of Jesus returned to Quebec in 1842. By 1845 a novitiate had been established in Montreal, but it was not until about seventy years later that "English Canada got its own novitiate in Guelph in 1913."[15]

When these English-speaking Canadians finished their novitiate studies, a juniorate was added at the same location in Guelph in 1915. During their juniorate at Guelph, "in an atmosphere of somewhat more concentrated attention than would be normal in a secular college,"[16] the Jesuit brothers studied Latin, Greek, English, and rhetoric and also worked the farm. Bernard Lonergan entered the Jesuit novitiate in Guelph "in the summer of 1922."[17] When Frederick Crowe moved to Guelph to begin his life as a Jesuit in 1936, Lonergan was already a priest and was working on his doctorate in Rome.[18]

During his novitiate Crowe spent "his two years of ascetical training"[19] under Joseph P. Monaghan, SJ (1884–1980). After the two further years of his juniorate Crowe first met Fr Bernard Lonergan at a retreat in 1940. Crowe writes: "I remember an evaluation he gave us fifteen years later, when fresh from our own juniorate studies, we sat at his feet one summer day and asked him to tell us (guru style, we would now say) what the value of Greek and Latin classics was. The response was forthright: the work of translation takes you behind words to ideas ... I do not remember where the conversation went from there."[20] Although he was impressed by Lonergan's erudition, Crowe did not form a close intellectual bond with Lonergan at this first meeting.

Following the classical studies of the juniorate, three years of scholastic philosophy studies began for Crowe in Toronto. Beginning in 1885,

Jesuit seminarians had studied philosophy at the Jesuit-run Collège de l'Immaculée-Conception in Montreal, and Bernard Lonergan taught there after returning from his doctoral studies in Rome in 1940. With the number of English-speaking vocations growing, however, the Jesuits founded the College of Christ the King (Collegium Christi Regis) in 1930 as a seminary of philosophy at 403 Wellington Street West, Toronto, Ontario. A faculty of theology was added in 1943, and the school was eventually called Regis College.[21]

Crowe studied philosophy at Regis College from 1940 to 1943. Since he had already completed a bachelor's degree in New Brunswick, he was able to use these three years at Regis to work towards a licentiate in philosophy. When Crowe finished his philosophy studies, however, Regis College did not yet grant their own degrees. His licentiate in philosophy was bestowed in 1943 from L'Immaculée-Conception in Montreal.

Having completed seven years of formation, Crowe set off for his three years of regency in Halifax, Nova Scotia. According to Crowe, regency was the period "between philosophical studies and theological studies, in which the young Jesuit was expected to teach, to coach athletic teams, to oversee student publications, to be prefect of dormitories, and in general to make oneself useful to the school or college in question."[22] During his regency, which began during the Second World War, Brother Crowe had "charge of the athletic equipment"[23] at the Jesuit college St Mary's.

His regency finished, Brother Crowe was sent back to Regis College to begin his theology studies in the fall of 1946. In the spring of 1947 a fortuitous event took place in Crowe's life. Bernard Lonergan was sent to Toronto principally to teach a course at the Pontifical Institute of Medieval Studies.[24] During that spring he lived at Regis College and there taught "a mini course, on Scripture and Tradition."[25] It was in that mini course that Crowe "first became a student of Fr. Lonergan."[26]

A Brief Sketch of Lonergan and Crowe's Interactions

Bernard Lonergan was transferred to Regis College as a full-time professor in the fall of 1947. As Crowe had taken that one course with Lonergan in his first year of theology studies, he was part of the first English-speaking cohort to study under Lonergan for all four of their theology years.[27] In his book *Lonergan*, while commenting on Lonergan's own doctoral dissertation, Crowe spoke about those years with his "master": "Setting out to give some account of this dissertation, I cannot myself avoid a very personal approach. I carry the freight of my own apprenticeship to Lonergan, four years when I sat as a disciple at the feet of a master, and this just at the time when he was fresh from his study of grace in Thomas and engrossed in his work on Thomist cognitive theory."[28] Crowe refers here to Lonergan's 1941–2 articles "St Thomas' Thought on *Gratia Operans*" and to Lonergan's 1946–9 *Verbum* articles on Aquinas's doctrine of intelligible emanation in the human mind.[29]

Soon after Lonergan's 1941 article on operative grace appeared, Crowe "tried to read the first paragraph of *Gratia Operans* but gave up."[30] Eventually, however, he read the articles with great interest, perhaps in the fall of 1947 when he took his second Lonergan course. He expressed his appreciation for them in this way: "Then I think of the Thomist psychology which, with all its defects, I found so deeply explanatory of and clearly verifiable in my religious experience that I cannot regard it as of merely archaeological interest."[31] During the second course with Lonergan on the theology of grace, it was not only *what* Lonergan was teaching that so attracted Crowe but also *how* it was taught: "I feel bound to say that this experience, of studying divine grace under Lonergan, was an experience of having a doctrine that had taken possession of its teacher. There was conviction in Lonergan's voice, even when he adduced proof texts in the ahistorical manner of older theology, even when the Scripture he read in proof was from the Latin Vulgate. Those texts rang with feeling."[32]

In 1949–50, his fourth year of theology under Lonergan's "tutelage,"[33] Crowe took Lonergan's class on the Trinity.[34] As in the course on grace, he was deeply impressed by the lectures: "They ended with a sweeping view of life and thought, exploiting the potentialities of the trinitarian categories of intelligence, word, and love. It was an exhilarating experience for me, and not only that: *as well it became an anchor through several years of change in a changing world conceived in the categories of a changing theology.*"[35] It is hard to overestimate the influence of Lonergan on Crowe's thinking about the Trinity, especially the psychological triad: intelligence, word, and love.

After he was ordained a priest in June of 1949, Crowe returned to Regis College in 1949–50 to work on his licentiate in theology. When he had finished his licentiate thesis under Lonergan, he was sent to Rome for his doctorate at the Gregorian University.[36] Like Lonergan had fifteen years earlier, Crowe then travelled to Amiens, France, for "a third year of novitiate," his final year of formation – "his year of tertianship, a short ten months but regularly a profound experience for Jesuits."[37]

Having completed this year in Amiens, Crowe was asked to teach theology at Regis College in Toronto. He would be taking the place of

Lonergan, who had been assigned to teach at the Gregorian University. When Charles Boyer, SJ, had visited Toronto in the fall of 1952,[38] Lonergan had learned that he would be going to Rome the following year. Years later he explained: "I worked at *Insight* from 1949 to 1953. During the first three years my intention was an exploration of methods generally in preparation for a study of the method of theology. But in 1952 it became clear that I was due to start teaching at the Gregorian University in Rome in 1953, so I changed my plan and decided to round off what I had done and publish it."[39] In a letter of December 1952 to Fr Crowe, Lonergan explained how much of *Insight* he had written: "About 12 chapters done. About 6 chapters to go ... Topics: insight in maths, empirical science, common sense, knowing things, judgment; objectivity of insight; nature of metaphysics; God; dialectic of individual consciousness (Freud) of community (Marx) of objectivity (philosophies), of religion. Had hoped to include theology, but impossible now that I am going to Rome in September."[40] Crowe was amazed to find the book finished by August 1953. That summer he had arrived in Toronto and "read the manuscript (not the Preface, and possibly not the Introduction) in early August, when the final sections had already been returned by the typists."[41] It was decided that Crowe would produce an impressive index for the book. For various reasons the publication of *Insight* was delayed until 1957.

Lonergan did not publish his second great masterpiece, *Method in Theology*, until 1972. In its early stages *Insight* was intended to become a book on methodology for theology. Crowe later expressed the connection between *Insight* and *Method in Theology* in this way: "*Insight* studied the operations that are the basis of method; work on method itself can begin in earnest now."[42] With his being sent to Rome in 1953, Lonergan decided that a book on theological method would have to wait.

In Crowe's opinion, the years of Lonergan's teaching of theology in Canada (1940–53) and in Rome (1953–65) were not wasted in terms of methodology. In those twenty-five years of actually teaching theology, Lonergan worked out the nature of theological method.[43] Moreover, he held graduate-level seminars on methodology in those years at the Gregorian University, as well as summer courses at places like Regis College.[44]

During the summer vacation of 1965 Lonergan was diagnosed with lung cancer and had to undergo life-threatening surgery. His superiors decided that he should recuperate in Toronto and not return to Rome. So, after twelve years of living in separate Jesuit communities, Lonergan and Crowe were back together. In the years immediately following his return to Toronto, Lonergan did not have to teach and instead worked on lectures and articles that would eventually take shape in *Method in Theology*.

Although Lonergan had been working on *Method in Theology* since 1965, Crowe only gradually appropriated the work. In the 1970s he was reprinting Lonergan's early Latin theology,[45] developing the Lonergan Center in the library of Regis College at its Bayview Avenue property,[46] and involved in the formation of a new ecumenical school of theology.

Ever since the Jesuits had helped to form the Toronto School of Theology (TST) in 1968, non-Catholic theology students had begun to take courses at Regis College. The college's location in Willowdale was inconvenient not only for Jesuits to travel to the other TST locations in downtown Toronto but also for their students to reach Regis College. So, discussions began about whether to move Regis College again. This whole affair with its personal difficulties became a great burden to Crowe.[47]

In 1975, out of dissatisfaction over the Jesuits' decision to sell the Bayview Avenue buildings and move to a downtown location, Bernard Lonergan asked to be transferred to Boston College. Crowe, by contrast, was in favour of relocating the school in order to be closer to the other schools in the ecumenical TST. The move would require living quarters to be apart from the college in separate houses with communities of smaller sizes.

With the 1976 move of Regis College, Crowe expanded the Lonergan Center in rented office space near the new location. In these years, 1975–6, he did not publish very much, partly because he was attempting to write a book about *Method in Theology*'s functional specialty of history. Crowe's archives show him working for many years on this book, which came out in 1978.[48] Between 1976 and 1978 Crowe was also involved in a theological commission dealing with the question of women's ordination to the ministerial priesthood.[49] All the while, he was still energetically teaching theology at Regis College, thinking more deeply about the problems of dogma and history, and trying to adapt his pedagogy to the changed student body of the 1970s.[50]

One of Crowe's long-time and most loved courses at Regis was called "The Word of God Communicated to Men,"[51] about the transmission of divine revelation. Through teaching that class Crowe came to think of revelation as primarily history itself, with the culmination of history occurring in the life, death, and resurrection of Jesus of Nazareth. He is God's "primary word" to us.[52]

The year 1979 brought a new opportunity for Crowe – a chance to reflect on the entire life's work of Lonergan. Various Jesuits were planning to celebrate Lonergan's seventy-fifth birthday. In particular, Gonzaga

University in Spokane, Washington, wanted to honour this milestone with a series of lectures. In 1972 Lonergan had given the first set of the St Michael's Lectures at Gonzaga, "where Fr. Lonergan's thought has been studied assiduously ever since the appearance of *Insight* in 1957."[53] Subsequent to Lonergan, E.L. Mascall, George Lindbeck, Joseph Komonchak, David Tracy, and Paul Ricoeur, also delivered lectures.[54] Gonzaga University thought it was fitting that the 1979 lecture "should return to the profound thinking of Bernard Lonergan."[55] Crowe was invited to deliver these lectures because "no one most probably is better qualified than the eminent theologian Frederick Crowe, SJ, the director of the Lonergan Center at Regis College, Toronto."[56]

Crowe delivered three lectures at Gonzaga on 5–7 October 1979. These lectures, prepared "as a whole and delivered as a unit,"[57] were subsequently published as *The Lonergan Enterprise*. The first and third of the lectures had featured "as a pair"[58] in an earlier lecture tour that year through seven cities of Australia. The Lonergan Centre in Sydney, directed by Fr Peter Beer, SJ, had worked with Fr Thomas Daly of the Melbourne College of Divinity to bring Crowe to Australia in order to celebrate Lonergan's seventy-fifth birthday. Crowe's central idea in the lectures was inspired by a letter of John Henry Newman.

After John Henry Newman had written his *Essay in Aid of a Grammar of Assent*,[59] he sent a copy to his friend Robert Dale. Dale replied to Newman's letter and spoke about the new theology that was needed: "No one, as far as I know, has ever done for Theology what Bacon did for physical science, and since I saw the announcement of your Essay I have been looking for its appearance with great curiosity and interest, for there are many passages in your writings which indicate that you had given very much thought to many of the questions that would be illustrated in a Theological *Novum Organon*."[60] In his reply Newman wrote: "You have truly said that we need a Novum Organum for theology – and I shall be truly glad if I shall be found to have made any suggestions which will aid the formation of such a calculus – but it must be the strong conception and the one work of a great genius, not the obiter attempt of a person like myself, who has already attempted many things, and is at the end of his days."[61]

Crowe began his 1979 lectures with these two passages from Newman's *Letters and Diaries*. He also quoted them at the end of his 1980 address to the University of St Thomas in New Brunswick. In that lecture Crowe went on to explain briefly their basic thrust. Francis Bacon had invented an inductive organon, "an instrument of mind,"[62] that was parallel to the instrument of mind that Aristotle had unknowingly invented by his logical works. This logical organon had served for over two thousand years "to systematize deductive thought and reduce the leeway of error."[63] Seeing the need for a new inductive instrument to guide experimental science, Francis Bacon "would do for experimental science what Aristotle had done for demonstrative thinking."[64] Crowe brings up Dale's letter and Newman's response because of the way in which they "saw the need for an analogous organon in the field of theology."[65] What Aristotle did for medieval science with his logical organon, and Bacon proposed to do for modern science with his own inductive tools, Crowe thought Lonergan had analogously done for modern theology.

In short, Crowe was deeply appreciative of Lonergan's work in general and valued the *Verbum* articles, *Insight*, and *Method in Theology*. He lived with and studied under Lonergan at the same time that Lonergan was working on the *Verbum* articles. Crowe came back from Rome in time to read *Insight* in manuscript form; he then grew in familiarity with the work as he produced the index. Finally, Crowe worked closely with Lonergan as he was writing *Method in Theology*. This sketch of their interactions has given a general sense of what Crowe thought was valuable in Lonergan's writings. But what in particular shaped his pneumatology?

The Influence of Lonergan's Writings on Crowe's Pneumatology

The Verbum *Articles*

As he began teaching Trinitarian theology in Montreal, Bernard Lonergan was troubled by the claim of Louis Billot, SJ, that the intellectual procession of a word is exactly parallel to what happens when an image proceeds forth "in the imagination."[66] In his "The Concept of *Verbum* in the Writings of St Thomas Aquinas" Lonergan sets forth his own interpretation of Aquinas. According to Lonergan, there are two main analogies in Aquinas for the way in which the Son proceeds from the Father: the intelligible emanation of a definition (or concept) and the intelligible emanation of a judgment. Both the definition and the judgment can be called inner words of the mind.[67] Crowe follows Lonergan in thinking that there is something fundamentally different about the way an inner word consciously proceeds from the mind and the way an image can proceed from the imagination.

The basic feature of an inner word, Crowe explains, is "the *rationally conscious expression* of understanding."[68] In the case of forming a concept, there is a kind of freedom from the imagination, in which "understanding has taken possession of itself, has expressed itself in the universal which is *simply* universal, the universal *common to many*, with the possibility of application to various instances."[69] According to Crowe, our "understanding expresses itself in a concept, and this expression is the 'emanatio intelligibilis [intelligible emanation].'"[70] What makes the intelligible emanation in the intellect different from the image proceeding in the imagination and from natural processes (such as heat emanating from fire) is that, in the expressing of our understanding, "we are intellectually conscious of what we are doing and of our sufficient grounds for doing it."[71] As Crowe will say, the process of expressing our understanding is "not only intelligible but also intelligent."[72] By *intelligent*, Crowe means an awareness both of the act and of the grounds for the act. "When we define," he comments, "not as parrots, but as intelligent men, we do so in virtue of understanding; when we judge not as bigots, but as rational men, we do so in virtue of reflection, and that 'in virtue of' does not indicate causation in the ontological sense."[73] In other words, while the emanation of the inner word is caused by the human intellect, the inner word is not merely a product or effect of the intellect. We consciously form inner words in virtue of our conscious acts of understanding.

In this way of conceiving the intelligible emanation of an inner word, Lonergan thought that he might have found the source of another theologian's trouble with the psychological analogy for the Trinity. Maurilio Penido, while not denying the authority in Catholic theology of the procession of a word from the human intellect as an analogy for the Son's eternal generation, had questioned the authority of the Holy Spirit's procession being understood by the analogy of a procession of love in the will. Lonergan writes: "By definition, the will is a rational appetite. Might it not be that the procession according to the will is to be grasped only in terms of an analysis of rationality and rational consciousness?"[74] Lonergan thought that enquiry into the distinctive way an intellectual word emanates would be a significant step to understanding better the procession of love in the will.

In his *Verbum* articles Lonergan argues that the procession of the Holy Spirit was not understood by Aquinas as a procession of love "from the will or any procession from something in the will, but the procession of love *in* the will *from* the intellect."[75] Crowe eventually sought to deepen this insight of Lonergan. He did so by investigating what Aquinas meant by *complacentia boni* (complacency in the good) and applying it as an analogy for the procession of the Holy Spirit. The uttering of an inner word of judgment gives rise to a conscious act of love that shares in the inner word's intelligibility. The procession of complacent love is also an intelligible emanation.

Crowe recognized the importance of the Thomist psychological analogy with its two intelligible emanations for understanding the two divine processions and the unity of the three persons. Lonergan was especially focused on the intelligible procession of the Son, whereas Crowe turned his attention to clarifying the procession of the Holy Spirit. But the question arises: Why are there two processions in God?

In 1949 Lonergan published his final article, *Imago Dei*, of the series, which became the fifth chapter of *Verbum: Word and Idea in Aquinas*. In it he explained the underlying point of the articles. "When Aquinas spoke of God as *ipsum intelligere* [the act of understanding itself]," Lonergan asks, "did he mean that God was a pure act of understanding? To that conclusion we have been working through four chapters. But to cap that cumulative argument, there comes the impossibility that Aquinas meant anything else."[76] After working through various possible meanings of *intelligere* to show that Aquinas could only have been thinking of the act of understanding, Lonergan writes: "It remains that *ipsum intelligere* is analogous to understanding, that God is an infinite and substantial act of understanding, that as the Father is God, the Son is God, the Holy Spirit is God, so also each is one and the same infinite and substantial act of understanding, finally that, though each is the pure act of understanding, still only the Father understands as uttering the Word."[77] The whole question of the divine knowing occurs after Aquinas has treated the divine substance (*Summa Theologiae*, I, qq. 2–13). In those questions on God's substance, Aquinas explains not so much what God is but rather what God is not. Aquinas admits that we do not know God's essence in this life. But in place of our knowing what God is, is it possible to use his infinite act of knowing as a kind of substitute in our thinking about God? In other words, can we treat God's act of intellect as a kind of property by which we have some analogous notion of what God is like?

In *Summa Theologiae*, part I, questions 14–26, Aquinas begins to discuss the divine operations that remain within God. He treats of God's intellect and will. Lonergan's position probably finds its inspiration in the way that Aquinas treats God's inner activity after treating what God is. We may not know what the essence of God is, but we can extrapolate from our experience of human acts of understanding to an infinite act of divine understanding. Instead of just thinking of God as the utterly simple, infinite act of existence, this procedure thinks of him as an unrestricted, infinite act of understanding. Would such a procedure help us grasp the unity between the questions on the one God in the *Summa* and the questions on the Trinity?

Bernard Lonergan thought that the *Summa Theologiae* marked a great advance in Thomas Aquinas's thinking about the Trinity. Lonergan writes: "Though Aquinas in his earlier works began from God the Father to treat next the generation of the Son and then the procession of the Holy Spirit, his *Summa Theologiae* eliminated even the semblance of a logical fiction of a becoming in God. The *Summa* treats first God as one, to turn to God as triune 'secundum viam doctrinae [according to the way of teaching].' In this presentation, the starting point is not God the Father but God; the first question is not whether there are processions from God the Father but whether there is procession in God."[78] According to Lonergan, Aquinas's treatment of the one God in questions 2–26 before he treats of the triune God (qq. 27–43) does not need a great apology. Lonergan goes on to say: "After establishing two processions in God, the existence of real relations in God is treated. Only after both processions and relations have been treated is the question of persons raised. The significance of this procedure is that it places Thomist trinitarian theory in a class by itself."[79]

Lonergan wrote in a similar way in his book *The Triune God: Systematics*. He begins his systematic account of the Trinity with the processions. In the third assertion of chapter 2, he turns to a discussion of the divine nature. The procession of the Word, that is, the generation of the eternal Son, raises the question of the divine nature. "Since generation results in a likeness of nature," Lonergan writes, "we have to consider the question: What is the nature of God?"[80] In this discussion he defends the importance of thinking of God's nature as intellectual because it provides an analogical understanding of what God is. Although we do not have the beatific vision in this life by which we would know what God is, "this in no way prevents us ... from ordering what we know analogically [of God] in such a way that some element of what we know analogically is first after the manner of a nature or essence."[81] Lonergan, to the chagrin of some Thomists,[82] looked to God's act of understanding for this element that provides the first element in our ordering of what God is. "In this sense," he writes, "the nature of God is God's act of understanding, upon which follows God's infinity and aseity and simplicity, and whatever else there is in God but unknown to us."[83] Lonergan then argues at some length for how God's infinity, aseity, and simplicity follow from the view that God's nature is primarily intellectual.

In these philosophical arguments Lonergan is considering *nature* as essence, from which all other aspects of God follow like properties. But then he turns to thinking of nature "in the sense of an intrinsic principle of operation."[84] Here again he concludes "that the divine nature is intellectual."[85] By our natural knowledge of God, Lonergan thinks that we can know that God is intellectual. That notion of God as intellectual, however, does not prove on its own that there are distinctions in God. Lonergan only accepts that there are distinct persons in God on the basis of revelation. "For although," he writes, "absolutely no real distinction can be posited in God according to our natural knowledge of God, still, as we come to know God through faith and theology, we discover real personal distinctions in God that are constituted through relations of origin."[86]

Reflecting on these personal distinctions within the Trinity, Aquinas himself had linked the origin of the persons to the divine nature. In his question on man as the image of God, Aquinas wrote: "The mode of origin is not the same in all things; rather the mode of origin in each thing is in accord with what befits its own nature: animate things being produced in one way, inanimate things in another; animals in one way and plants in another. It is evident, therefore, that the distinction of divine persons is in accord with what befits the divine nature."[87] After quoting this passage, Lonergan immediately quotes a line from Prima pars, question 93, article 6, of the *Summa Theologiae*: "The uncreated Trinity is distinguished on the basis of the procession of the Word from the Speaker and of Love from both."[88] Aquinas went on to discuss the way a word and love proceeded in the rational creature. But these finite processions within the image of God are analogous to the processions of the Word and the Holy Spirit. Since the origins of those persons "are according to the emanations of intellectual consciousness, we must conclude," Lonergan writes, "that the divine nature is intellectual."[89]

Crowe knew these texts in Aquinas and Lonergan and found them persuasive. In his own course notes on the Trinity, Crowe asks: "What grounds the relation of origin between the Father and Son, and what grounds the relation of origin between the Spirit on one side, and the Father and Son on the other?"[90] Drawing on Lonergan, Crowe adds: "The answer, in its final formulation, will be that the divine nature is 'rational' (we have no better single word for it at the moment), so that in God there is One who from the fullness of infinite understanding utters a Word, this Word is also One who is divine, and from him flows a Love that is likewise One who is divine; thus the one infinite 'rational' nature 'grounds' the distinct 'characteristics' of three divine persons who are, nevertheless, but one God."[91] Crowe's use of the words *ground* and *rational* echoes Lonergan's *Verbum* articles. A "basic contention" of those 1946–9 articles was "that the human mind is an image, and not a mere vestige, of the Blessed Trinity because its processions are intelligible in a manner that is essentially different from, that transcends, the passive, specific, imposed intelligibility of other natural process."[92]

But then Lonergan makes use of the word *ground* in talking about the procession of a word in human consciousness: "Any effect has a sufficient ground in its cause; but an inner word not merely has a sufficient ground in the act of understanding it expresses; it also has a knowing as sufficient ground, and that ground is operative precisely as a knowing, knowing itself to be sufficient."[93] The point is that our concepts and judgments proceed from our awareness of the sufficiency of our understanding. We grasp the reason that this has to be the definition of a circle, for example. In terms of the judgment, we grasp, for instance, the sufficiency of the evidence for affirming the truth. Inner words do not proceed automatically like images in the imagination.

Lonergan then introduces a single term to summarize what he wants to say in his *Verbum* articles: "We may say that the inner word is rational, not indeed from the derived rationality of discourse, of reasoning from premises to conclusions, but with the basic and essential rationality of rational consciousness, with the rationality that can be discerned in any judgment, with the rationality that we now have to observe in all concepts."[94] Lonergan later uses the words *reflective rationality*[95] to express the way in which inner words (definitions and judgments) consciously and intelligently proceed in us.

By 1965–6 Crowe did not want to separate this dynamically conceived divine nature from the psychological analogy. The divine nature so conceived helps us to understand why there are two processions and three divine persons. Crowe speaks of the "doctrine of a 'rational' God who is *Dicens, Verbum,* and *Amor* [Speaker, Word, and Love]."[96] He saw Lonergan's teaching on the divine nature as filling out the trajectory of Augustine and Aquinas. For this reason, the title of the fifth chapter of *The Doctrine of the Most Holy Trinity* is "The Psychological Analogy: The Divine Nature Such as to Be *Dicens, Verbum,* and *Amor*."[97] Crowe loved the following line of Lonergan's: "The Augustinian psychological analogy makes trinitarian theology a prolongation of natural theology, a deeper insight into what God is."[98]

For Crowe, Lonergan both clarified Aquinas's notion of the two processions in God and brought the question of the procession in God to "its clearest formulation and proper order."[99] According to Crowe, "the ultimate question to which the analytic mind came in the course of history ... was the following: Why are there processions in God? What kind of 'nature' is it that, though infinite, has Son proceeding from Father, and Spirit from both, while the Father himself proceeds from no one?"[100] Crowe articulates here in 1965–6 what he had begun to hold in 1949–50. Thinking of God's nature as dynamic will stay with

Crowe for the rest of his life and deeply shape the third stage of his pneumatology.

Insight: *A Study of Human Understanding*

In his 1957 review article "The Origin and Scope of Bernard Lonergan's *Insight*," Crowe talked about how, for many, reading *Insight* would be "the beginning of a new and extended intellectual experience."[101] He said that *Insight* would give to many readers "a new orientation."[102] Crowe was convinced that the book was in fundamental continuity with the best of Catholic philosophy, while at the same time taking a remarkable step forward. On the one hand, his "own tentative view is that *Insight* is destined to take a place among the great books of modern thought, but it might be rash at the present time to assign it a more precise ranking."[103] On the other hand, he connected Lonergan's work with the Thomist revival that began under Pope Leo XIII. In Crowe's mind, *Insight* was not "intended as a totally new line of thought but as a development of Thomism according to the Leonine *vetera novis augere et perficere*."[104]

Crowe's review begins with the main theme of *Insight* and then takes up the relationship between *Insight* and Thomas Aquinas's thought. The goal of the book is to help readers towards "the full perfection of self-knowledge"[105] on the basis of which there follows a "consequent ontology."[106] Crowe was persuaded that Lonergan had uncovered the basic structure of human knowing with its three interrelated levels. These three levels provide a basis for grounding Thomistic metaphysical analysis.

Crowe was not shy in comparing Lonergan's achievement to the partial successes of Sigmund Freud in the area of self-knowledge and Martin Heidegger in the area of ontology. Lonergan's method in *Insight*, according to Crowe, fits with other twentieth-century proposals: "Postpone metaphysics and take our departure from the subject, in the present case, from the dynamism and immanent laws of cognitional activity itself."[107] Crowe was persuaded that Lonergan had "worked out in full detail"[108] what Freud and Heidegger had proposed in the realm of self-knowledge and metaphysics.

Insight's original subtitle was an "Essay in Aid of a Personal Appropriation of One's Own Rational Self-Consciousness."[109] In our consciousness, in our awareness of ourselves and our knowing activity, Lonergan was saying, we can discover an unchanging but dynamic *structure* of operations. What is this structure? In his 1965 essay "Neither Jew Nor

Greek, but One Human Nature and Operation in All," Crowe gave a useful summary of Lonergan's *Insight* as a "748-page introduction" to "the notion of structure."[110] Since this summary gives us a good take on Crowe's Lonergan, it is worth quoting at length:

> In the beginning is experience: I hear and taste and feel and smell and, most of all, I see. So of course does my dog; but there is the difference between me and my dog that I get ideas about my experience; more basically, there is in me a wonder, a capacity to seek the intelligibility of experience; it is this wonder that gives rise to ideas. Sooner or later, however, in the self-correcting process of learning, I discover that my ideas are not always right, that error abounds when I accept my ideas uncritically, that ideas in general are just *possible* explanations of the data and, if I am to be rational, I must institute a further inquiry, I must reflect on the correctness of my ideas; it is this reflection that gives rise to rational truth and knowledge of the real. So there are three levels: experience (data, presentations of sense, representations of imagination), understanding (ideas, thoughts, suppositions which are possible explanations), reflection (grasp of evidence grounding judgment and knowledge). And the dynamism which operates the transition from level to level is manifested in a twofold question: the question for understanding which turns experience into something to be understood, the question for reflection which turns the idea into something to be investigated for its truth. Furthermore, within each of the two higher levels there is the extremely important element of formulation, the Thomist twofold *verbum*: on the level of understanding, ideas are formulated into concepts (transition from the engagement with the particular to release from the particular into universalization); on the level of reflection, grasp of evidence is formulated in judgments (transition from subjective grounds of affirmation to objective judgment and the "public" character of knowledge, the possibility of communication).[111]

Crowe's summary of the structure of human knowing lends itself to figure 1.

In the first stage of his development Crowe maintained that Lonergan's Thomism, with his interpretation of a twofold inner word and its emphasis on insight into phantasm, led Lonergan to grasp the "cognitional process in its dynamism and immanent conditions of unfolding."[112] From Aquinas's largely theoretical account of knowing, Lonergan was able, in his own words, to piece together "a sufficient number of indications and suggestions to form an adequate account of wisdom in cognitional terms."[113] Crowe draws our attention to a reference to science in an important passage of *Insight*: "The contribution of

The dynamism that operates the transitions between levels, and the question that manifests this dynamic wonder	Levels of cognitional activity	Name of level with operations on that level	Element of formulation – Thomist twofold verbum
Further inquiry – question for reflection? *Is my idea/ concept correct?*	3	*Reflection* (grasp of evidence grounding judgment and knowledge)	→ judgments
Wonder about what is experienced → gives rise to questions for understanding and ideas → *What is this all?*	2	*Understanding* (I get ideas, thoughts, suppositions which are possible explanations about my experience)	→ concepts
	1	*Experience* (I hear and taste and feel and smell and, most of all, I see; i.e., data, presentations of sense, representations of imagination)	

Figure 1 Crowe's account of the three levels of thought

science and of scientific method to philosophy lies in a unique ability to supply philosophy with instances of the heuristic structures which a metaphysics integrates into a single view of the universe."[114] The way scientists proceed – starting with data, formulating hypotheses, and testing for verification – provides the instances to which Lonergan is referring. The method of modern science, as it has developed in the centuries after Aquinas, illustrates the threefold structure of human knowing.

Crowe understood that Lonergan was then grounding his explicit metaphysics "on cognitional activity."[115] As this dynamic structure of operations is "unchanging,"[116] it gives philosophy "permanent stability and removes it from the possibility of radical revision."[117] The metaphysical principles of all material reality could only be revised by an appeal to experience, to understanding, or to judgment. In trying to refute the structure of our knowing, one ends up supplying "an instance of the unchanging structure of cognitional activity."[118]

Four years after *Insight* was published, Crowe wrote an article in 1961 defending the way in which Lonergan aligns the threefold structure of human knowing with the three metaphysical principles of proportionate being: potency, form, and act. The article, "St Thomas and the Isomorphism of Knowing and Its Proper Object," sought to present evidence in Aquinas's writings that supports Lonergan's claim of an isomorphic relationship between knowing and what is known. Lonergan's argument, according to Crowe,

> is that human knowing is structured in a set of three related acts and that the contents of those acts must be similarly structured: human knowing in its proper field, is a unification of experiencing, understanding, and judging; and so what is known in this field will be a parallel unification of a content of experience, a content of understanding, and a content of judging. Further, knowing is objective; the pattern of cognitional contents is not just notional but reflects the ontological pattern of what is known. And so, corresponding to experience, understanding, and judgment in the human subject, we have potency, form, and act in the proportionate object of his knowing.[119]

In 1957 Crowe had been aware of the many intellectual influences on Lonergan's thought, yet he was still convinced that Thomas Aquinas's philosophy was the basis of *Insight*.[120] On this foundation, however, Lonergan had built a larger structure. In a word, Crowe thought that Lonergan had reached "up to the mind of Aquinas" as few others had.[121]

Taking someone through Crowe's remarkable but complicated argument for finding isomorphism in Aquinas would require a whole chapter. Such analysis is not important for Crowe's pneumatology. What is relevant is the fact of Crowe's appropriation of Lonergan's notion of levels of thought. If the classes that Crowe took with Lonergan and the theology of the *Verbum* articles persuaded Crowe to take his theology seriously, *Insight* gradually convinced him about the need for a new first philosophy. Crowe found in Lonergan a defence for Thomistic metaphysics rooted in a verifiable cognitional theory.

In his "Neither Jew Nor Greek, but One Human Nature and Operation in All" Crowe makes the following remark: "We need then a critical awareness, an appropriation and evaluation of our own powers of intelligent grasp and reasonable affirmation of the universe of being; we need also an awareness and appropriation of our power for harmonious accord with the universe, but the emphasis of this article has been on the cognitional side rather than on the affective."[122] Crowe's reference to a *harmonious accord* is an allusion to his series of 1959 articles, "Complacency and Concern in the Thought of St Thomas."[123] There Crowe argued that, corresponding to our judgments of existence, there exists an affective complement. He had identified this affective acceptance of what is with Aquinas's notion of *complacentia boni*.

Crowe thought, I will argue, that Lonergan's *Insight* had not delineated enough the affective dimension of life. Crowe's work on an affection that complements the judgment of being was an attempt to expand Lonergan's thought. Crowe thought that we could become aware of this power of complacency with what is. He also wanted to use this harmonious accord, this first moment of love, as an analogy for the procession of the Holy Spirit.[124]

The whole question of affectivity raises an important question for Lonergan's levels of knowing. How does love fit with these levels? Does it belong as an extension of the third level? Does it belong on a level above the third? As we will see in later chapters, Crowe eventually accepted the idea that love belongs in a fourth level of consciousness. This issue of love within a fourth level of consciousness brings us to the third book of Lonergan's that especially influenced Crowe, *Method in Theology*.

Method in Theology

As Crowe had immediately written a review of *Insight* in 1957, so he wrote a review of *Method in Theology* in 1973.[125] He admitted, however, that the review would not necessarily "reveal the essential Lonergan";[126] it would "rather show what is at the centre of my interests and consciousness."[127]

The review begins by explaining the genesis of the book, and then Crowe states his "view on the central and most comprehensive difference between Lonergan's thinking at the present time and that of the 'earlier Lonergan': the shift from exploring cognitional process to exploring values and the fourth level of consciousness."[128] Crowe even adds that this shift from an emphasis on intellect to an emphasis on love is the "criterion" by which one might "divide his thought so far into two periods."[129] He thought that this later Lonergan had emerged not with the publication of *Method in Theology* but with a shift in Lonergan around 1965.

Lonergan's concern with methodology, however, goes back to the 1930s, and Crowe traced some of this history in his 1991 book *Lonergan*.[130] For our purposes, what has to be emphasized is Lonergan's 1965 breakthrough to the idea of functional specialties. Drawing on the three cognitional levels (experience, understanding, judgment) and adding a level that moves the subject beyond knowing to a *decision* as the fourth level of consciousness, Lonergan was able to explain eight distinct and interrelated tasks in theology. "From the structure of consciousness," Crowe notes, "we move to the specialties they organize. The four levels, and the two directions in which one may move through them, give the eight functional specialties."[131]

The eight functional specialties are distinct but interrelated stages in the whole process of theology, which Lonergan divided into two phases. In the first phase there are the stages of *research, interpretation, history,* and *dialectic.* In the second stage we pass through the stages of *foundations, doctrines, systematics,* and *communications.* Crowe explains how Lonergan ties the functional specialties to the four levels of consciousness: "Thus, on the four levels of the upward development of consciousness we have research corresponding to experience, interpretation corresponding to understanding, history corresponding to judgement, and dialectic corresponding to decision. And, on the same four levels but in a downward movement, we have foundations, doctrines, systematics, and communications on the levels, respectively, of decision, judgment, understanding, and experience."[132] Crowe's description of Lonergan's functional specialties is illustrated in figure 2, showing the four levels of operations in the middle column.

Corresponding to human experience, understanding, judgment, and decision, we have the functional specialties of *research* into data that is experienced in the fonts of theology; understanding of that data in *interpretation;* judgment about what is changing in the data through *history;* and then an analysis of the differences, *dialectic;* leading to a decision, a personal commitment about which of the competing histories to

First phase of theology	Levels of consciousness	Second phase of theology
Dialectic	Decision	Foundations
History	Judgment	Doctrines
Interpretation	Understanding	Systematics
Research	Experience	Communications

Figure 2 Two phases of methodical theology

follow. The second phase begins with the fourth level of decision and moves downward through the levels of judgment and understanding to experience.

This second phase of theology, according to Crowe's interpretation, presupposes religious conversion and the gift of grace. Based on one's conversion, *foundations* look within human interiority in order to better articulate *doctrines*. Since conversion involves a decision for God, *foundations* are placed at the level of responsible decision.[133] Then one moves to the level of judgment and works out the *doctrines* that need to be articulated.[134] A *systematics*, corresponding to the level of understanding, is then able to work out a way of putting these doctrines together. And this leads to a return to the level of experience as we try in *communications* to bring the Gospel to others on a level of their experience.

What Crowe came to see was that these two phases of theology contained the seeds for "one of the last of [Lonergan's] great general ideas,"[135] the two paths of human development. In 1976 Lonergan explained: "Human development is of two types. There is development from below upwards: experience, understanding, judgments of fact, judgments of value. This is the way we appropriate, make things our own. On the other hand, there is development from above downwards, the benefits of acculturation, socialization, education, the transmission of tradition."[136] In *Insight*, Lonergan had focused on three levels of thought and on the development from experience, through understanding, to knowledge of what is. By the time of *Method in Theology* he had determined four levels of consciousness. In addition to the questions "What is this?" "Is it correct?" there arises the question "What is the worthwhile or valuable thing to do?" This is the question of responsibility and decision.[137]

Soon after *Method in Theology* Lonergan began to speak of the general movement from experience to understanding to judgment to values as a development from below. He contrasts that movement with an interior movement that begins, to continue the metaphor, "from above downwards." Lonergan will even say that the development that begins from above is prior: "The structure of individual development is twofold. The chronologically prior phase is from above downwards."[138]

Crowe first mentions the two ways of development in passing during a lecture at the 1976 Lonergan workshop: "Fr. Lonergan has recently emphasized that 'human development is of two quite distinct kinds.' There is 'development from below upwards,' and this will be my concern ... The other kind is 'from above downwards,' the result of the 'transformation of falling in love' ... *I leave it aside, however, in this paper*, well aware that in so doing I may seem to commit the folly of those who build just half a ship."[139] In 1979 Crowe again mentions the two paths, claiming that they are "unexplored" and that his own reflections on them are "rudimentary."[140] But in 1981, after more careful research, he was able to compare the two ways of development to the two phases of theology that Lonergan had worked out in *Method in Theology*: "This twofold scheme is new, though it stands in continuity with *Method* ... for it derives directly from the contrast between the two phases of theology, and almost comes to explicit formulation at one point."[141] Crowe did not think that Lonergan had thematized the two paths of development when he wrote *Method in Theology*. Yet he thought that it was implicit in the way Lonergan set up the two phases of theology with their respective movements between stages.

Crowe was convinced that the later Lonergan had appeared around 1965. As Crowe had followed the method of reading Aquinas that Lonergan laid out in *Verbum*, as he had tried to follow the method that Lonergan laid out in *Insight*, so he continued to follow the method that Lonergan presented in *Method in Theology*. In 1985 Crowe published his book on the two paths of development that had been first sketched out in *Method*. That book, *Old Things and New: Strategies for Education*, focused on the application of Lonergan's idea for teachers. The third stage of Crowe's pneumatology (1985–2000), however, is marked by the application of Lonergan's two paths to a theology of the Holy Spirit.

Conclusion

This chapter has introduced the main ideas in Lonergan's writings that influenced Crowe's own thought and especially his pneumatology. The dates of Lonergan's publications (1946–9, 1957, 1972) do not exactly correspond to the three stages of Crowe's pneumatology (1953–68, 1969–84, 1985–2000). It took time for Crowe to assimilate certain aspects of Lonergan's own developing thought. But there is a correlation between Crowe's appropriation of the central ideas in these three Lonergan works and the three stages in Crowe's thought.

The *Verbum* articles stressed a dynamically conceived divine nature. There are two processions in God because God's nature can be thought of as a kind of intellectual dynamism that unfolds in an act of infinite Speaking (the Father), an infinite Word of truth (the Son), from which is spirated an infinite act of Love (the Holy Spirit). Trying to unpack the nature of an analogous act of love in us as it applies to the Holy Spirit was the focus of the first stage in Crowe's own pneumatology (1953–68).

In his 1957 book, *Insight*, Lonergan clearly distinguished three levels of cognitive activity. Crowe thought that Lonergan had uncovered the basic three-level structure of human knowing by which counter-positions – positions involved in some fundamental confusion – could be refuted and a true metaphysics could be grounded. But this structure in *Insight* gradually gave way in Lonergan's writings to four levels of consciousness. Thinking about levels of human consciousness in relation to the missions of the Son and the Holy Spirit dominates the second stage of Crowe's pneumatology. In that second stage (1969–84) Crowe used aspects of Lonergan's "philosophy of interiority"[142] to think about the way in which love could precede knowing. In so doing, he tried to articulate how the mission of the Holy Spirit could precede that of the Son.

In his 1972 book, *Method in Theology*, Lonergan brought together his four levels of consciousness to explain a two-phase notion of theology. Crowe became fascinated by the two sides of theology. As he read Lonergan's writings after *Method in Theology*, he became convinced that Lonergan was making explicit what had been implicit in *Method*, namely that human development has, generally, two paths of development: from below upward and from above downward. These two paths become the main preoccupation of Crowe's Lonergan studies in his third stage of pneumatology. In that stage (1985–2000) Crowe proposes, without rejecting the traditional ordering (Father, Word, Holy Spirit), a complementary inverse ordering beginning with the Holy Spirit (Holy Spirit, Word, Father).

Lonergan's ideas on divine rationality in *Verbum*, the levels of consciousness in *Insight*, and the two paths of human development in *Method in Theology* deeply influenced his fellow Canadian Jesuit and student Frederick Crowe. Crowe embraced these ideas, explored them, and expanded them. Out of these influences emerged specific questions about the Spirit.

PART I (1953–1968)

Searching for the *Proprium* of the Holy Spirit

2 Appropriating Aquinas on Love

Proprium *Emerging as a Theme*

In dealing with the account in Genesis of the seven days of creation, Thomas Aquinas makes the following statement: "The Person of the Holy Spirit is suggested in the *complacentia* [complacency] by which God sees that what he has made is good."[1] Aquinas is trying to explain the role of the three divine persons in creation. He ingeniously links a line repeatedly used in Genesis 1 ("And God saw that it was good") with complacency and the Holy Spirit.

The Catholic theologian who has done the most work on Aquinas's doctrine of *complacentia* is Frederick Crowe. Crowe's remarkable 1959 study, "Complacency and Concern in the Thought of St Thomas,"[2] continues to generate interest both among interpreters of Aquinas and among those grappling with the nature of love. Crowe argued that, for Aquinas, *complacentia* is the first act of love and thus the most basic act of will. In his influential book *By Knowledge and by Love*, Michael Sherwin, OP, praised Crowe for drawing attention "toward the centrality of *complacentia* in Aquinas' mature theory of love."[3]

Crowe's interest in *complacentia* was twofold. He thought that complacent love was neglected in contemporary culture and philosophy. He wanted to make available this aspect of Aquinas's thought in the hopes of engaging and healing the culture of his day. Second, Crowe thought that that Aquinas's doctrine of complacency helped us to understand what was distinctive about the Holy Spirit within the Trinitarian life.

In the first stage of Crowe's pneumatology an overarching question emerges: What is the *proprium* of each divine person? "The proper name [*nomen proprium*] of any person," Aquinas explains, "signifies that through which the person is distinguished from all others."[4] For Aquinas, "essential" divine love is common to the Father, Son, and Holy Spirit. Only when love is taken as "proceeding Love"[5] can love be a proper name for the Holy Spirit.

But what is love? According to Crowe, love in its most basic form is complacency, a passive affective acceptance of what is. In his articles "Complacency and Concern" Crowe tries to establish this thesis about love as an interpretation of Aquinas, but also as a truth verifiable in one's own consciousness. In so doing, he argues that complacent proceeding love, in its procession from a rational judgment, provides theologians with the most fitting analogy for the Holy Spirit's eternal procession.

What Is Complacency?

For a first approximation of what Crowe means by *complacency*, it is useful to glance briefly at some of his best descriptions. Many of the following quotations are taken from the third of his "Complacency and Concern" articles (in chapter five of *Three Thomist Studies*), written by Crowe without the use of scholastic terminology in the hopes of dialoguing with contemporary philosophers.

- "Complacency is ... the affective correspondence with being in which the being of things we know pleases us" (*Three Thomist Studies*, 153).
- "This pleasure is not sensible gratification; it is consent to being, harmony with all that is, peace with the universe" (153).
- "It is the human spirit at rest in relation to its object, at the end of process" (153).
- "It does not need explanation through any attraction or inclination or tendency" (153).
- "It is enough that the good is and that we come to know it is and have the power to joy in its being" (153).
- "Psychologically it is a coming to rest, a fruition ... in the tranquil possession of the good that is" (154).
- "The natural complement of the truth" (154).
- "Affective contemplative charity which is at rest in its object" (155).
- "It is a correspondence which is restful and fulfilling and is operated, not by conscious effort laboriously executed, but at least in the first instance by natural spontaneities" (175).
- "To the boundless intellectual curiosity of children and its natural satisfaction with the truth there corresponds a natural complacency and sheer delight, an initial universal joy, in the things that are" (176).

Crowe repeatedly links complacency with what is, with being, with all that is. Complacency is the affective complement or response to our coming to know something.

Crowe contrasts complacency with another kind of attitude that human beings take towards what is not yet but could come about through our efforts. "The human mind is not limited," he writes, "to affirming existence; it can also advert to what is lacking, what is not, and it is fertile too in invention, in creating ideally what may be."[6] From this aspect of our knowing, there arises in us "a new type of love: the *intentio boni* [intending the good], desire, tendency. There is then a transition from complacency to concern, from passivity to activity."[7] Crowe gives a description of this transition: "The passive actuation which is complacency in an ideal end becomes the principle of operations for achieving the ideal."[8] As a person realizes that the ideal is achievable, another aspect of love emerges. In short, "love has two quite distinct but complementary roles ... The fundamental division, prior to all question of the self, seems to me to be this: in one role love is passive, quiescent, complacent; in the other it is active, striving, tending toward an object."[9] He calls this other role of love *concern*.

Crowe takes over Paul Weiss's notion of concern: "A concern – and each being has a concern – is a 'way of reaching from the concrete present into the abstract future,' enabling the being to focus on that future ... 'in the shape of a limited, pertinent possibility.'"[10] If complacency "consists in an approval of the good without any reference to action,"[11] concern regards the good as an end to be actually attained.

While *complacency* is an English cognate for Aquinas's *complacentia*, *concern* does not have an exact cognate in Aquinas's doctrine of love. According to Crowe, the idea of concern "corresponds quite accurately, I think, to the *intentio finis* [intending the end] of the *Prima secundae*, but it would multiply confusion to use here the many-faceted *intentio*."[12] Since *intentio* in Aquinas has so many meanings, and the word *intention* also has different meanings within contemporary philosophy, Crowe opted for the word *concern* to describe love's role as the principle of our striving for an end.[13]

Crowe recognizes, however, that his translation of the Latin *complacentia* as "complacency" has its drawbacks. *Complacency* in contemporary English has connotations of irresponsible self-satisfaction. It sometimes means unwarranted contentment with the status quo. It means acceptance of what should not be accepted. These connotations are "poles apart from Thomist *complacentia*."[14] According to Crowe, the word *complacentia* (complacency), however, "has the root sense of a concept I take to be altogether basic in Thomist psychology of the will, and I think we must just accept its unwelcome connotations as part of the unavoidable limitations of language."[15] *Serenity*, and not *complacency*, is the word Crowe began to prefer to use around 1969 when translating *complacentia boni*. But even this word is unsatisfactory.[16] My own preference is *loving acceptance*.

In chapter 4 of *Three Thomist Studies* Crowe tries to verify his thesis about complacency in seven controverted areas of Aquinas's scholarship. In doing so, he tries to integrate his distinction of two attitudes of willing or loving with "the rest of Thomist thought."[17]

Although Aquinas has a doctrine of love as complacency, Crowe thinks that he gave most of his explicit attention to love as concern. Crowe writes: "The doctrine of love as tendency claimed attention throughout his career; the doctrine of love as complacency, explicit enough at times, was nevertheless kept more or less on the periphery of his thought."[18] There is one place where Crowe thinks that complacent love is not on the periphery of Aquinas's thought: the treatise on the passions in the Prima secundae of his *Summa Theologiae*.[19] Here, for example, are three of Aquinas's most important remarks on complacency from that treatise.

> And similarly the adjustment of sensitive appetite or of will to something good, that is to say, their *very complacency* in the good [*complacentia boni*], is called sensitive love, or *intellectual or rational love* ...[20]
>
> Thus also the desirable gives to the appetite, in the first place, a certain adjustment to itself, which is a complacency in the desirable, from which follows all movement towards the desirable ... the *first change* of the appetite by the desirable is called love, which is *nothing else* than a *complacency* in the desirable [*complacentia appetibilis*] ...[21]
>
> The very aptitude or proportion of the appetite to good is *love*, which is *nothing else* than a *complacency* in the good [*complacentia boni*].[22]

The treatise on the passions, the movements of the sense appetite, is found in *Summa Theologiae*, part I-II, questions 22–48. As is well known, Aquinas repeatedly extends the discussion in these questions to the movements of the will, the rational affective faculty whose object is presented by the intellect. The will's first change is called complacency. Aquinas explicitly speaks of complacency as an intellectual or rational love. According to Michael Vertin, Crowe's article focuses not on the passion or emotion of complacency but on "rational love, the basic form of willing."[23]

Crowe speaks of complacency as coming to "the center" of Aquinas's thought in the questions on the passions.[24] By this metaphor of moving an idea from the periphery to the centre of one's thought, Crowe means that Aquinas in the Prima secundae actually focused on and consciously tried to explain the role of this passive moment in the will. In that section of *Summa*, however, as Aquinas searched for the suitable word for this idea, "the context did not demand or favour a thoroughgoing treatment, and the doctrine was never developed beyond an inchoate stage."[25] But how can Crowe say that the idea was coming to the centre of Aquinas's thought and yet was at an inchoate stage?

A useful contrast, perhaps, could be found in St Francis de Sales's *Treatise on the Love of God*.[26] Crowe refers to St Francis in "Complacency and Concern,"[27] and Francis clearly distinguishes two moments of love that form a single whole.[28] Early in book 1, St Francis de Sales says: "The complacency and the movement towards, or effusion of the will upon, the thing beloved is properly speaking love; yet in such sort that the complacency is but the beginning of love, and the movement or effusion of the heart which ensues is the true essential love, so that the one and the other may truly be named love, but in a different sense: for as the dawning of the day may be termed day, so this first complacency of the heart in the thing beloved may be called love because it is the first feeling of love."[29] According to de Sales, both complacency and the subsequent "movement towards" the beloved are properly called love. One is the beginning, the other is the completion. Aquinas leaves the discussion of complacency in an inchoate stage because he does not relate it explicitly to love as a tendency. The same cannot be said of St Francis de Sales's discussion.

Given the influence of Francis de Sales on Jean-Pierre de Caussade, SJ, it is interesting that Crowe also draws attention to de Caussade. According to Crowe, the best avenue of all for approaching the Thomist idea of *complacentia boni* may be found "in Jean-Pierre de Caussade's *abandon* to divine providence."[30] Self-abandonment (abandon) to divine providence "is, in its primary sense, an acceptance of the will of God, a submission to it."[31] De Caussade's prime example is Mary's response to the angel: "Let it be to me according to your word" (*The Holy Bible*, revised standard version, Catholic edition, hereafter cited as RSV, Luke 1:38).

This doctrine of self-abandonment rests on the belief that everything that happens in the world is willed by God or at least allowed by God. In so far as "in all things God works for the good of those who love him" (Romans 8:28), all that God commands or allows is somehow working for our happiness. Part of our mission is to accept what God allows to happen to us. Of course, such acceptance of "the concrete events of history"[32] is not easy and requires effort. But the "loving abandonment"[33] eventually elicited can be seen as a passive conforming to what is. Crowe thinks that this ability to accept God's will is a dimension of our affective life. He, therefore, disagrees with all those who think of the basic act of the human will as merely an impulse, a tendency towards union, an attraction.

Crowe is partly responding to the Jesuit Pierre Rousselot (1878–1915). According to Crowe, Rousselot, in 1908, "raised an agitation that has not yet subsided by setting up a dichotomy between what he called the physical and the ecstatic concepts of love."[34] The distinction between these two loves has to do with whether there is any thought of the self in the moment of love. In the 1930s, following a similar distinction, the Swedish Lutheran bishop Anders Nygren published a two-part study of love, *Agape and Eros*.[35]

Crowe discusses Nygren at greater length in chapter 5 of *Three Thomist Studies* and sees a certain parallel between Nygren's interpretation of the Christian views of Eros and the common scholastic notions of love. Within scholastic circles Crowe thought that the "dominant notion of voluntary activity has taken the will as an appetitive faculty whose essential act is an inclination manifested in tendency: the will regards an end, and its activity is process towards that end."[36] This common scholastic understanding of love, as an "inclination manifesting itself in a tendency"[37] towards the good, corresponds in some significant way, he thinks, with what Nygren presents as the historical understanding of Eros as a love concerned with what one does not yet have. Eros is our basic, self-seeking act of love, in contrast to God's basic act of self-giving love, *agape*, Nygren claims.

Crowe, however, criticizes the dominant scholastic view of human love as a "process towards"[38] or as an inclination manifesting itself in a tendency. He mentions several texts taken from one of the major commentators on Aquinas, John of St Thomas (1589–1644), that express the scholastic view of love he is trying to resist. "The intellect," John of St Thomas writes, "draws the object to itself ... but desire is allured and drawn by the object, and thus its object is its attractive force."[39] In this view, objects are received by human beings through *the intellect*. We go out to the object, in the way of motion, through *the will*. Crowe does not want to deny that the will's love is the principle of tending towards the good, but he thinks that St Thomas's teaching and his own verification of this teaching in his experience of love give a more complex account of voluntary activity.

Around the same time that Nygren wrote his first part of *Agape and Eros*, the French Dominican Henri-Dominique Simonin argued that St Thomas Aquinas's later position viewed love "not so much as a term giving tranquility as a movement whose cause is a form received in intellect and whose act is variously described as *consonantia, inclinatio, proportio*."[40] Aquinas's thinking, therefore, underwent a development away from the view of love as a form in the will to "the view that will's nature is to tend to a term."[41] Crowe, however, "holds that there is a certain exaggeration in Simonin's thesis."[42] According to Crowe,

Simonin fails to recognize that "the idea of love as a completion and lulling ('apaisement') of the will has not disappeared in the later works of St. Thomas, nor indeed has that of formation. Desire is tendency and movement, but love, like delight, implies presence already of the good and hence a state of rest."[43] In other words, love as rest and love as tendency need to be accounted for in Aquinas's mature writings.

More recently, Michael Sherwin has argued that between the *Commentary on the Sentences* and the second part of the *Summa Theologiae*, Aquinas replaced "the language of form with the language of *complacentia*."[44] While Sherwin acknowledges Crowe's important emphasis on *complacentia*, he criticizes his basic conclusion: "The synthesis Crowe seeks between receptive and active aspects of love (between 'complacency' and 'concern') are already present in Aquinas."[45] Sherwin thought that Crowe himself failed "to recognize the primary meaning of *inclinatio* in Aquinas. Like H.-D. Simonin and Pierre Rousselot, Crowe reads *inclinatio* as primarily signifying a motion or impulse. For Aquinas, however, *inclinatio*, primarily signifies a *principle* of motion. It is the appetitive orientation of the appetite toward its object."[46] In terms of *inclinatio*, Sherwin raises a real question about interpreting Aquinas. Are we meant to identify *complacentia* and *inclinatio*? Crowe does not think so.

Crowe, however, raises a real and slightly different question: can we speak of love not so much as the principle of motion but rather in its original moment of spiration in the will? The root sense of complacency in Aquinas, Crowe maintains, "indicates that will, before being the faculty of appetite, of process to a term, is the faculty of affective consent, of acceptance of what is good, of concord with the universe of being, and that the basic act of will is to be understood only if it is regarded not as an impulse to a term, or even the principle of process to a term qua principle, but simply as itself a term."[47] Prior to love being a principle of our tending towards the good, Crowe is saying, it is itself the end-point of a process that begins in the senses and the intellect. In general, he writes, "willing basically is the end of a process, a quiescence; only secondarily is it the initiation of another process."[48] Complacency, according to Crowe's reading of Aquinas, is the affective completion of a process of receiving reality.

Crowe denies that the intellect simply takes in what is, and the will then goes out to what is. There is an affective dimension to both our reception of being and our moving towards the good. Before love can be a principle of tending towards a good that *is not yet*, there must be a more passive moment of reception in the will regarding *what already is*. This is Crowe's hypothesis about the way in which Aquinas envisages the will's basic act of love.

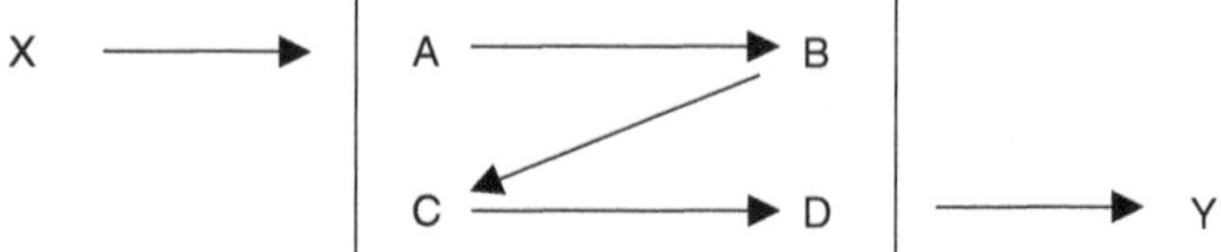

Figure 3 Diagram for understanding the act of complacent love
Source: Frederick E. Crowe, *Three Thomist Studies*, 90.

Crowe has a diagram to illustrate what he is saying about the way that an act of will can be the end of a process (see figure 3). The diagram is adapted from the diagram that Bernard Lonergan used in his course on grace.

The key letter in the diagram is *B*. It represents both the act of complacent love and the passive act of willing the end (*velle finem*). *B* is first of all a passive act that depends on *A*. *A* is "the judgement on the good as end, specifying the act of willing the end."[49] The two vertical lines distinguish the realms of human intellect and will. *X* stands for "the influence of the sensible world"[50] on the human powers of intellect and will.[51]

On the far side of the diagram, *Y* stands for our subsequent activity in the world. That activity flows from taking counsel about what to do (*C*) and coming to a decision (*D*). The diagonal line from *B* to *C* shows the influence of the willing of the end on our intellectual search for the means to that end. "D," Crowe writes, "is the election of some means to the end, the act in which will is *mota et movens* [moved and moving], reducing itself from potency to act."[52]

In point of fact, therefore, Crowe wants to say that *B* in the diagram is both the act of complacent love and the act of concerned love. But how does *B* go from being an affective complacency to being a principle of taking counsel (alone or from others) for a future action? Is there a change on the side of the will between what *we* could call *B1* (the passive moment of complacent acceptance) and *B2* (love as principle of motion)? Or is Sherwin right in saying that the one act of love is both passive and active? In other words, are we calling *concern* this one unchanging act of love when something extrinsic to *B* takes place? In this case, the taking counsel for the means would extrinsically give a new name to *B* without any change happening to the will. God does not change, for example, when he begins to be called *Creator*. He can be called Creator because of some change extrinsic to him, namely, creation having taken place.

Crowe does not think that the shift of will between what I have called *B1* and *B2* is merely an extrinsic denomination. He insists that a further judgment takes place beyond the initial *A* judgment of the intellect.

This "further judgment makes us aware that the good which is not yet can be effected through our own efforts and by appropriate means, and then the will responds with the first indeterminate *intentio finis* [intention of the end]."[53] In other words, through further judgments new aspects of the object emerge.[54] These new judgments account for shifts in the will from being complacent to being concerned. But where is the judgment to be placed in the diagram that explains how *B* changes? It is hard to say, and Crowe himself did not think that these articles of his were the final word on the transition between complacency and concern.[55]

Maybe this lack of integration in the diagram is fitting, given Crowe's interpretation of Aquinas's own position. Crowe admits that if his "tentative position on the historical side is correct, St. Thomas never really integrated these two modes of love with one another, or brought them together in sharp confrontation, or employed them as a scheme in the systematic articulation of his works."[56] Like Aquinas in his lack of integration of these two ideas on love, Crowe distinguishes complacency and concern but leaves questions unanswered in his diagram about where we should place the further judgment that gives rise to concern.

In this book on Crowe's pneumatology, it is not necessary to settle these disputes about Aquinas's own position. It is not necessary even to follow Crowe in his fascinating and complex argument for his interpretation of Aquinas. It would require another book, I think, to do justice to his position on these two roles of love: complacency and concern. What is fundamental, however, is to grasp Crowe's own acceptance of two distinct roles of love.

Crowe's article "Complacency and Concern" tries to show how his distinction between the two roles of love is a "recurrent duality"[57] in Aquinas and implicitly underlies many other questions in his mature writings. One of those questions is Aquinas's view of the mode of the Holy Spirit's procession. Crowe argues that the passive role of love, love as complacency, is the best analogy for the way in which the Holy Spirit can be understood to be proceeding Love in God.

Application of Complacency to the Doctrine of the Holy Spirit

There is one text in Aquinas's treatise on the Trinity in the *Summa Theologiae* that is especially important for Crowe's thesis as it applies to the procession of the Holy Spirit. In *Summa Theologiae*, part I, question 37, article 1, in trying to explain how love is proper to the Holy Spirit, Aquinas speaks of a "certain impression ... of the thing loved in the affection of the one who loves."[58] Instead of speaking of love as an impulse towards the loved object, Aquinas uses the language of *impression*, or imprint, when he is talking about the Holy Spirit. Crowe thinks we can interpret this impression of love as *complacentia*.

Where else is love described as an impression? In *Summa Theologiae*, part I-II, question 28, article 2, Aquinas says that the loved thing (*amatum*) is impressed in the affections of the lover (*amans*) "through a certain complacency."[59] The complacency is an impression in the will. But this is almost exactly how Aquinas spoke about the proceeding love that serves as the psychological analogy for the Holy Spirit's procession. The two texts are worth looking at side by side (table 1).

While Aquinas does not explicitly use the word *complacency* when he speaks of the impression of love in *Summa Theologiae*, part I, question 37, Crowe thinks that the questions on the Holy Spirit in the Prima pars should be read in light of his teaching on *complacentia* in the Prima secundae. What Crowe finds so fascinating is that the analogue for the Holy Spirit in question 37 is not love as a tendency towards what is not yet. The love that is used as an analogy for the Holy Spirit is an impression that is produced in the lover from an intellectually conceived word.

According to Aquinas, love must "proceed from a word. For we do not love something except inasmuch as we apprehend it by a conception of the mind."[60] This conception of the mind is an inner word, a *verbum*. "There is no procession of love," Aquinas argues, "except as following upon [*in ordine ad*] the procession of a word."[61] While human love normally originates from a word of the mind, the word itself "has a principle from which it proceeds."[62] An inner word is spoken on the basis of understanding, as "a conception of the thing understood" that "proceeds from knowledge [*notitia*] of the thing."[63] Later on in the *Summa*, in explaining how the image of the Trinity is found in the human

Table 1 Parallel discussions of love as an impression in the will

Language	*Summa Theologiae*, I, q. 37, art. 1	*Summa Theologiae*, I-II, q. 28, art. 2
Latin	Ita ex hoc quod aliquis rem aliquam amat, provenit quaedam *impressio*, ut ita loquor, rei amatae *in affectu amantis*, secundum quam amatum dicitur esse in amante.	Amatum continetur in amante, inquantum est *impressum in affectu eius per quandam complacentia*.
English	So when anyone loves an object, a certain impression results, so to speak, of the thing loved in the affection of the lover; by reason of which the object loved is said to be in the lover.	The loved object is contained in the one who loved inasmuch as there is an impression in his affection by a kind of complacency.

soul, Aquinas writes: "The image of the Trinity, first and principally, is to be found in the acts of the soul, that is, inasmuch as from our knowledge [*notitia*], we form an internal word by thinking; and from this word, we break forth into love."[64] Thus, by means of a psychological analogy, Aquinas illustrates the Catholic belief that the Holy Spirit proceeds from the Father and the Son. The Holy Spirit is eternally the Love that proceeds from the Speaker (*Dicens*) and the Word spoken.[65]

In this human analogy Crowe thinks that love proceeds from an inner word as a term. Think back to the line from *A* to *B* in the diagram, figure 3. Love as proceeding from an inner word brings a process of receiving reality to a close. Crowe thinks that complacency especially captures this aspect of love. Complacency, as he understands it, is a response to an inner word, a judgment of what is. "It is under this aspect," Crowe writes, "that love corresponds to and provides an analogy for the procession of the Holy Spirit in the Trinity, where the Third Person is a term bringing the divine processions to a close and is certainly not a Love for an object good to-be-made, to-be-done, to-be-attained, or to-be in any way that involves a not-yet."[66] The Holy Spirit does not exist only inasmuch as creation takes place. The Holy Spirit eternally is, whether or not the Trinity creates.

This completeness of the inner Trinitarian life does not mean, however, that creation is not in some way related to the Holy Spirit. Aquinas will even say, "The Father and the Son love each other *and us* by the Holy Spirit or Love proceeding."[67] According to Aquinas, the Son and the Holy Spirit have an eternal *respectus* (relation) to creation. "It is not true," Aquinas writes, "that all names implying a relation of God to creatures are said from time."[68] The Son, the Word, is "expressive not only of the Father, but also all creatures."[69] Aquinas insists that the name, Word, "principally is imposed to signify a relation to the Speaker, but consequently it signifies a relation to creatures, insofar as God, by understanding himself, understands every creature."[70] For Aquinas, there is one eternal Word. In that one Word which the Father begets, "the Father speaks himself and every creature, inasmuch as the begotten Word sufficiently represents the Father and every creature."[71] Pivoting on this understanding of the Word's relation to creation, Aquinas argues that in God there is only one proceeding Love. Just as the Father speaks himself and every creature in the Word, so "he loves himself and every creature by the Holy Spirit, inasmuch as the Spirit proceeds as love of the first goodness."[72] In other words, there is a way in which the Holy Spirit eternally is notionally related "to any possible world, but it is conceived subsequent to the internal constitution of the Trinity."[73] In the Holy Spirit the Father has complacency not only in contemplating the Son but also in contemplating all that can *possibly* be made through the Word.

Even if one grants Crowe the Thomistic basis for his way of explaining the procession of the Holy Spirit as complacent proceeding love, what does one do with the texts in Aquinas where the Holy Spirit is spoken about as a tendency, an impulse towards the loved thing? Crowe has a way of putting these texts to work for his own theory. He refers us back to the ways in which Aquinas first introduces the procession of the Holy Spirit in *Summa Theologiae*, part I, question 27, article 4.[74] Aquinas speaks of the procession of love first in terms of an "inclination." Unlike the procession of the intellect, the procession of the will does not bring forth a likeness. Instead, the procession of the will is better conceived as having the aspect of "impelling and moving." Since, in general, "spirit is named from a certain vital motion and impulse," the proceeding Love in God should be called Spirit. Aquinas explains how "from love someone is said to be moved or impelled to do something."[75]

In other words, Crowe maintains, love as an inclination manifesting itself in tendency is often used by Aquinas to explain the procession of the Holy Spirit. At the same time, Aquinas also speaks about the Holy Spirit's procession in language that harmonizes with complacent love. Crowe therefore asks, "Which of the two is to be retained and exploited in the Trinitarian analogy?"[76] He wants to hold onto the psychological analogy. He wants to keep analogies of love for the procession of the Holy Spirit. Crowe finds two analogies in Aquinas. His answer to his own question is unequivocal: "Clearly, the Holy Spirit is to be conceived on the analogy of the *complacentia boni*."[77] In fact, in 1959, Crowe wants us to give up using love as tendency to explain the Holy Spirit's procession. "Nor is there any loss," he writes, "to Trinitarian theory through discarding the notion of love as tendency."[78]

To those who object that he is discarding the very analogy used frequently by Aquinas, Crowe responds by explaining that "St. Thomas felt obliged to assign a scholastic sense to the word 'Spirit' and did so in terms of tendency, but we can drop that attempt today and so avoid the incongruity of comparing the Holy Spirit with an impulse *ad aliquid faciendum* [for doing something]."[79] Why does Crowe think that it is incongruous to compare the Holy Spirit to an impulse to do something? He is afraid that such an analogy suggests that the Holy Spirit's existence is explained by his relation to creation. Crowe thinks that we, basing ourselves on the revelation of the Trinity, "can conceive divine Understanding uttering an eternal Word and the Word issuing in eternal Love; and this proceeding Love, *amor notionalis* [notional love], is entirely contained within the Trinity, is a term of the internal processions, and is not to be explained by relation to the created universe."[80] What is distinctive about the Holy Spirit's procession? What is truly proper to the Holy Spirit? In the Thomist psychological analogy, Crowe insists, "the distinctive character of Love here is its rational procession from the Word."[81]

In God there is only one Word. In the eternal begetting of the Word "the Father speaks himself and every creature."[82] The eternal Word of the Father "expresses and manifests even non-beings,"[83] that is, beings that will not be created but possibly could be made. According to Aquinas, however, the Word proceeds primarily as expressive of the Father and "quasi-secondarily"[84] as expressive of creatures. In like manner, the Holy Spirit proceeds primarily as the Love that flowers forth from the Father speaking the Son and "quasi-secondarily"[85] as a Love of creatures that are expressed in the Word.

While there is one inner Word in God, analogous inner words are multiplied in us. We form judgments about both what is and what ideally could be. Following upon these judgments – judgments of actual existence or of possible existence – Crowe thinks that an act of complacency is spirated. But the primary meaning of complacency for Crowe is an affective response to an affirmation of actual being. It is precisely in its clear passive dependence on a judgment of being, an inner word, without any reference to action, that complacency serves as an excellent analogy for the Holy Spirit's eternal procession from the Word.

Conclusion

Before writing his long article "Complacency and Concern in the Thought of St Thomas,"[86] Frederick Crowe was interested in the Holy Spirit's eternal procession as an intelligible emanation. The emanation of the Son and the Holy Spirit had served as the focus of his Trinitarian theology teaching in Toronto during the 1950s and was the aspect of Lonergan's course that had grabbed his attention at the time of his own theology studies.[87] During the years in which he worked out his theory of complacent love (1954–9) Crowe had begun to make the question of the mode of the Holy Spirit's procession his own. The Holy Spirit's *proprium*, his eternal personal "character," is proceeding complacent Love. This analogy of an affective response in the will to *what is* ensures that the Holy Spirit's eternal existence depends on the utterance of the Father's Word and not on what God actually creates.

3 Basil Helps to Extend the Search into the Economy of Salvation

If we have anything intelligent to say in our final chapter on the Trinity in the world, anything relevant, anything worthwhile, it will be due to this beginning made by Basil.

Frederick Crowe, The Doctrine of the Most Holy Trinity

In letter 236, St Basil of Caesarea writes about the need to distinguish the three divine persons, "for, if we do not consider the particular properties [*charaktêras*] of each ..., but merely confess God (in each) on the ground of the common essence, *it will be quite impossible to give a sound exposition of faith.*"[1] Crowe places great importance on this quotation from St Basil. "I hope," he tells his theology students, "this statement of Basil's will strike a spark in the reader; at least may he not set it down as a trifle within the range of any child's intelligence."[2] Crowe then refers to the personal impact of this passage on his own mind: "For my part, I do not know of any passage in the fathers that I read with such a moving sense of assisting at a great evolution in the understanding of our faith."[3] He will even speak of "this beginning made by Basil" as "the acorn from which our trinitarian treatise has grown."[4]

The very last line of Crowe's 1965–6 course notes reads: "Once you commit yourself to the principle of St. Basil, you cannot consistently abandon it till you have applied it to the whole range of human history and human institutions that are affected by the entry into the world of Father, Son, and Holy Spirit."[5] In other words, Crowe came to think that one could extend Basil's search for the character of each divine person from a consideration of the eternal mystery of the Trinity to the character of each divine person in the economy of salvation.

When Crowe taught the Trinity course in 1961–2, he wrote a short set of thirty-page notes for his students, and there is no focus on Basil's principle in them. When Crowe taught the Trinity class in 1965–6, he wrote his monumental *Doctrine of the Most Holy Trinity*. This chapter studies *The Doctrine of the Most Holy Trinity* to show how Basil's principle has now become Crowe's. I look first at how his 1965–6 notes studied more deeply the eternal personal properties of each of the Three, and second at how he applied this principle to the way in which each of the Three is present in the world. If Crowe's 1959 article "Complacency and Concern" is a search for the eternal *proprium* of the Holy Spirit, Crowe's final chapter of *The Doctrine of the Most Holy Trinity* is his search for the *proprium* of the Holy Spirit in the world.

Background to Crowe's 1965–6 *Doctrine of the Most Holy Trinity*

The Doctrine of the Most Holy Trinity has two parts: a *via analytica* and a *via synthetica*.[6] In the first part (chapters 1–5) Crowe analyses the historical development of Trinitarian doctrine from the testimony of the Scriptures to the account of the Trinitarian processions in terms of a psychological analogy. The idea of dividing the first part of the treatise into five chapters was taken from Lonergan's fifth thesis of the *Pars dogmatica* in which he explains the order of the *via analytica* in almost exactly the terms used by Crowe: "Thus, we proceeded historically from the missions of the divine persons to their consubstantiality, thence to their relative properties, to the procession of the Holy Spirit from both Father and Son, and finally to the psychological analogy in St. Augustine."[7]

Crowe's five historical chapters match neatly Lonergan's description of the analytic part of Trinitarian theology. The analytic part of Crowe's treatise begins with what was first for us – the sending of the Son and Spirit as recounted in the Scriptures. That same part concludes with what is first in itself – the divine nature as rational and giving rise to intelligible processions of Word (Son) and Love (Holy Spirit). Table 2 compares Lonergan's description of the way of analysis and Crowe's first five chapters.

In contrast to the *via analytica*, Crowe's synthetic way reverses the order of ideas. The synthetic or systematic view begins with what is first in itself (*prius quoad se*), God's inner life understood through the psychological analogy, and ends with what is first for us (*prius quoad nos*), the missions of Son and Spirit. Starting with the principle of a dynamically understood divine nature, Crowe's synthetic part (chapters 6–8) offers a systematic understanding of Trinitarian doctrine by means of one analogy, *per modum unius* (*by means of a single principle*).[8] Thus, the second half of Crowe's treatise, corresponding to Lonergan's Pars systematica, can be seen in table 3.

Table 2 A comparison of Lonergan's *via analytica* and the first five chapters of Crowe's *Doctrine of the Most Holy Trinity*

Lonergan's description of the *via analytica*	Crowe's principal divisions of part 1, "Development of Trinitarian Dogma: Analytic Process of History"
"We proceeded historically from": Revelation of the missions of *the divine persons*	Chap. 1: From Old Testament Yahweh to New Testament *Father, Son, and Holy Spirit*
To their *consubstantiality*	Chap. 2: Father, Son, and Holy Spirit as *consubstantial*
Thence to their *relative* properties	Chap. 3: One God in three persons distinguished by mutual *relations*
To the *procession* of the Holy Spirit from Father and Son	Chap. 4: Relations by origin – *processions* in God
And finally to the psychological analogy in St Augustine	Chap. 5: The psychological analogy – the divine nature such as to be *Dicens, Verbum,* and *Amor* (Speaker, Word, and Love)

Table 3 Division of Part 2 of Crowe's *Doctrine of the Most Holy Trinity*

Part 2	Systematic overview: *omnia per modum unius*
Chap. 6	Divine nature as rational; processions; relations; persons in God
Chap. 7	The three divine persons in the world – general structures
Chap. 8	The "trinification" of the human world

Notice how the four topics covered in chapter 6 (Divine nature as rational; processions; relations; persons in God) are the same four topics that are covered in chapters 2–5. In chapter 6, however, those topics are discussed in the inverse order. In chapter 2 Crowe's historical analysis showed how the Church moved from reflecting on God sending the Son and Spirit to considering the idea that the Father, Son, and Spirit are consubstantial persons. In chapters 3–5 Crowe follows the history of how the Church developed the idea of these persons being distinguished according to mutual relations, of these relations being founded on eternal processions within God, and finally of these processions being grounded on a dynamically conceived "rational" divine nature.

Having gone through his long analysis of history, Crowe is able to discuss these same ideas more quickly from the systematic prospective. Chapter 6 begins with a consideration of the divine nature as rational, on the basis of which we can understand the existence of divine processions. Then, on the basis of divine processions, we can understand the idea of real subsisting relations. From relations, we can form a better understanding of divine persons. In other words, Crowe inverts and condenses the materials of chapters 2–5 into a single chapter.

Crowe can cover all this material in one chapter of less than twenty pages because he has the four chapters (150 pages in the Latin text) of Lonergan's *De Deo Trino: Pars systematica* to which he can refer his students for the same material. He encouraged them to spend as much time as possible with that work and to view his own chapter 6 as a means of helping them "over a few hurdles" in Lonergan's work.[9]

The biggest reason for Crowe's compromise on the length of chapter 6 was "simply [his] practical recognition of what can be done in a seminary course on the Trinity today."[10] By 1965 Crowe thought that with the majority of his students he could not "go deeply into the theory of the Trinity."[11] He was up against a "real practical problem"[12] of what the majority of his students were interested in and could handle. Crowe realized that the psychological analogy could only be properly understood after "prolonged reflection."[13] He did not think that his own chapter 6 was sufficient to provide them with such understanding, and he was worried that an imperfect understanding would yield bad results in their grasp of how the Three are present in the world. Given the restraints of his seminary course at Regis College, however, Crowe did not think he could spend any more time on theoretical questions dealing with God in himself.

In the final two chapters of *The Doctrine of the Most Holy Trinity*, Crowe moves from what is first in itself (God's eternal life) to what is first for us, God's presence in the world. Chapter 7 of *The Doctrine* deals with what must be true about God's inner life for divine persons to be present in the world. His final chapter deals with the human need for the Three to be in the world. Unlike Lonergan, however, who spent only a quarter of his systematic part on the divine missions, Crowe spends 60 per cent of his systematic view on the way that the Father, Son, and Holy Spirit are in the world.

Crowe did not think he was alone in emphasizing the divine missions. Speaking of various advances in the twentieth century in Catholic Trinitarian theology, Crowe cites Lonergan's work on consciousness as an example of a specific development. "Likewise," he adds, "in the study of the divine missions, a great deal of work has been done, with broad theories developed to conceive the whole supernatural area in synthesis, and this we shall take up in chapter seven."[14] He thought that his treatment of this question was thus part of a larger movement within twentieth-century Catholic Trinitarian theology. He writes: "I should say that the chief effort, at least in extension if not in intension, has been in the field of practical application; application, first of all, to the mystic life (this effort goes back to the middle ages); application, then in much more everyday matters, so that we have studies or articles on the Trinity in relation to every angle of life, fraternal charity, morality, the sacraments, etc.; this we shall see in chapter eight."[15] Crowe, unfortunately, does not extend his treatment of the divine missions to all these everyday matters. In a way, he takes a short cut.

He concludes *The Doctrine of the Most Holy Trinity* by showing how all of theology could be restructured according to a Trinitarian framework. Crowe proposes that all the materials of theology could be attached to treatises on the "individual persons of the Trinity."[16] He links the sacramental and institutional aspects of our faith with the established and traditional study of the incarnate Word, *de Verbo Incarnato*. He links, in contrast, "the charismatic and individual in the church"[17] – grace, prayer, the gifts of the Holy Spirit, new movements in the Church – with a proposed new treatise: *de Spiritu dato* (on the given Spirit). Finally, Crowe sketches the way in which "everything that comes under the heading of the eschatological"[18] can be subsumed under a new treatise on the hoped-for Father (*de Patre sperato*). Insofar as all of the Christian life is studied in these areas of theology, Crowe offers his students a general way of relating everyday life to the presence of the three divine persons in the world.

Conceiving the Personal Properties of the Three in the Godhead as Never Before

Knowledge of the psychological analogy for the Trinity was not something Crowe thought his students could have simply by reading books, even Lonergan's books. The psychological analogy for the Trinity had to be experienced, understood, and verified in a personal way by each student. Only by grasping for oneself and in oneself what it means to speak an inner word and to love on the basis of that word does one properly understand what Augustine, Aquinas, and Lonergan were talking about in their psychological analogies.

Crowe thus begins the systematic overview by helping us locate the relevant psychological acts in our consciousness that provide the analogies for the three persons of the Trinity (chap. 6, sec. 1.1). Once he explains what we mean by intelligible emanation of a word from an act of understanding (sec. 1.2) and of love from that word (sec. 1.3), he tries to help the students grasp that the term of each procession is *God* (sec. 1.4). He does this by a series of analogies that assist someone in approaching an infinite limit. At stake in these limit examples is the question of divine simplicity. Divine simplicity means that all that is in God is God. The psychological analogy enables one to understand the way in which the Word, Speaker, and Love are distinct from one another. But this analogy also helps one to grasp how the three divine persons are so intelligibly related and united that their distinction does not violate the divine simplicity.

When Crowe turns to the question of how the eternal *Amor* (Love) proceeding in God is also God, he mentions Lonergan's argument and the Thomist argument.[19] Right before these references he speaks of "our analogy." Here, "in the context of our analogy," is his argument for why proceeding Love in God is God:

> When intellect knows itself, it is present to itself in a similitude of itself, and in God this "similitude" is God. Now in loving, the one loved is also present in the will by dynamic presence, or, as I would prefer to say, by affective presence. That is, the *amari* or being loved of the one loved and the *amare* or loving of the lover are one; as the *amatus* [one loved] is integral to the *amari* [being loved], so he is to the *amare* [loving]. Well, then, in God's love of the infinite goodness that he is, God is present to self in his own love of self, and this affective presence is not just affective presence; it is God.[20]

Note Crowe's use of the first person here. He is aware, I think, of the uniqueness of his position on complacency. He also prefers the words *affective presence*. Crowe has slightly developed his language since 1959, but he is still thinking about this divine proceeding love as complacent love. Nevertheless, his preference for the phrase *affective presence* is the fruit of his "Complacency" studies through which he more profoundly appropriated "our power for harmonious accord with the universe."[21]

Crowe has developed not only his thinking about the Holy Spirit but also his understanding of the procession of the Son. He writes: "The uttered Word has a real orientation to Love; the will is a rational appetite, it embraces the good that is rationally affirmed and, by the same token, the rational affirmation looks towards the love that proceeds from it."[22] Crowe is trying to explain how the psychological analogy helps us understand the divine persons as real relations. The classic problem is that the name Holy Spirit does not seem to imply a relation to another, like the terms *Father* and *Son* imply. Through thinking of the Son and the Spirit according to their names, Word and Love, Crowe suggests that their mutual implication of one another is clearer. As a rational affirmation looks forward to its affective complement, so the eternal Word is eternally oriented towards the Love that proceeds from himself. Thus, Crowe uses this orientation in our knowing and loving to explain the relation of the Word and the Spirit to each other: "The orientation is real, the procession is real, hence the principle and term are really related to one another, so that, when Love proceeds eternally in God, there is a real relation between this proceeding Love on one side and, on the other, the Word and the One uttering the Word who together are the principle of proceeding Love."[23] Note in this quotation how Crowe distinguishes the One uttering the Word, the Word, and the proceeding Love. He wants there to be a kind of intelligible implication of the other two persons in the proper name of each divine person.

It is important to recognize that the analogy on which he relies does not appeal to divine attributes absolutely considered. Crowe insists that the Holy Spirit is proceeding Love and not simply love. The absolutely considered divine attributes, for example, love or truth, are not immediately relevant for his Trinitarian theory. This distinction between essential names and proper or notional names is especially important for Crowe's thinking about the Father.

Crowe insists on speaking of the Father as the One uttering the Word. He never says that the Father is analogous to the act of understanding absolutely considered. To understand (*intelligere*) is common to all three persons. Truth (*veritas*), in its absolute aspect, is common to all three persons. Love (*amor*), absolutely considered, is common to all three persons. The divine persons share the same essence, and that essence is understanding itself, truth itself, love itself. But the Father alone is the "*Intelligere dicens Verbum*"[24] (Understanding speaking a Word). The Son alone is the "*Veritas dicta*"[25] (Truth spoken). The Spirit alone is "*Amor procedens spiratus*"[26] (spirated proceeding Love). God the Father is analogous to an act of understanding, not absolutely considered but as an act of understanding that generates a true word. God the Son is analogous to an act that expresses that understanding. God the Holy Spirit is analogous to the basic act of love grounded on the expression of God's infinite understanding.

Crowe has argued that we have intelligent acts like these within our conscious life. "But," he writes, "the three acts in us are not just three acts, they are joined to one another by rationality, by processions, by origins; the *intelligere* is *intelligere dicens verbum*, the *verbum* is *veritas dicta*, the *amor* is *amor procedens*."[27] In this section of his treatise Crowe uses the unity of these three analogous acts in us for ordering our ideas about God. Crowe is placing first the ideas that are required to understand other ideas. In this case, processions are needed to understand how there can be relations in God.

On the basis of his articulation of the psychological analogy Crowe has worked out distinct properties for each of the three divine persons.

The persons are distinguished by these relative properties. Crowe is thus using the psychological analogy to understand more fully the real relations in the Trinity. He is seeking to answer the question that Basil posed: What truly distinguishes the divine persons?

Moving Away from the Term Spiration

Crowe explores the relations that follow upon the two divine processions when they are "understood according to the likeness of the intelligible emanations of a word from a speaker and love from both."[28] From the relations he studies the persons in themselves and then as they are in the world. Crowe, however, has three difficulties with using the Thomistic terminology for relations in God. "Traditionally," he writes, "these relations are called: paternity and filiation (the mutual relation of Father and Son), and active and passive spiration (the mutual relation of Father and Son on one side, and Holy Spirit on the other)."[29] Since Crowe is seeking to understand these relations by starting with the eternal processions, he finds the terms *paternity, filiation*, and *spiration* "quite awkward."[30] For Crowe, they are non-psychological terms; paternity does not seem to suggest a way in which the first person can be related to the second and third persons by one relation; and they do not indicate how the Word as a real relation can be related simultaneously to the first and third persons.

According to Crowe, the first difficulty with the traditional terms stems from their "emerging in the analytic sequence as 'defensive' doctrine."[31] The doctrine of relations, he explains in chapter 3, developed as the Church tried to defend the distinction of three persons in God.[32] The focus at the time, however, was not on "conscious intellectual activity."[33] Since Crowe wants to understand the whole Trinitarian doctrine by the analogy of "conscious intellectual activity," he finds the traditional names for relations difficult to wield.

Crowe has a second, more fundamental, difficulty with the traditional terms. *Paternity, filiation*, and *spiration* (active and passive) "do not indicate the ground in the first person for a relation to both the second and third persons."[34] *Paternity* expresses the Father's orientation to the Son. *Spiration* expresses his orientation to the Holy Spirit. Instead of thinking of the Father in relation to the Son and then subsequently in relation to the Spirit, Crowe wants a name for the Father that would explain how he can be related to the Son and the Spirit by one real relation. Crowe finds such a concept in the psychological analogy: "'Fatherhood' points only to the Son and not to the Spirit. But Understanding uttering a Word points to Love as well, for it is not coldly speculative understanding that is in question here, but an understanding of the divine goodness and beauty and harmony; so the Word that is uttered is not an abstract concept but the full expression of that goodness and beauty and harmony, a Word, therefore oriented towards Love."[35] In the texts of Aquinas Crowe has support for finding a ground in the psychological analogy for the relationship of the first person to the Son and the Spirit. "The Son is the Word," Aquinas noted, "but not just any word. He is a Word spirating Love" (*Summa Theologiae*, I, q. 43, art. 5, ad 2). In other words, in speaking the Word that brings forth Love, the Father is oriented not only to the Son but also to the Spirit. The terminology of *a Speaker of a Word* seems to express, in contrast to the traditional name of *paternity*, the grounds for the Father, the Speaker, being related to the Son and the Spirit.

The third awkwardness that Crowe finds in the traditional names of the four real relations – paternity, sonship (filiation), active spiration, and passive spiration – is closely related to the second awkwardness. "The traditional names," he writes, "do not indicate the unity of the ground of relationship in the second person to the first and third; filiation and active spiration convey two different ideas."[36] *Filiation* or *sonship* conveys the idea of one who comes forth, after the manner of an image, from another with the same nature as the one from whom he came forth. The Son is of the same nature as the Father and is his perfect image. *Filiation* is passive. *Active spiration* is the idea of the Son bringing forth a breath of love. These two ideas are supposed to be applied to the same divine person. When the second person is conceived as subsisting filiation, his being the principle of the Holy Spirit seems to be added on to what he is as the Son. Crowe is not at all denying the importance of the concept of eternal sonship. It played a vital role in the development of Trinitarian theology. "But," he adds, "if you conceive the second person as the uttered Word, *Veritas dicta*, you can understand this one characteristic as ground for a relation both to the One uttering the Word and [to] the Love that necessarily follows from such a Word."[37] Crowe believes that God has revealed himself as three eternal divine persons. The Holy Spirit, in this sense, is necessary to the inner life of God. Since Crowe believes that the Spirit proceeds eternally and without change from the Father and the Son (by what must be a kind of eternal necessity),[38] he likes the analogy of a truth spoken precisely because love will flow from that word by moral necessity.

Two points must be noted here. First, Crowe is alive to the potentially confusing aspect of traditional Thomistic Trinitarian theology in which there are *four* real relations and *three* subsisting real relations. Active spiration, according to Lonergan, does not constitute a subsisting person, as it is "not really distinct from paternity or from filiation."[39] Crowe wants to find a *characteristic* that conveys both the passive orientation that the Son has to the Father and the active orientation that the Son has to the Spirit. Second, Crowe finds in Lonergan's account of the psychological analogy the clue to this problem. The spoken Word exists as *from* the Speaker and *the source* of proceeding Love. Conceptually, the Word is related to the Father in one way and to the Spirit in another. But in actual fact the Word is related to the other two persons by one real ordering. According to the human analogy, "in the one word there is spoken a true good, which as true arises from the speaker and as good is ordered to the spiration of love."[40] The existence of the second person as Word cannot, therefore, be separated from the existence of the Spirit as Love. Like a speaker who speaks a concrete word to bring forth a loving response, so the Father's speaking of the Word necessarily brings forth the Holy Spirit too. A relation, according to Lonergan, is defined as "the order of one to another."[41] The psychological analogy helps us understand how there is a "single system of relations"[42] in the Trinity. In the concept of a spoken Word, the Son is simultaneously and really referred to the Father and the Spirit "by a single real relation."[43]

Crowe thinks that this account of the Word provides "a new answer to the question: How many real relations are there in God?"[44] He notes that the four relations mentioned by Aquinas are not the only answer given by medieval theologians. According to Crowe, John Duns Scotus taught that each divine person has a "real relation of similarity, equality, and identity towards the other two,"[45] resulting in at least eighteen real relations in God and possibly twenty-three (if the four relations of origin and a relation of "disparity of origin" are included).[46] On the basis on the psychological analogy, however, Crowe thinks that one can argue for only three real relations.

When one approaches the question of relations from the testimony of the Scriptures, the obvious place to start is with the terms *Father* and *Son*. Jesus of Nazareth expressed a unique relation that he had towards the Father: "No one knows the Son but the Father and no one knows the Father but the Son" (Matthew 11:27). What distinguishes the Father in God? He is the one who brings forth the Son. The Son is Son because of his unique relation to the Father. Crowe thinks, however, that once we move to the idea of an eternal generation of this Son *by way of intellect*, a deeper understanding can occur about his unique characteristic. Sonship is not necessarily the clearest way of conceiving his distinctiveness within God. In the prologue of his gospel, John called him the Word: "In the beginning was the Word, and the Word was with God, and the Word was God" (John 1:1).

The Father does not proceed. The Word proceeds from the Father and has another proceeding from him: the Holy Spirit. The Holy Spirit

does not have someone proceeding from him. Sonship, Crowe maintains, does not capture this uniqueness of the Word in the same clarity
as *uttered Truth* does. He is approaching Basil's question with what he
has learned from the psychological analogy. A better understanding of
real relations can be gained from the psychological analogy. In chapter 6
of *The Doctrine of the Most Holy Trinity* Crowe says: "It seems to me
simpler and more accurate to say there are simply three real relations
in God, one in each person towards the other two, the one ground of
relation determining the relation as one in each case despite the multiplication of terms."[47] According to Crowe, the eternal procession of
the Word, understood according to the likeness of an intelligible emanation, becomes the ground or foundation for understanding the real
relation that is the Word.

Not only does Crowe think that it is simpler and more accurate to
talk about *three* real relations, but also he thinks it is "more concrete. For
'paternity' is a kind of abstraction, regarding the ground of the Father's
relation to the Son, but prescinding from the ground of his relation to
the Spirit."[48] Lonergan taught him that science always heads towards
the understanding of the real, and the real is concrete. "Sciences,"
Crowe writes, "reach their perfection in application to the concrete."[49]
What is concrete in God? The three distinct persons. Crowe tells his
students: "You can speak of either three or four real relations in God
and be correct, for you can count four prescinding from aspects that are
one in the concrete, or count three if you take a more concrete view."[50]
Unfortunately, while he criticizes the traditional terminology of four
real relations, he could have spent more time developing and explaining, it seems to me, his more concrete view of the three real relations.

In the rest of chapter 6 of *The Doctrine of the Most Holy Trinity* Crowe
turns to questions of persons in God. In this way, he is trying to follow
the order of St Thomas Aquinas in the *Summa Theologiae*. Aquinas began
with processions in God (I, q. 27), next took up relations (I, q. 28), and
then moved to the divine persons in general (I, qq. 29–32). Crowe, after
treating "persons in God" (sec. 3.1), tries to enrich Aquinas's doctrine
with Lonergan's insights into what it means for a person to be a subject
(sec. 3.2) and how we can speak of intersubjectivity in God (sec. 3.2).

In section 3.1 of chapter 6 Crowe explains the origin of many different
ways to consider a divine person. First, he speaks about how the name
was introduced into Catholic thought by Tertullian. Next, Crowe takes
us through various proposed definitions of the word *person* in Augustine, Boethius, Richard of St Victor, and Thomas Aquinas. He characterizes this line of development as a *logical* consideration of *person*, with the
basic final definition being "subsistens distinctum in natura rationali"[51]

(a distinct subsistent in a rational nature). Crowe then explains how these various definitions were given metaphysical elaboration by "Scotus, Capreolus, and the renaissance scholastics" who sought "to explain the constitution of a person."[52] Out of these theories, debates arose regarding what really does constitute a person. From these and many other debates, Crowe suggests that "thinkers turned in the next stage to cognitional and psychological studies as more empirical than the metaphysical field."[53] But that trend, that turn towards the subject, he claims, "was copied in the fields of experimental and depth psychology and so the question of the person also came to be treated almost exclusively in psychological terms."[54] Crowe aptly notes that these modern approaches generated vast debates not unlike those of the earlier metaphysical theories. As philosophers turned to cognition and psychology to get behind and beyond the metaphysical debates, so, Crowe thinks, "the vogue is now to turn to more literary forms of thought, to the concrete interpersonal relationships familiar to us all, to artistic sketching and phenomenological description."[55] He does not think that any of the five approaches has to be rejected, including the logical and the metaphysical. Each approach has something to contribute and answers a different kind of question. All the approaches can be seen as part of a heuristic approach to articulating fully what a person is.

After his historical summary of the notion of person Crowe turns to the idea of "persons as subjects" (sec. 3.2). He gives a very brief survey of the history of the post-Kantian distinction between subject and object. What Crowe means by *subject* is "conscious person."[56] He then refers to various views of consciousness among contemporary Catholic and Protestant theologians. His preference is for Lonergan's account of consciousness: "internal experience, strictly understood, of oneself and one's acts."[57] Crowe then explains how this notion can be analogously applied to each of the three divine persons in the inner Trinitarian life.

In section 3.3 Crowe takes up his last issue in this chapter, "the Divine Persons and the Intersubjective." He notes that a divine person is only a subject "by intersubjectivity. He is distinct from the other persons in God only by relation to them, by being turned towards them; his being is being-towards-another."[58] This is a beautiful section in which Crowe uses his psychological analogy to talk about the joy of the Father and the Son in the Trinity. The Father's joy is in uttering his Word. Crowe compares it to the joy that we have in some great idea. The Son's joy is in being spoken by his Father. Crowe compares it to the joy we have in being able to formulate this great idea. Presumably, the Holy Spirit is their mutual joy.

At the end of chapter 6 Crowe has a fourth section, in which he summarizes in Latin the thesis of the chapter (sec. 4.1), states some remaining theoretical problems (sec. 4.2), and gives a bibliography (sec. 4.3). In his Latin summary he gives many useful definitions, including those of *intelligible emanation, subject,* and *consciousness.*

Crowe admits that chapter 6 is a compromise. In it he discusses from the systematic viewpoint what he had discussed in four chapters from the historical or analytic viewpoint ("three equal persons in God, of distinction of the persons by relations of origin, of origin by the twofold procession of Word and Love").[59] But he is not sure what else he can do in the current situation of training in which seminaries allot only one course to the Trinity. Nevertheless, Crowe's understanding of only three real relations in God was a conscious effort to help his students in 1965 to answer for themselves Basil's question, What distinguishes the three divine persons from each other?

Discerning the Personal Properties of the Three in the World

Crowe began his 1965 Trinitarian treatise by discussing in chapter 1 the economic Trinity as manifested in the scriptural accounts of the sending of the Son and the Spirit. The move in chapter 2 occurs from what is first for us (the experience of the incarnate Son and the experience of the Holy Spirit at Pentecost) to what is first in itself, the consubstantiality of the Three. This discussion of the eternal life of the Trinity continues in chapters 3–5 and into chapter 6. Finally, in chapters 7 and 8 Crowe returns to the Trinitarian persons in the economy of salvation, but he does so with all the understanding that has been made possible by the *via analytica* and the *via synthetica.* These two final chapters are not short and show Crowe's great interest in this question of the Trinity in the world.

Chapter 7 of *The Doctrine of the Most Holy Trinity* deals with what it would mean for the Three to enter "*any* world the Trinity entered."[60] It deals first with the general metaphysical problem of how God can be said to enter the world at all (sec. 7.1). Secondly, Crowe applies "the content determined by our psychological analogy and so consider[s] the Father in the world as *Dicens,* the Son in the world as *Verbum,* and the Holy Spirit in the world as *Amor.*"[61] He uses Basil's word *character* in the title of this section (sec. 7.2): "Each of the Three in the World with His Proper Character." Finally, he says a few things concerning "the new society that results from their presence in the world" (sec. 7.3).[62]

In chapter 8 Crowe introduces his neologism *Trinification.* His point is that when God communicates himself to us, it is the triune God who does so. The chapter discusses the human *need* for the triune God and the triune response to this need. Crowe discusses first our need as images of God for understanding, truth, and love (sec. 1.1). He also discusses our need for the Trinity to take away the loneliness of our human spirit (sec. 1.2). These two needs structure God's response (sec. 2.1). Finally, these questions lead him into a discussion of how historically God has responded to our need for Trinification and the stable structure that this Trinification has established for understanding ourselves and history (sec. 2.2–3).

The Presence in the World of the Father, Son, and Holy Spirit as Exemplars

By 1965 Crowe was interested in the presence of not only the Son and Spirit in the world but also the Father. He said that it was "a new and extremely difficult question: whether he is in the world in a way that is proper to himself and is not common to all Three. It is a new question."[63] Crowe credits Maurice de la Taille with introducing the question in his 1928 article "The Hypostatic Union and Created Actuation of Uncreated Act." "Here," Crowe writes, "for the first time (as far as I know), these three items of revelation were seen as 'instances' of a kind."[64] In talking about these items, Crowe refers to the hypostatic union, sanctifying grace, and the light of glory.

The three items of revelation come out more clearly in the original French title of de la Taille's article: "Actuation créé par Acte incréé: Lumière de gloire, grace sanctifiante, union hypostatique" (Created actuation by Uncreated Act: Light of glory, sanctifying grace, hypostatic union). Crowe does not think that de la Taille dreamed "of a one-to-one correspondence between these three facts and the three persons of the Trinity."[65] In other words, de la Taille did not uniquely relate the light of glory, sanctifying grace, and the hypostatic union to the presence of Father, Son, and Holy Spirit in the world. According to Crowe, de la Taille "makes only the most casual reference to the Spirit's role in sanctifying grace, and none at all to a possible role of the Father, i.e., special to the Father, in the light of glory."[66] Nevertheless, Crowe himself thinks that a one-on-one correspondence can be made between these three created actuations and the three divine persons. The idea suggested to him by de la Taille's work, however, would look something like table 4.

While Crowe does not think that de la Taille completely made this correspondence, he thinks that Lonergan made it "in his course on grace at Regis College in 1950–51, and put [it] into print in his *Divinarum*

Table 4 Crowe's alignment of the persons of the Trinity with three created realities

Persons of Trinity	Father	Son	Holy Spirit
Corresponding created actuations are due to a special role of the three persons	Light of glory	[Hypostatic union]	Sanctifying grace

Personarum ... (p. 214) in 1957."[67] Crowe is referring to what is now called Lonergan's "four-point hypothesis."[68] Lonergan formulated this hypothesis about the four real relations in this way:

> If one asks about the supernatural character of the formal terms, it is pertinent to note the following. First, there are four real divine relations, really identical with the divine substance, and therefore there are four very special modes that ground the external imitation of the divine substance. Next, there are four absolutely supernatural realities, which are never found uninformed, namely, the secondary act of existence of the incarnation, sanctifying grace, the habit of charity, and the light of glory. It would not be inappropriate, therefore, to say that the secondary act of existence of the incarnation is a created participation of paternity, and has a special relation to the Son; that sanctifying grace is a participation of active spiration, and so has a special relation to the Holy Spirit; that the habit of charity is a participation of passive spiration, and so has a special relation to the Father and Son; and that the light of glory is a participation of Sonship, and so in a most perfect way brings the children of adoption back to the Father.[69]

How is this fourfold connection possible? Lonergan gives this answer: "Just as God by the divine intellect knows the four real relations, so also by the divine intellect, together with the divine will, God can produce beings that are finite yet similar [to the four real relations] and absolutely supernatural."[70] Figure 4 summarizes Lonergan's teaching in this regard.

Lonergan is working from certain created realities that are, in some sense, external to God (*ad extra*) and *not* absolutely identical with the divine essence: the *secondary act of existence* of Christ's human nature; the created *sanctifying grace* infused into the essence of the human soul that makes a creature just and pleasing to God; the created *habit of charity*; and the created *light of glory* by which a creature is able to see God face to face. Lonergan correlates these respectively to the four real relations in God: *paternity* (the relation of the Father towards the Son); *active spiration* (the relation of the Father and the Son towards the Spirit); *passive spiration* (the relation of the Holy Spirit towards the Father and the Son); and *filiation* (the relation of the Son towards the Father). The difference, Crowe claims, lay in the fact that Lonergan's approach "was through the created terms *ad extra*," whereas his "approach is through *the persons themselves*."[71]

Lonergan left ways to think of our participation in the four real relations. Crowe admits, in chapter 7 of his *Doctrine of the Most Holy Trinity*, that this view of Lonergan's "was the creative idea behind our generalized theory" for how the three persons are in the world in their distinctive characteristics.[72] Crowe prefers, however, to think of "the Three as present"[73] to us in a way proper to each person (see table 5).

The real divine relations that ground external imitation of the divine substance	The four absolutely supernatural realities made known by revelation	It would *not* be inappropriate to say that one of these respective realities is a created	These different created supernatural realities have, therefore, a
Paternity	*Christ's secondary act of existence*	participation of **paternity**	special relation to the *Son*
Active spiration	*Sanctifying grace*	participation of **active spiration**	special relation to the *Holy Spirit*
Passive spiration	*Habit of charity*	participation of **passive spiration**	special relation to the *Father and Son*
Filiation (Sonship)	*Light of glory*	participation of **sonship**	special relation to the *Father*

Figure 4 Lonergan's four-point hypothesis

Table 5 Crowe's explanation of the three divine persons as present in a proper way

The three divine persons	Present in the world in a special, personal way, proper to each, and not had by the others in this way, quoted from Crowe, *The Doctrine of the Most Holy Trinity*, 167
Father	"It seems a reasonable hypothesis ... the Father as present ... to the saints in the beatific vision."
Son	"As present ... to all men as Man among them and their Brother."
Holy Spirit	"As present to the church ... (generally interpreted as a special mode of inhabitation in the souls of the just)."

Without totally abandoning the four-point hypothesis, Crowe admits that his preference for thinking of the three divine persons as present according to their distinctive personal properties is related to his preference for talking about three real Trinitarian relations rather than four: "In chapter six I argued briefly that we should talk of *three* trinitarian relations rather than of four, that we count four only by prescinding from an aspect that is concretely one with the aspect considered; naturally the doctrine of chapter seven should be coherent with that of chapter six, and so I prefer not to speak here of *four* relations and their participation in created grace."[74]

While Crowe speaks of the Father as present in a proper way the beatific vision, the Son as present in a proper and special way as man, and the Holy Spirit as present in a proper and special way in the souls of the just, he also has another way of speaking of the three as present in the world with their proper characters. Lonergan argued that the four utterly supernatural realities or graces "that are never found unformed"[75] (light of glory, grace of union, habit of charity, and sanctifying grace) were created as likenesses of the four real relations. This idea of likeness lies behind Crowe's own idea that the personal properties of the Three are the *exemplars* of the created understanding, truth, and love that we need and that come to us through the presence of each of the Three as individual persons.

Presence of Each of the Three in the World in a Proper,
Unique, and Personal Way

One looks for the words *divine missions* in the synthetic or systematic part of Crowe's 1965–6 treatise, and instead one finds the phrase *the presence of the Three in the world*. Where one hopes to find discussion of the sending (*missio*) of the Son and the sending of the Spirit, one finds talk of the "being-in-the-world" of the Son and Spirit and Father. Crowe consciously makes this substitution. He says in his Latin *thetica* for chapter 7: "pars 2a fundatur in eius asserto XVII, sed 'esse-in-mundo' substituitur loco 'missio.'"[76] (The second part is founded on his assertion 17 [in Lonergan's *The Triune God: Systematics*], but "being-in-the-world" is substituted in place of "mission.")

In chapter 7 of *The Doctrine of the Most Holy Trinity* Crowe takes up the question of a personal and proper presence of each of the Three in the second section, "Each of the Three in the World with His Proper Character."[77] His goal is to find the way in which each divine person is present as an individual person that is exclusive to that person. He does not want us to forget "that the fundamental idea of our whole 'system' is supplied by the psychological analogy, that the personal 'character' of Father, Son, and Holy Spirit is defined for us by the divine rationality which 'moves' God to utter a Word and breathe forth Love; so this aspect of the Trinity in the world has certainly to be treated."[78] Crowe is still talking about the entry of the Three from the side of the Three themselves. He will discuss the relevance of their entry for us in chapter 8. Crowe summarizes the second section of chapter 7 as follows: "In the second section of chapter seven we determined the general features of trinitarian entry into the world. The Father will come as Understanding, the Son as Word, the Spirit as Love; they will be in the world, each with his *own proper character*, and this will be meaningful for those rational creatures to whom they come."[79]

At this point, when Crowe speaks of the Father coming as Understanding, he is not talking about something generally given in this earthly life. As he says a bit later, "The Father we conceive to be really in the world as divine Understanding expressing itself, not in the world of earthly life but in the world where my knowledge 'will be whole, like God's knowledge of me' (1 Cor 13/12)."[80] When he says that the Three enter this world, he means to include the world of heaven.

Crowe immediately points out that the created understanding of God's essence, for example, that is produced as a consequence of the entry of the Father into our world is not produced by the Father alone. "Not that each [person]," Crowe writes, "will produce in the images of God that psychological act which he is in the Trinity and for which he stands in the *imago Dei*, but in ways that go beyond the perspective of efficient causality their presence as Understanding, Truth, and Love will be meaningful."[81] Earlier, Crowe spoke about there being room "for a relation of our understanding to infinite Understanding in the world, of our truth to infinite Truth in the world, and of our love to infinite Love in the world – a relation to them as exemplars, as subsistent persons, as constitutive of the meaning of our universe, and perhaps in other ways."[82] Crowe does not want to say that all human love is *efficiently* produced in us by the sending of the Holy Spirit. He does not want to say that all truth is efficiently produced by the Word alone being sent. But he does want to say that divine love in us finds its exemplar in the Holy Spirit, and truth finds its exemplar in the Son.

What is an exemplar? Aquinas links exemplars with imitation: "an exemplar, if properly considered, denotes causality regarding the things modeled upon it, since in imitation of the exemplar something else is made."[83] An exemplar, in this context, can mean a "pattern, model, example."[84] The Son and the Spirit are subsistent Truth and Love, according to the psychological analogy. As subsistent Truth, the Son is the pattern, model, example for the creation of all other truth. As subsistent Love, the Spirit is the pattern, model, example by which God creates all other love. Finite truth and love are imitations of the eternally uttered Word and proceeding Love.

Crowe thinks that the sources of the Catholic faith "show the Word in the world, and indeed in the world as Word," and "show the Spirit in the world, with some indication that he is here as Love."[85] He also feels that the same sources "indicate a really special relation of our knowledge to the divine Word, and a really special relation of our sanctification to divine Love."[86] The Son and the Spirit, therefore, are present to us in unique and proper ways during this life.

Crowe thinks that "what is true of our special relation to the Word and Love on earth would be true *a fortiori* of our relation to Understanding in heaven."[87] He repeats the point that the understanding given to us in heaven will be produced by all three persons, but still it is possible that the Father will be present to us in a unique and personal way in the beatific vision as an exemplar cause.

Trinitarian Response to Our Need for Trinification

Crowe has a hypothesis that the Father has a special role to play in the beatific vision. As the Son has a role to play by being sent into our world in the flesh, and the Holy Spirit has a role by being sent into our hearts, so the Father also has a role in the created order. That role occurs in heaven where "we might conceive that in the light of glory, where the Father is present to us and we are joined to him by a grace which is an imitation of the divine filiation, we are sons of God in a new sense and brothers of his Son in a new sense."[88] Crowe even speculates that the beatific vision will bring the Son to us in a new sense. "Here on earth he is our Brother as human, as one of us; there in heaven he is our Brother as divine, because we share in his divine filiation."[89] The result of this new sharing in divine filiation is a new sharing in the Holy Spirit. When we share in the Son's divine filiation in heaven, "the Father has a new reason for giving us the Love which is the Holy Spirit; just as he loves his Son, as it were, twice, first eternally as God and then temporally as Man, so he will love us twice, first as men joined to his Son in human fellowship, and then as Gods (*inquantum possibile* [inasmuch as it is possible]) joined to his Son in divine fellowship."[90] Eternally, there is an order of origin among the persons of the Trinity. The Father is the origin of the Son, and the Father and the Son are the origin of the Holy Spirit. Crowe is saying that the order in which we encounter the persons in heaven will follow this ordering.

Crowe thinks that in heaven we will still be related to the divine persons in their personal distinction. In the vision of God, Crowe proposes, the Father makes "his Son present to us also and [gives] his Spirit in a new way."[91] But Crowe does not think that this was the historical order in which the persons were present to us.

The Father does not come to earth in the way that the Son and the Spirit do. The Father's "coming is coincident with our receiving the light of glory and reaching our destination."[92] But if the eternal Truth brings truth into this world, how can the Father also not be present on earth in a proper way? In the psychological analogy, truth depends on understanding. How can the Truth here and now be present in a proper way without the One who is eternal Understanding also being present? Crowe answers this objection by pointing out that "we can have truth without its proper principle in our understanding, as when we believe in another, trusting his understanding."[93] He is talking about the way in which faith supplies now what beatific understanding will provide in heaven. We have the truth because we accept in faith the word of another's understanding. Then, once we have truth, "we can also have love. Son and Spirit can therefore be in our world as Truth and Love (to which correspond faith and charity) without the Father being in our world as Understanding."[94]

Crowe strongly insists on the Son's presence as Truth before the Spirit's presence as Love. The Trinitarian entry into the world has special events in "748 and 781 A.U.C. (if indeed they were sent at those dates)."[95] He is talking about the manifest presence of the Son and the Spirit in Palestine. It "was thousands of years after the creation of man" that God sent his Son and Spirit "in manifest presence to our world."[96] Crowe does not deny the presence of the Holy Spirit in the Old Testament period. This is clear, he thinks, from Old Testament saints. Still, he does not think that the manifest presence of the Spirit took place until Pentecost. Before that point "he was in the world incognito."[97]

This raises a question. The Son was made man somewhere around 4 BC (748 AUC). Does this mean that the Spirit was "in the world without the Word?"[98] The problem arises from the idea that nothing is loved by the will that is not first known by the intellect. The coming of the Holy Spirit into the heart brings charity in the will. There is a "charity that the presence of the Holy Spirit gives."[99] If there are acts of charity in the will, there must be some corresponding faith in the intellect.

Crowe makes an interesting basic distinction between faith and charity. "Charity," he says, "has a concreteness that does not allow the distinctions possible in intellectual operations; as there can be judgment of faith without our own understanding, so there can be implicit judgments (heuristic anticipations) and explicit judgments."[100] On the side of the intellect, there is a whole set of distinctions that can be made and applied to the faith of those who lived before the Word became flesh. Crowe quotes John 1:10: "He was in the world; but the world ... did not recognize him."[101] Crowe interprets this to mean that in the period of the Old Testament there were signs for the people that the Word was in the world. These prepared them for his manifest coming. Through these signs there was implicit faith "in the Word incarnate" that "could fulfill the conditions on the side of intellect for the charity that the presence of the Holy Spirit gives."[102]

Crowe knew that his students might be uneasy with his conviction of the Spirit's presence in the Old Testament period. "You may have wished," he writes, "when I spoke of the Spirit being given in the OT, to challenge me with John's statement: 'the Spirit had not yet been given, because Jesus had not yet been glorified.'"[103] Crowe responds first by referring to several passages from Luke as well as to a text in Hebrews and 2 Peter. The Holy Spirit is the "agent in the conception of Jesus" (Luke 1:35); descends from heaven "at the baptism of Jesus" (Luke 3:22); spoke "through the OT prophets" (Hebrews 3:7; 2 Peter 2:21); and came upon "Simeon in the temple" (Luke 2:25). Crowe's point is that the Holy Spirit is active before the death, resurrection, and ascension of Christ. Whatever John 7:39 means, it cannot rule out the presence of the Holy Spirit before Christ's glorification. "Some distinction has to be made," Crowe writes, "and the simplest explanation seems to be that John is speaking of the manifestation of the Spirit as distinct from the Son, a distinction that is clear when he comes in power though the Son has returned to the Father."[104] Crowe thinks that John contributed to the life of the early Church by bringing out the Son's and the Spirit's distinction. As part of this contribution, John "insists also on the order of the Son's going and the Spirit's coming."[105]

But why did the Son and the Spirit come in the way they did? Why did the Spirit come at "Pentecost and not someone else"? Why did he "come in the way he did and not some other way?"[106] When Crowe answers this question, he does so with the term learned from Basil, referring to the Holy Spirit's "eternal personal 'character.'"[107]

Recalling his 1959 articles in *Theological Studies*, "Complacency and Concern in the Thought of St Thomas," Crowe makes this distinction: "The Spirit is Love and love is first of all a peace and harmony and rest in the enjoyment of what is, and then it is an unrest and a desire and striving for what is not (*complacere* and *intendere*)."[108] But then, unlike in "Complacency and Concern in the Thought of St Thomas," Crowe applies *all* of this description of love to the Love proceeding in God. According to Crowe, "all this the Spirit is in God, the term of Understanding and Word as the divine *complacere* [being complacently in love], the principle of divine creativity as *intendere* [tending] (*Creator Spiritus*)."[109] The key words here are *term* and *principle*. In figure 1 in the last chapter we saw how Crowe conceived of a moment in the human will, *B*, that is first of all the term or end-point of a receptive process. That same act of will, *B*, can become the principle of another process, a process of bringing about what is not yet. In other words, Crowe's emphasis on the analogy of complacent love for the mode of the Holy Spirit's procession does not now rule out the possibility that the analogy of concerned love also applies to the Holy Spirit. "The Holy Spirit is eternally complacent love and concerned love, restful love and restless love. This divine restfulness therefore is what the Spirit will be in the world, that is to say, he will represent acceptance of what is and harmony with the universe of being, he will find his role in relation to that of the Son, bringing men to the truth, not as revealer of new truth but as hearing the Son with love and obedience."[110] Crowe then takes up the restless aspect of the Spirit's presence in our world: "furthermore, as representing the divine unrest he will be the principle of growth in the new being, keeping the freshness of youth in the church and continuously renewing it (Vatican II, *De Ecclesia*, c. 1)."[111]

Crowe later will speak of the role of the Holy Spirit as counteracting "the tendency to petrification" in the institutional Church.[112] The Holy Spirit is thus the "principle of perpetual rejuvenation in the church."[113] He admits that the Holy Spirit "does indeed stand for the acceptance of the word of God and for harmony with all that is, but what we are is largely potential, so he stands also for the emergence of new understanding and new forms in the church."[114]

Crowe illustrates this role of the Holy Spirit by a comparison of the ways in which the virtues and the gifts of the Holy Spirit operate in us. The virtues, according to Crowe, "are a form, and an interior principle of right conduct."[115] By contrast, the gifts of the Holy Spirit (wisdom, understanding, knowledge, counsel, piety, fortitude, and fear of the Lord) should not be thought of as "forms and are not an interior principle of right conduct."[116] Crowe quotes Lonergan who said that the gifts "link us dynamically with the sole source of absolute perfection."[117] The seven gifts link us with the Holy Spirit himself and exist in the soul as dispositions "to follow external guidance and direction of another."[118] Crowe's memorable example illustrates how both the virtues and the gifts help to guide us, but in different ways: "Think of a football player running interference; as a runner, he has a *virtue*, an internal principle, the full expression of whose potency would be running at the greatest possible speed; but as running interference, he is at the disposal of the ball-carrier, and the best speed is not necessarily the fastest possible but is governed by an external principle."[119] In football a lead blocker cannot get too close to the ball carrier or too far ahead. In either case, he will not be helping the ball carrier to avoid the other team's defence. This person running interference must constantly follow the guidance of the ball carrier. He adjusts himself to the movements of the one with the ball behind him.

In this analogy the Holy Spirit carries the ball, and we are blocking for him. Crowe writes: "Well, the gifts put us at the disposition of the Spirit, to be governed according to his wisdom and love, and not simply according to the forms or virtues or patterns intrinsic to us. And in this way the Spirit continually rejuvenates the church."[120]

Crowe was writing these words towards the end of the Second Vatican Council. He knew of the struggles within the Church for and against changes to the liturgy and the life of the Church. His thinking about changes is guided by his Trinitarian pneumatology:

> If we remember that truth is the guide, that law is the intelligibility of the good, that love without order is a rudderless ship, and at the same time recognise that our truth is only partial, that what is a good law today is not necessarily a good law tomorrow, that the urge to love is to establish an ever better and better order, then we may be able to read "the signs of the times" (Vatican II, Decree on Ecumenism), be acquitted of the Protestant charge that we resist the Lordship of the Spirit (see G.S. Hendry, *The Holy Spirit in Christian Theology*, 1965, revised ed.), and still be true to the Catholic doctrine that the Spirit proceeds eternally and temporally from the Word that expresses divine Understanding.[121]

Conclusion

Although at the beginning of his teaching career Crowe was more interested in the intelligible emanations, his main interest by the end of this first stage, under the influence of St Basil, lay in the presence of the Three in history. He was convinced that the Spirit was at work in the changes coming with the Second Vatican Council and in the ecumenical movement. By 1966, in his article "Development of Doctrine: Aid or Barrier to Christian Unity," Crowe could write: "One [preliminary] question is why a novice in the field of ecumenism should presume to speak to you on that subject [ecumenical relations between Christians] at all. My answer is partly to lay the blame on the Holy Spirit, who all too clearly means to involve everyone, expert or novice, in the ecumenical movement. Something wonderful, pentecostal, challenging, is going on in regard to Christian disunity, and we cannot evade the responsibility laid on us by the Spirit."[122] It was Crowe's effort to discern this unique role of the Holy Spirit in the Church's life in the mid-1960s that also helped him accept what he had largely dismissed in 1959, namely, the analogy of concerned love for the procession of the Holy Spirit. The Holy Spirit in the world stands for harmony, but also the restless renewal of the Church. The Spirit must, somehow, have this restless character in eternity.

PART II (1969–1984)

Reversing the Relation of the Two Divine Missions

4 Who Provides the Context, the Son or the Spirit?

The Spirit proceeds from the Son and works in the context of the Son.

Frederick Crowe, "Son and Spirit in the Church"

On the contrary, God first sent the Spirit, and then sent the Son in the context of the Spirit's mission.

Frederick Crowe, "Son of God, Holy Spirit, and World Religions"

Did God first send the Son or the Holy Spirit into the world? Between 1968 and 1984 Crowe changed his position about the relation of the two divine missions. In 1968 he said that the Son was sent first and provided the context for the Spirit's mission. In 1984 he maintained that the Spirit was sent first and provided the context for the Son's mission. Why did Crowe change his mind?

Two aspects of Crowe's position need to be distinguished. There is the question of which person was sent first, the Son or the Spirit, but there is also the question of the context for the missions. Crowe changes his mind first about which person was sent first. In 1968 he said that the Son was sent first because truth preceded love. From 1972 on, however, the idea of the Spirit being sent first was implicitly operative in his thinking. It took Crowe a long time to publish his idea that the Spirit was communicated first. He said it explicitly only in 1983 and then in a footnote. On the basis of this prior gift of the Spirit, however, Crowe claimed that the Holy Spirit's mission even provided a context for the mission of the Son.

In the first stage of his development Crowe explains that the Holy Spirit finds "his role in relation to that of the Son, bringing men to the truth, not as a revealer of new truth, but as hearing the Son with love and obedience."[1] Finding the role of one person in relation to another is very close to what Crowe means by working in the context of another.

By 1984 Crowe had changed his mind and placed the Son's mission in relation to the Spirit's. The Holy Spirit's prior mission eventually provides for Crowe a divine rationale for sending the Son. The gift of the Spirit is the gift of Love. This Love needs to be declared in order for God and humanity to be fully in love. The Son's mission is to declare the Love that has already been bestowed.

Crowe thought about the question of the *order* of the two missions when he was taking Lonergan's class on the Trinity, and it found its way into his own notes on the Trinity. Lonergan's later writings (post-1965), however, seem to call into question the very foundation of Crowe's earlier position on the order of the missions (Son first) and provide an analogy for reassessing the context of the two missions.

Chapter 4, following his methodology in *Theology of the Christian Word*, looks at this stage of Crowe's pneumatology in three parts. First, we look at the question of the relation of the missions in his earlier thought; second, we trace how the question of reversing the context of the Spirit's mission emerged for Crowe; and, finally, we will examine Crowe's way of answering this question once it had become thematized.

Background: The Relation of the Divine Missions in Crowe's Earlier Thinking

In the first stage of his pneumatology Crowe largely followed the position of his teacher, Bernard Lonergan, on the relation of the divine missions to one another. In his textbook *De Deo Trino: Pars systematica* Lonergan asked, "Are the divine missions ordered to each other?"[2] Lonergan follows Aquinas in thinking of the order of the missions within time as founded upon the order of the eternal processions. The order of the divine processions is understood according to the psychological analogy. "There is no procession of love except in an order to the procession of the Word," writes Lonergan.[3] From the order of the eternal processions, Lonergan reasons to an order in the missions. For him, the missions add a created effect to the processions, but the missions are *constituted* by the eternal divine processions and divine relations.

Lonergan also thinks that the missions are ordered to one another according to their created effects or consequent terms.[4] He tries to show that "the fact that a divine person sends or is sent cannot have the correspondence of truth through the divine perfection alone."[5] "Appropriate external terms"[6] are also required for it to be true to say that the Son and the Spirit are sent into the world. The appropriate external term, the consequent condition, of the sending of the Son, according to Lonergan, is the created human nature assumed by the Word. The consequent term of the Holy Spirit's mission is "the gift of sanctifying grace."[7]

Lonergan follows Thomas Aquinas in seeing that God's love in some respects is not like human love. God's love is not responsive to a pre-existing good. His love causes the good that is in creatures.[8] Speaking to God, the human author of the book of Wisdom prays: "for thou lovest all things that exist" (RSV Wisdom 11:24). Referring to this passage, Aquinas says that there is a difference, however, between the general love that God has for all things and the "special love" that he has for the rational creature.[9] That special love causes in us a "participation in the divine good" that draws us "above the condition of nature."[10] Since Aquinas thinks of this sharing in the divine goodness as something contingent and external to God, he maintains that this grace is not just the favour (*gratia*) by which God considers that we are just and pleasing to him. Aquinas speaks of this grace as a supernatural quality within the essence of the soul[11] and calls it *gratia gratum faciens*, the grace that makes us pleasing.[12]

Lonergan connected the special love that was spoken about by Aquinas in *Summa Theologiae*, part I-II, question 110, article 1, with the mission of the Holy Spirit. The Holy Spirit, according to Aquinas, "procedit ut Amor"[13] (proceeds as Love). He is Love taken notionally in God and not as the essential love that is common to all three persons. Aquinas says that the Father and Son "love themselves and us by the Holy Spirit or proceeding Love."[14] As proceeding Love, the Holy Spirit can be understood also as Gift. Lonergan draws our attention to this passage in Aquinas: "A gift is not called a gift from the fact that it is actually given, but inasmuch as it has the aptitude to be able to be given."[15] In other words, the Holy Spirit can be called gift *eternally* because he is the divine person eternally *apt* to be given. He is apt to be given because he proceeds as Love, and love is the "first thing we give to someone."[16]

Lonergan reads these texts of Aquinas from the Prima pars and the Prima secundae together to mean that the special love that the persons of the Trinity have for certain created persons leads to the sending and giving of the proceeding Love. Lonergan puts a strong emphasis on sanctifying grace, habitual grace, as the consequence in us of this sending of the Holy Spirit. This appropriate external effect has a special connection to the person of the Holy Spirit, and this connection also serves to explain for him the order that exists between the mission of the Son and the mission of the Spirit.

Lonergan begins with Galatians 4:4–6: "God sent his Son ... so that we might receive adoption as children. And because you are children, God has sent the Spirit of his Son into your hearts crying, 'Abba, Father'" (*The Holy Bible*, new revised standard version, hereafter cited as NRSV). He comments: "From these words it seems we must understand that the mission of the Son is to make us children of God by adoption; and that the mission of the Holy Spirit is in accord with the adoption."[17] Lonergan then spells out the connection in terms of the Holy Spirit as proceeding Love: "The Holy Spirit is sent as a special and notional divine love. The special divine love is that according to which the just are loved as ordered to the divine good. But since God does everything in accord with the order of justice, this special love itself supposes a special reason. And this special reason cannot be other than God's own Son, who is both mediator and redeemer."[18] The Son's mission provides the special reason or the context for the sending of the Holy Spirit. Lonergan then explains how the incarnation leads the Father to love human beings with the same love with which he loves his Son made man. Lonergan appeals to the baptism of Christ, with the descent of the Holy Spirit, as evidence that the Father loves the Son *as man* by the Holy Spirit. If the Father loves the man Christ Jesus with the special love, he can also love other men with that special love. Lonergan quotes Christ's words in John 17:23, "You have loved them even as you have loved me" (NRSV). Connecting these words of Christ to the Holy Spirit, he draws this conclusion: "if the Father loves us as he loves his own Son, he surely loves us and gives to us by the Holy Spirit."[19]

Lonergan speaks of the Son's mission as "the first mission [*prior ... missio*]."[20] Once the Son has reconciled us to the Father, the Spirit's "consequent mission ... is to each one of the just, who have been reconciled."[21] He finds support for his position in St Paul: "This Spirit he poured out richly through Jesus Christ our Saviour, so that, having been justified by his grace, we might become heirs according to the hope of eternal life"[22] (NRSV Titus 3:5–7). The Holy Spirit is sent to justify us by the gift of sanctifying grace. But the Spirit is only sent to us because of the incarnation and redemption. The ultimate end of each mission is the same, Lonergan insists. The ultimate end is drawing us into the life of heaven for the glory of God the Father.

There is one other important element to Lonergan's doctrine of the missions for understanding Crowe. In his *De Deo Trino*, Lonergan goes on to ask, "Is it appropriate that the divine persons be sent, the Son visibly and the Spirit invisibly?"[23] Earlier on, he focused on the incarnation of the Son (the visible mission) and the sending of the Holy Spirit into our hearts (an invisible mission). But now he asks about an *invisible* mission of the Son and a *visible* mission of the Spirit. There had long been reflections on the invisible mission of the Son (the way the Son seems to be sent to us by the gift of wisdom) and the visible mission of the Spirit (e.g., in tongues of fire at Pentecost).[24] And so Lonergan asks, "Is the Son also sent invisibly and the Holy Spirit visibly?" He answers yes. In terms of the various *visible* missions of the Holy Spirit, Lonergan thinks that these are best understood in relation to the Spirit's invisible mission. He sees the dove at the baptism of Christ, the bright cloud at his transfiguration, and the wind and the tongues of fire at Pentecost as sensible manifestations of the Holy Spirit's "invisible mission."[25]

With regard to the Son's invisible mission, Lonergan claims that the ways in which the Son is sent invisibly are *appropriated* to him according to some likeness. Effects of grace that have more connection with the intellect are appropriated to the Son because these effects are analogous to the Son's procession. Effects of grace that have more connection with the will are appropriated to the Holy Spirit who proceeds as Love.[26]

Lonergan, therefore, has two different senses of the invisible mission of the Holy Spirit. Very briefly in "Question 31," in volume 12 of *The Collected Works of Bernard Lonergan*, he speaks about an appropriated invisible mission of the Spirit linked with the effects of grace on the will itself. He also speaks at greater length, as we have seen, of an invisible mission that brings sanctifying grace to the *essence* of the soul. Lonergan wants to hold, it seems to me, that the invisible mission of the Holy Spirit that brings sanctifying grace is not a simple appropriation but is proper to the Holy Spirit.

Crowe knew these questions in *De Deo Trino*. Referring to question 28, he summarizes Lonergan's account of the way in which God rationally makes us lovable:

> His method of making us lovable is tricky (see BL, *The Mystical Body of Christ*, also *DDT*, II, q. XXVIII: "Utrum ... missiones inter se ordinentur"). He loves his Son with an eternal Love in heaven. Now suppose that the Son becomes Man; will God not have the same Love for him in his human state as he does in the eternal? But, if he loves his Son, he must also love his Son's friends; and, if the Son is Man, all men will be his friends in the solidarity of the human race and human fellowship. In this way the cunning God is able to trap himself into making us lovable (sending his Son to be our Brother), and thus making it rational for him to bestow his Love (sending his Spirit into our hearts).[27]

In this argument, the Spirit is clearly sent *in the context* of the Son's mission. Even if the Holy Spirit is sent into men's hearts before the Incarnation, it must be in view of the Incarnation. Granting the Incarnation as the basic rationale for why God gives us the Spirit, Crowe takes up several questions related to the working out of these missions in history.

One question has to do with God the Father not entering this world in a manifest way. As we saw in the previous chapter, Crowe thinks that the Father does enter our earthly world but in the beatific vision through the light of glory. Given the importance of the psychological analogy for understanding the Trinity, however, it seems unfitting for the Word and Love to enter the world without their ground, the Understanding that speaks the Word. "It is true," Crowe writes, "that there cannot be truth if there is no understanding at all, but we can have truth without its proper principle in *our* understanding, as we believe in another, trusting *his* understanding."[28] The understanding here must be Jesus of Nazareth's beatific vision or immediate vision of God. In Christ's human understanding, God the Father is made present in this world. Our grasp of truth by faith rests on Christ's understanding. Thus, Crowe adds, "When we have truth, we can also have love. Son and Spirit can therefore be in our world as Truth and Love (to which correspond faith and charity) without the Father being in our world as Understanding."[29]

A second problem was precisely the presence of the Holy Spirit in the time before the Incarnation. Crowe was convinced that the Holy Spirit was at work in the Old Testament: "it seems clear that God gave his grace to the saints of the OT and that, giving his grace, he gave his Spirit of love."[30] But how can the Spirit of love be in the world without the Word of truth being in the world? "It might seem," Crowe writes, "that faith is the presupposition of charity, and the charity that corresponds to the presence of the Spirit requires the faith that corresponds to the presence of the Word."[31] Truth and faith correspond to the presence of the Word. Charity (along with sanctifying grace) corresponds to the presence of the Spirit. In these "primitive times" before the Incarnation, Crowe explains, "the Spirit came *incognito* and did his work in secret while he awaited the time when the fullness of the Word could be manifested."[32] The Spirit of Love was present before the Word, the Son, was present *in his fullness*. The Word's presence in primitive times was partial. The Word's presence, Crowe thinks, corresponds to the way in which we can make all kinds of intellectual distinctions between implicit and explicit judgments. The Word was present before the Incarnation as the full truth can be present heuristically and by anticipation through implicit judgments. This idea of heuristic anticipations explains how the Holy Spirit was present in the world as Love before the Father sent his Son born of a woman.

Crowe was committed to several ideas, therefore: the Holy Spirit was really present in the Old Testament; charity corresponds to the sending of the Spirit. But he also would not accept that charity could be in the will without truth in the intellect. In this life such truth requires faith, and so faith precedes charity. As the Son enters our world as Truth, his mission precedes the mission of Holy Spirit, who enters our world as Love.

For Crowe to abandon this position of the Son's mission providing the context for the Spirit's, he needs two changes in his thinking. First, he needs to find a way to think of the mission of the Holy Spirit as providing a rationale for sending the Son. Second, he needs to rethink the order of faith and love in our souls. If he wants to hold on to the idea of the Holy Spirit entering this world as Love (which he will always cling to) and wants to think of the Spirit as being sent first, then he will need to be able to think in general of love as preceding truth. In 1969 Crowe makes this very move.

The Need to Rethink the Relation of the Missions

In March 1968 Lonergan gave a lecture at the Thomas More Institute in Montreal in which he said: "There remains the fourth topic, faith. I would describe faith as the knowledge born of religious love."[33] He admitted that such a consideration of faith provided "a basis for ecumenical dialogue." He wanted "to point to a horizon common to all Christians and acceptable in some respects to all men of good will."[34] A few months later, building on earlier discussions,[35] Lonergan first used the exact phrase *falling in love* as related to the love of God, in his October 1968 paper "Theology and Man's Future."[36] He speaks in a similar way of "falling-in-love" in his 1969 article "The Future of Christianity."[37]

Crowe was not far behind Lonergan in using the language of "falling in love" to describe what must come before faith. In the fall of 1969 Crowe wrote that "the faith by which a believer says, 'God is my Savior,' is the spontaneous result of his falling in love with God."[38] For the first time in his writings Crowe voices the view that love precedes faith. Earlier in this same essay he explains how theology, as a work of human understanding of our faith, is the third activity in a process that begins with love. From love, the truths of faith are believed; and from faith, theology emerges as we seek understanding. Crowe insists that on earth the "structure of our created finite activity as pilgrims"[39] follows that order.

In God's eternal, unchanging life, however, Crowe still thinks, the "process" is the reverse. The Father as infinite Understanding speaks a Word of truth, the Son. From this Word of truth, infinite Love (the Holy Spirit) eternally emerges without change. Although Crowe has begun to think that the structure of our finite activity as pilgrims reverses this immanent Trinitarian order, he still thinks that these three acts in us (love, believing [judgment], understanding) are respectively related to the same three divine persons (Holy Spirit, Son, Father). Even though love is first in our activity as pilgrims, Crowe still assigns it as the analogue of the Holy Spirit: "As the gift of the Spirit is the divine falling in Love with us, so our response is a falling in love with God (charity) which enables us to believe (articles of faith) and belief in turn supplies a basis for pondering and reaching dim understanding (theology)."[40] This believing and theological understanding are fittingly connected with the Son and Father: "As the Word appeared briefly in a limited district, so our articles of faith are piecemeal and partial. As the Understanding is not yet, so our theology is only analogical understanding, and analogy, as Aquinas says, is a similarity of that type which involves a still greater dissimilarity. So we live in hope."[41] Crowe has not abandoned the Thomistic psychological analogy in which created love follows an inner word expressing an act of understanding,[42] but he has already accepted an idea of love as preceding knowing that will lead him later on to think that the Holy Spirit is the first person sent to us.

Nevertheless, in 1969 Crowe may not have recognized this implication for the missions when he writes: "The order, however, is fixed: Love follows from the resources of the Word, and works in the context of the Word, not outside it."[43] As the Holy Spirit proceeds eternally from the Word, so the Holy Spirit's mission follows upon the mission of the incarnate Word. Furthermore, the Holy Spirit "works in the context of the Word." Crowe has not yet integrated his older theology of the missions with his new ideas about the priority of religious love.

A few months after the appearance of Crowe's article "The Pull of the Future," Lonergan gave a paper in St Louis in February 1970, "The Response of the Jesuit as Priest and Apostle in the Modern World."[44] In it he stresses the interpersonal nature of love: "Being in love is not just a state of mind and heart. It is interpersonal, ongoing; it has its ups and downs, its ecstasies and quarrels and reconciliations, its withdrawals and returns; it reaches security and serenity only at the end of a long apprenticeship."[45] Lonergan then uses the example of a man and woman in love. "If a man and woman were to love each other," he writes, "yet never avow their love, then they would have the beginnings of love but hardly the real thing. There would be lacking an interpersonal component, a mutual presence of self-donation."[46] Lonergan then lists what would be lacking in such a situation of unexpressed love: "There would not be the steady increase in knowledge of each other. There would not be the constant flow of favors given and received, of privations endured together, of evils banished by common good will, to make love fully aware of its reality, its strength, its durability, to make love aware that it could always be counted on."[47] After explaining the analogy, Lonergan applies it to God's ways of loving humanity:

> What is true of the love of intimacy, also is true of the love of God. Though God is one, he is not solitary. The one God is three persons: Father, Son, and Spirit. The Father is not only the light in which there is no darkness but also love, *agápe* (1 John 1:5; 4:8, 16). The Son is his Word, through whom all things were made (John 1:3), sent into the world to manifest the Father's love for the world (John 3:16; 1 John 4:14–16). The gift of the Spirit is what floods Christian hearts with God's love. United in Christ through the Spirit, Christians are to love one another (*koinonía*), bear witness to God's love (*marturía*), serve mankind (*diakonía*), and look forward to a future consummation when their love of God will not just be orientation to mystery but coupled with a knowledge of God similar to God's knowledge of them (1 Corinthians 13:12).[48]

The manifestation of love in the Son is like the avowing of love between spouses at their wedding. The implication is that the falling in love between a man and woman is analogous to the gift of the Holy Spirit.

In this same paper of 1970 Lonergan talks about the Holy Spirit in connection with the salvation of those who do not know the manifestation of God's love in the Son. Referring to St Paul, Lonergan writes,

> "God wills all men to be saved (1 Timothy 2:4)." And theologians have concluded that he gives all men sufficient grace for salvation. Just what this sufficient grace is, commonly is not specified. But it is difficult to suppose that grace would be sufficient if it fell short of the gift of loving God above all and loving one's neighbour as oneself. So I am inclined to interpret the religions of mankind, in their positive moment, as the fruit of the gift of the Spirit, though diversified by the many degrees of social and cultural development, and distorted by man's infidelity to the self-transcendence to which he aspires.[49]

Lonergan does not think that every aspect of the religions of mankind is positive and beneficial. The gift of sanctifying grace, the consequence of being sent the Holy Spirit, orients people to God. But this inner gift of the Holy Spirit can lead to distorted religious practices as non-Christians try to express in various outward ways the love they have received.

Having made the point about the Holy Spirit and world religions, Lonergan returns to talking about the gift of the Spirit in relation to the Son and the Father. "There is a notable anonymity to this gift of the Spirit," Lonergan writes.[50] He brings up Christ's words in John's gospel to explain this anonymity. "Like the Johannine *pneuma*, it blows where it wills; you hear the sound of it, but you do not know where it comes from or where it is going (John 3:8)."[51] According to Lonergan, "what removes this obscurity and anonymity is the fact that the Father has spoken to us of old through the prophets and in this final age through the Son (Hebrews 1:1–2)."[52] In light of such quotations, in which the Son is sent to remove the anonymity of the Spirit's presence, it is hard to escape the idea that for the later Lonergan the Spirit is sent before the Son. But it is worth noting that Lonergan includes the prophets as part of the way in which the Father removes this anonymity. Before he sends his Son, the Father is already speaking about his love for his people.[53] The gift of the Spirit before Christ, therefore, is not without some outward avowals of love.[54]

In *Method in Theology* Lonergan twice refers to his analogy of human love. The first time is in chapter 4 ("Religion") in a section called "The Word." Lonergan uses *word* to mean "any expression of religious meaning or of religious value."[55] An "outer" religious word is the word that enters the world of signs and symbols, the world of judgment and decision, the world mediated by meaning. The "inner" word is the "prior word"[56] of love that God speaks to the human heart and seems less conditioned by historical situations. "Religion is the prior word God speaks to us by flooding our hearts with his love," Lonergan writes. "That prior word pertains," he adds, "not to the world mediated by meaning, but to the world of immediacy, to the unmediated experience of the mystery of love and awe."[57]

Lonergan then defends the need for outer words in religion. He claims that the outer word "has a constitutive role."[58] He explains: "When a man and woman love each other but do not avow their love, they are not yet in love. Their very silence means that their love has not reached the point of self-surrender and self-donation. It is the love that each freely and fully reveals to the other that brings about the radically new situation of being in love and that begins the unfolding of its life-long implications."[59] Lonergan then applies this analysis of human love to our love for God. "What holds," he writes, "for the love of a man and a woman, also holds in its own way for the love of God and man."[60] He thinks that eventually people who have been given the gift of God's love need objectifications of that inner gift. In particular, the person needs "the word of tradition that has accumulated religious wisdom, the word of fellowship that unites those who share the gift of God's love, the word of the gospel that announces that God has loved us first and, in the fullness of time, has revealed that love in Christ crucified, dead, and risen."[61] In their outer words, Lonergan explains, "the religious leader, the prophet, the Christ, the apostle, the priest, the preacher announces in signs and symbols what is congruent with the gift of love that God works within us."[62]

Lonergan makes it clear, however, that the word that comes from the prophets of Israel and Jesus of Nazareth is not on the same level as the objectifications of this gift of inner love that we find in other religions. "There is," he writes, "a personal entrance of God himself into history, a communication of God to his people, the advent of God's word into the world of religious expression. Such was the religion of Israel. Such has been Christianity."[63] Like the inner word that is outside of historical conditions but is from God, the outer expressions of Judaism and Christianity are from God. In these two cases, Lonergan explains, "God's gift of his love is matched by his command to love unrestrictedly, with all one's heart and all one's soul, and all one's mind and all one's strength. The narrative of religious origins is the narrative of God's encounter with his people. Religious effort towards authenticity ... become[s] an apostolate ... Finally, the word of religious expression is not just the objectification of the gifts of God's love; in a privileged area it is also specific meaning, the word of God himself."[64] How does this gift of love, this inner word, this prior religious word relate to Lonergan's earlier thought on sanctifying grace, the consequent term of the mission of the Holy Spirit?

In chapter 11 of *Method in Theology* Lonergan writes, "It is this other-worldly love, not as this or that act, not as a series of acts, but as a dynamic state whence proceed the acts, that constitutes in methodical theology what in a theoretical theology is named sanctifying grace."[65] Drawing on the New Testament's teaching on grace, theoretical theology uses the categories of metaphysical psychology to explain the relation that grace has to the human soul. Sanctifying grace is thus distinguished from other kinds of grace and understood objectively as an entitative habit, perfecting the essence of the soul and bringing about justification. Methodical theology further transposes "the ancient faith," Crowe explains, "on the basis of interiority, into expressions for our time."[66] The perspective in methodical theology begins from our conscious operations of mind and heart as they are experienced in "a process of conversion and development."[67] What is it like, from the side of the subject, when justification takes place? We do not have direct experience of the essence of the human soul, but we do experience changes in our awareness during a religious conversion. On the basis of descriptions of this other-worldly love, of this "dynamic state, manifested in inner and outer acts, ... special theological categories are set up."[68] Although it begins with description, methodical theology uses categories derived from consciousness in an explanatory way by relating these new expressions of the ancient faith to each other.[69] The perspective of theoretical and methodical theology is different, but the prior inner word of love, according to Lonergan, is identical in reality to sanctifying grace.[70]

Not long before Lonergan connects the inner word of love with sanctifying grace in chapter 11, he alludes to the analogy of human love that he used in chapter 4. He is explaining the transcultural basis for the categories of a methodical theology: this gift of sanctifying grace as experienced. Lonergan writes:

> Similarly, God's gift of his love (Rom. 5:5) has a transcultural aspect. For if this gift is offered to all men, if it is manifested more or less authentically in the many and diverse religions of mankind, if it is apprehended in as many different manners as there are different cultures, still the gift itself as distinct from its manifestations is transcultural. For of other love it is true enough that it presupposes knowledge – *nihil amatum nisi praecognitum* [nothing is loved unless it is already known]. But God's gift of his love is free. It is not conditioned by human knowledge; rather it is the cause that leads man to seek knowledge of God. It is not restricted to any stage or section of human culture but rather is the principle that introduces a dimension of other-worldliness into any culture. All the same, it remains true, of course, that God's gift of his love has its proper counterpart in the revelation events in which God discloses to a particular people or to all mankind the completeness of his love for them. For being-in-love is properly itself, not in an isolated individual, but only in a plurality of persons that disclose their love to one another.[71]

As in chapter 4, Lonergan speaks of a disclosure of love that takes place in the events of the Old and New Testaments. Such disclosures are the counterparts to an interior gift of God's love.

By June of 1972 Crowe is quoting chapter 4 of *Method in Theology*. That summer he gave a long lecture, "Eschaton and Worldly Mission in the Mind and Heart of Jesus," at Villanova University on the question of Christ's beatific or immediate vision of God.[72] In one part of the paper he tries to show that in Christ "the immediate knowledge of God is the principle of his love and obedience, whereas in us the love of God and our obedience to him form the principle of our faith."[73] Crowe then has a long footnote about the relationship of the "early Lonergan to the later Lonergan."[74] He interprets the later Lonergan as follows: "in our human condition on earth he sees falling in love with God as prior to faith in the traditional sense."[75]

Crowe goes on to argue that the order of the divine persons in the eternal life of Trinity (Father, Son, and Holy Spirit; *or* Understanding, Word, and Love) is reversed in the communication of divine persons to those who are being led back to God. "That is," Crowe writes, "the Holy Spirit is given to enable us to believe in the Son who will lead us to the Father."[76] He thinks that the inversion is "Lonergan's position."[77] "This inverse order," Crowe writes, "is paralleled in the field of the virtues: charity floods our hearts and enables us to speak the truth of what is revealed; this truth we then try to understand in the painful and inadequate achievements of theology."[78] In God, the order of the divine persons is Understanding speaking, spoken Truth, proceeding Love. In our religious life as pilgrims on earth, Crowe interprets Lonergan as teaching that the order of analogous psychological acts is inverted: love, truth, understanding.

In the text of the talk Crowe puts forward this position both as Lonergan's position and as his own. He adopted this position of the Spirit as coming first through his interaction with the later Lonergan. Lonergan's writings about the priority of the gift of God's love (as understood by Crowe) before faith (judgment) led Crowe to this interpretation. If religious love (charity) is prior to faith, then the Spirit's presence is prior to the Son's, Crowe had begun to recognize. From the first stage of his pneumatology he has been committed to the idea that the Spirit is "in our world ... as Love."[79] He insists that it is "charity that the presence of the Holy Spirit gives."[80] Crowe wants to think of the Holy Spirit entering the world and bringing complacent and concerned religious love as a fruit, a consequence, of his presence in our souls. When he finds Lonergan placing religious love before faith, he interprets this as the Holy Spirit leading us to the Son.

In June 1974, during the Lonergan Workshop at Boston College, Crowe gave a talk entitled "Lonergan's New Notion of Value." In it he set out what he thought were the general lines of contrast between the Lonergan of *Insight* and the Lonergan of *Method in Theology*. Crowe writes: "There is a distinction between the way the operations of conscious intentionality go forward 'ordinarily,' that is, from the empirical through the intellectual and rational to the responsible level, and an exception to this 'ordinary' process which occurs in God's gift of his love in religion. In this exceptional case, deliberation and intellectual activity are not prior to the fourth level; they are subsequent."[81] Instead of the fourth level arising out of the three prior levels (experiencing, understanding, judgment), the fourth level becomes the prior level in a kind of downward dynamic movement beginning from God's love.

Following Lonergan's lead, Crowe gave up his exclusive use of faculty psychology's theory of intellect and will.[82] He tried to accept Lonergan's intentionality analysis with its four levels, but he still wanted to hold on to love as the sign of the Spirit's presence. By locating love within the fourth level, Crowe had a stronger ground for thinking of the Spirit as preceding the Son in the world.

Having found a way to invert *the order* of the missions, Crowe began to think about the question of reversing *the context* of the missions. The occasion was a request to contribute an essay for a Festschrift in honour of his colleague at Regis, a fellow Jesuit, and a Scripture scholar, David Stanley.[83] To honour of his friend and build on an insight he had had at the first Karl Barth Colloquium,[84] Crowe took up the question of how the Scriptures can offer such power and consolation to those who did not have a scholarly knowledge of the texts.

On the one side, modern critical scholarship presents itself as necessary for understanding the Scriptures. On the other side, such scholarship "is not a practical device for my prayer life," Crowe writes.[85] He had gone a long way in accepting the findings of modern critical scholarship. He was very open to those who greatly limited Christ's actual references to himself, for example.[86] But at the same time, there is "the experience of many of us who treasure this holy book, and have copies as marked up as a school boy's manual – so often handled that they are ready to fall apart at the binding."[87] How can people seem to have such an unenlightened understanding of the text and benefit so much from it?

Crowe's basic answer is that the meaning of the texts "mediates Jesus, who in turn by the meaning he has mediates the transcendent world of his Father."[88] Crowe uses Lonergan's notion of mediation to explain what he means. Lonergan's basic account of the world mediated by meaning is quoted at length by Crowe:

> Finally, there is the notion of mediation. Operations are said to be immediate when their objects are present. So seeing is immediate to what is being seen, hearing to what is being heard, touch to what is being touched. But by imagination, language, symbols, we operate in a compound manner; immediately with respect to the image, word, symbol; mediately with respect to what is represented or signified. In this fashion we come to operate not only with respect to the present and actual but also with respect to the absent, the past, the future, the merely possible or ideal or normative or fantastic. As the child learns to speak, he moves out of the world of his immediate surroundings towards the far larger world revealed through the memories of other men, through the common sense of community, through the pages of literature, through the labors of scholars, through the investigations of scientists, through the experience of saints, through the meditations of philosophers and theologians.[89]

Crowe takes this idea of a child's world of immediacy and thinks about it for the religious person approaching the Scriptures. The world of immediacy for such a person, he considers, is not just a matter of his or her immediate surroundings. "The religious subject's world of immediacy," Crowe writes, "is constituted interiorly by the gift of God's love, by the love which floods our hearts through the Holy Spirit who is given to us."[90] How did Crowe make this connection? He found it in chapter 4 of Lonergan's *Method in Theology*: "Before it enters the world mediated by meaning, religion is the prior word God speaks to us by flooding our hearts with his love. That prior word pertains, not to the world mediated by meaning, but to the world of immediacy, to the unmediated experience of the mystery of love and awe."[91] In quoting Lonergan, Crowe seeks to make the point that the mediation of Jesus by the Scriptures is "not between a null point that we are and the infinity that God is."[92] Instead, the mediation "is between God and human subjects already in love with God, already experiencing immediately the mystery of love and awe."[93]

Why would God want people to encounter his Son in the flesh if they already had the immediate presence of God through the gift of his love in the Holy Spirit? "The answer seems to be," Crowe writes, "that the divine reality is mediated for imagination, thought, judgment, and decision. The mediation is for the divine reality as objectified, and that is a distinct and necessary step for the sort of beings we are."[94] The sending of the Son to live a human and historical life is a distinct and necessary step. The implication is that the Spirit's gift is also a distinct and necessary step. What Crowe is struggling with is the relationship between the inner word and the outer word as expressed in *Method in Theology* and the connection of that pair to the missions of the Spirit and the Son.

Crowe repeatedly speaks of a person who is "already" experiencing the mystery of God's love before the divine reality has been mediated through the Scriptures to him. To the problem of the power of the Scriptures he is applying the basic idea of the Spirit's priority that he has been thinking about for several years. But what we also see in this passage from Crowe is the *emergence of a new question*. It is one thing for the Spirit to be given first and lead us to the Son; the Spirit, thus considered, finds his mission in the context of the Son's mission. It is another thing to see the Son's mission in relation to the Spirit's prior mission. For example, consider what Lonergan said in his 1974 paper "Mission and Spirit": "Without the visible mission of the Word, the gift of the Spirit is a being-in-love without a proper object; it remains simply an orientation to mystery that awaits its interpretation. Without the invisible mission of the Spirit, the Word enters into his own and his own receive him not."[95] Without the Spirit's invisible mission the Word is not accepted by those to whom he is sent. The Spirit is sent, Lonergan is saying, in order to enable us to hear the Word. This line of thinking fits with Crowe's 1968 ideas of the Spirit being sent in the context of the Son's mission. The Spirit is sent to help us hear the Son.

Lonergan also says, however, that the mission of the Son is the "interpretation" of what took place in the gift of the Spirit; in other words, what has been happening within people in terms of God's love is declared and explained by the mission of the incarnate Word. By including this idea of interpretation, Lonergan seems to be opening the door for Crowe's later 1984 suggestion that we need to reverse the *order* and *context* of the divine missions. If the Son interprets what God is already doing in the Spirit, then the Son, it seems, is sent in the *context* of the Spirit's mission. The purpose of the Son's mission is understood in the light of the prior mission of the Spirit.

In his 1975 essay "The Power of the Scriptures" Crowe has already begun to adopt some of Lonergan's later ideas about reversing the order and context of the divine missions. The gift of the Spirit in our hearts is vital to our relationship with God but somehow needs the mediation of the Scriptures. The divine reality also has to be mediated in an outer way to bring forth a decision from us. The outer word of the Scriptures mediates the mission of the incarnate Son and completes what began with the gift of the Spirit.

Crowe quotes a long passage from Lonergan's *Method in Theology* in support of the idea of God mediating himself through something like the Scriptures:

> By its word, religion enters the world mediated by meaning and regulated by value. It endows that world with its deepest meaning and its highest value. It sets itself in a context of other meanings and other values. Within that context it comes to understand itself, to relate itself to the object of ultimate concern, to draw on the power of the ultimate concern to pursue the objectives of proximate concern all the more fairly and all the more efficaciously ...
>
> One must not conclude that the outer word is something incidental. For it has a constitutive role. When a man and woman love each other but do not avow their love, they are not yet in love ...
>
> What holds for the love of a man and woman, also holds in its own way for the love of God and man.[96]

Following Lonergan's lead in *Method in Theology*, Crowe is stressing the way in which outer words are necessary for us to be in love with God.

We might experience the love of God, but until this love is objectified, we are not in love with God. This 1975 essay marks the first time that Crowe explicitly refers to Lonergan's analogy of God's love for us, based on the love of a man and a woman. He introduces the analogy but skips over the details of what Lonergan says about this love. It is as though Crowe was struck by this analogy but was unclear about what to do with it.

Crowe thinks that this idea of a religious word that is already present when a religious person approaches the outer word of the Scriptures "is the most fundamental point" he has made about the way in which the Scriptures mediate "Jesus who in turn mediates God."[97] At the same time, he adds that this point "is the most undeveloped to date, and I have to leave it with these rather cryptic indications of its relevance."[98]

Crowe admitted that his reason for leaving the essay's key point "underdeveloped" was that he "was already committed rather heavily."[99] He was especially dedicated to trying to implement *Method in Theology*. This implementation required institutional changes, recruitment of theologians to take part, and Crowe's own intellectual efforts to understand and communicate the method of the later Lonergan.

As part of that program Crowe began to work on a book that would apply Lonergan's notion of history, as a distinct functional specialty or task of theology, to a topic that Lonergan had worked on for many years: the transmission of Revelation. The book, *Theology of the Christian Word: A Study in History*, was finished in 1977 and published the following year. Although the question of the reversal of the contexts for the missions had begun to emerge by 1975, his *Theology of the Christian Word* was a return to questions that Crowe had been thinking about for a long time during his teaching assignments but was now viewing in the light of Lonergan's *Method in Theology*. *Theology of the Christian Word*, nevertheless, shows a growing appreciation of Lonergan's analogy of human love as applicable to the divine missions.

In the seventh chapter of *Theology of the Christian Word* Crowe writes, "I do not propose to study the trinitarian basis of the Son/Spirit complementarity, but simply to investigate how it works out in a theology of the word spoken on earth to the human race."[100] In other words, Crowe is seeking in this chapter to provide a Trinification of the transmission of revelation by focusing on the roles of the Son and the Spirit in God the Father's plan. To speak of their complementarity is to speak of the relation of the mission of the Son and the Spirit.

Crowe thought that there were "two ways of being one-sided in our approach to this question"[101] of the complementarity of the two sendings. "The older way," he writes, "showed a concern with the need for the Spirit: If the Son is Savior, what need have we for more?"[102] In contrast to the older way, of being one-sided over the question of the missions, there was a newer way. "The newer form," Crowe writes, "put with a similar one-sidedness, would ask about the need for the Son: If the Spirit is the gift of God to all his children, and a sufficient gift for salvation, what need have we of the Son?"[103] He does not think that we should start with one mission and then ask about the need for another. He thinks that we need to start with the unity of God's plan. When we start with God's plan, "then the two sendings are joined in the unity of a response to a single need, and the two forms of God's word [are joined] in the unity of one communication."[104]

This mention of God's plan is a veiled reference, I think, to Lonergan's analogy of human love. That analogy provides a way of understanding God's plan for the two missions as part of one communication of love: love bestowed, love declared, love consummated.[105] Besides the veiled reference to this way of understanding God's communication of himself in love, there is one explicit reference to Lonergan's analogy towards the end of chapter 7. Crowe is distinguishing Lonergan's use of the terms *outer word* and *inner word*. The *outer word* applies above all to language about religion. "This 'outer' word," Crowe writes, "is not to be regarded as something merely incidental to religion; on the contrary, it has a constitutive role to play. For love that is not avowed, 'has not reached the point of self-surrender and donation'; this holds true for the love of man and woman, and it holds true 'in its own way for the love of God and man' (113)."[106] By quoting Lonergan, Crowe shows that he is thinking about this analogy from *Method in Theology*. The context of *Theology of the Christian Word*, however, was not the place for Crowe to develop it. He is writing about the communication of the outer word of God across time.

Crowe claims that there are various ways to examine the Son-Spirit complementarity in the transmission of God's word, but he studies it in terms of interiority. "Interiority," he writes, "is made known to us by way of experience, specifically, inner experience as contrasted with outer experience, the inner experience that we have come to name consciousness."[107] By *interiority*, Crowe seems to be talking about "interior sources of knowledge."[108] Interiority "stands for the subjective and individual factor"[109] involved in knowing. There is an individual and subjective factor involved when we hear and accept the word of God. There is an individual and subjective factor to our handing on that word to others. The role of the Spirit is to provide the subjective and individual "condition for the possibility"[110] of hearing God's ultimate Word, the Son. The Holy Spirit stands "as the interior *complement* to the outer word that the Son is."[111]

Whence is Crowe deriving this idea of complementarity? This idea, "though it had forerunners at the Reformation, seems only now to be emerging in that precise form."[112] The person in whom Crowe thinks this idea emerged especially was Bernard Lonergan. He draws on Lonergan's *Method in Theology* to explain how an inner word of the Holy Spirit relates to the outer word that God speaks in history.

Some years later Crowe gave the keynote address at a symposium in honour of Bernard Lonergan at the University of Santa Clara. The theme of the symposium was "Religion and Culture." At one point in the lecture he addressed the problem of why Lonergan did not write much theology after he published *Method in Theology*; he did not, in other words, show us how he would restructure theology in light of his own eight functional specialties. Crowe maintains, however, that Lonergan did leave a "number of hints and some fairly firm guidelines for that renewed theology."[113] He mentions three areas of theology: divine grace, Christology, and the Trinity. In terms of the Trinity, Crowe has a couple of sentences that are important for his own understanding of the divine missions: "For the Trinity, there are scattered clues in the discussions of various workshops, with some published indications as well. And we have even a new and very important area of theology in the inner and outer word of *Method*, and the relation of this pair to the missions of the Son and Spirit."[114] It was this relation between the inner and outer words and the two missions that especially interested Crowe. He added in a footnote, "I have developed this relation a little in my 'Son and Spirit: Tension in the Divine Missions.'"[115]

We saw Crowe struggling with this relation in his 1975 essay "The Power of the Scriptures." In his 1978 book *Theology of the Christian Word* he tried to situate Lonergan's notion of an inner word within the history of reflection on the Christian word of God. In the mid to late 1970s a new question emerged for Crowe about the relation of the two divine missions. In 1983 he tried to develop Lonergan's theology of the missions and finally said explicitly that the Spirit was sent first. In November 1984 Crowe went even further in reversing the ordinary way that we think about the relation of the two missions.

Full Thematization of the Reversal of the Missions

In 1978 Crowe was insistent on "two forms of God's word in the unity of one communication."[116] He wanted to think of the two sendings in the light of how God must have conceived their unity. In 1983 he quoted *Method in Theology's* analogy of how being in love required both falling in love and avowing that love.[117] Crowe thinks that Lonergan uses this analogy to explain "the ways of God in sending his Son and his Spirit."[118] God gives his Holy Spirit to all peoples. In this way he and they fall in love with each other. Crowe quotes Lonergan's interpretation of "the religions of mankind in their positive moment as the fruit of the gift of the Spirit."[119] The Father's declaration of love in his sending of the prophets, and finally the Son, has taken away the "notable anonymity of this gift of the Spirit."[120]

Crowe takes the quotation about human love from *Method in Theology* and links it with a passage from Lonergan's 1970 essay "The Response." He is clarifying what he thinks Lonergan has been saying implicitly for years: God loves us by the gift of the Spirit; he avows his love by the sending of the Son. The reversal of the missions appears nearly complete, therefore. In the first stage of his pneumatology Crowe thought that God sent the Spirit because he "trap[ped]"[121] himself through the sending of the Son. The Son's mission formerly justified the sending of the Spirit. Now the Holy Spirit's mission explains the Father's avowal of love in the Son's mission.

Crowe defends this idea of the two missions with passages from St Paul and St John and quotes Romans 5:8: "Christ died for us while we were yet sinners, and that is God's own proof of his love towards us."[122] He also quotes 1 John 4:8–9: "God is love; and his love was disclosed to us in this, that he sent his only Son into the world to bring us life." "Our view," Crowe then says, "is linked with the New Testament and traditional theology, but does give us a new perspective, from which the members of the great world religions are not so much anonymous Christians as they are anonymous Spiritans."[123]

Having sketched out what a systematic theology would require, Crowe looks at how we should reread the history of the divine missions. His interpretation is that the Son's mission was known to us first. But what is first for us is not necessarily first in itself, Crowe explains. What is actually first in itself is the mission of the Spirit. We only learned of this prior mission of the Spirit through the subsequent mission of the Son. Crowe states: "God, 'falling in love' with the human race, will also be drawn to 'avow' his love. The 'falling' is the gift of the Spirit, actually given from the beginning."[124] The Spirit's mission leads the Father to send the Son. Crowe implies that the Son's mission finds its place in relation to the love bestowed in the sending of the Spirit. "The 'avowal' [i.e., the sending of the Son] took place at a particular time and place, when the 'angel Gabriel was sent ... with a message for a girl ... the girl's name was Mary' (Luke 1:26–7)."[125] Crowe thinks that we are made aware of this avowal of love first. "Only slowly," he adds, "do we come to realize that the Spirit was long before given incognito, and continues to be given, even to those who have not heard of the Son or the Gospel."[126]

It is only at this point, in a footnote, that Crowe finally writes: "In this view, the self-communication of God follows an order that is the reverse of the order of processions. In the divine being the Father is the 'first' person, the Son and Spirit 'second' and 'third'; but the Spirit is communicated *to us* first, the Son second and the Father last of all."[127] What was somewhat implicit in the 1970s has now become explicit. The Spirit is communicated first.

Once Crowe has accepted that the Spirit is communicated to us first, he can ask the question of the relation of the missions of the Son and the Spirit in a new way. If the Spirit is already present in those to whom the Son is sent, does he still find his role in relation to the Son? Would it be better to think of the Son as sent in the context of the Spirit's mission? Does the presence of the Spirit as given by God provide a rationale for sending the Son in the flesh?

In November 1984 Crowe answered these questions in the affirmative, reaffirming what he had said in the prior year: "We have simply to reverse the order in which we commonly think of the Son and Spirit in the world."[128] But he also wrote, "God first sent the Spirit, and then sent the Son in the context of the Spirit's mission."[129] Crowe's claim in November 1984 about the context of the missions goes beyond simply saying that the Spirit is communicated first to us.

At the beginning of his 1984 Chancellor's Lecture given at the annual convocation of Regis College, Crowe explained the origin of his lecture. As the previous year's convocation address had discussed ecumenical relations between various Christians, he thought that a follow-up lecture on the wider ecumenism of Christianity and world religions would be appropriate. But Crowe also explained the "personal reason" for his choice of topic.[130] When Fr Monet, the then president of Regis College, had asked him to give the address on some aspect of Lonergan's thought, Crowe had just read the following line in Brian Hebblethwaite's *The Problem of Theology*: "Lonergan's insistence on the role of religious conversion ... renders theological judgments undiscussable across the borders of different world religions."[131] According to Crowe, "that coincidence" of the previous year's talk on ecumenism and his reading of a line that critiqued Lonergan's usefulness for ecumenism "proved decisive."[132]

Lonergan's health had been on the decline. A year before, he had been moved by Crowe from Boston to the Jesuit infirmary in Pickering, Ontario.[133] Fr Monet proposed that the Chancellor's Lecture honour Lonergan's "nearly eighty years in the service of the gospel and his long association with our college."[134] The convocation address was set for the evening of 26 November, the Monday after the Solemnity of Christ the King. That morning, however, Lonergan died. And so

Crowe's address on Lonergan's contribution to wider ecumenism took on an added poignancy that evening. His lecture had two main parts. In the first he explained his basic thesis on the need to reverse the order of the divine missions. The second part of the lecture drew out the implications for "the wider ecumenism of the world religions."[135]

In 1983 Crowe had briefly mentioned the idea of "anonymous Spiritans." He followed Lonergan in thinking of the world religions, in their positive moments, as the fruit of the Spirit. These moments were expressions of the inner gift of grace, he thought. Instead of looking to the mission of the Word and the various seeds of the Word scattered among these religions in their outer words as a basis for ecumenical work, Crowe wanted to turn to the mission of the Holy Spirit. He thought that Lonergan's later ideas about the priority of the gift of the Spirit and the religious conversion that the Spirit enabled gave a common foundation for wider ecumenism. Crowe writes: "What I am affirming, then, is our religious community with the world religions in some true and basic sense of the word, community, if not in the full sense of a common confession of faith, a common worship, and a common expression of hope in the eschaton. This community is effected by our common religious conversions, which in Lonergan's view, is our common orientation to the mystery of love and awe through the indwelling of the Holy Spirit who is given to us."[136] Crowe thinks that such an understanding of the world religions should shape our approach to non-Christian religious persons: "We do not, therefore, go to the world religions as strangers, as to heathens, as to pagans, enemies of God. For we are one with them in the Spirit, and expect to find in them the fruits of the Spirit. If these fruits seem often to be lacking, we will reflect that they are far too often lacking in ourselves also, though we have the outer word of doctrine and the sacraments deriving from the Son."[137]

Crowe refers us, in a footnote, to Lonergan's *Method in Theology* and Lonergan's 1970 paper "The Response of the Jesuit as Priest and Apostle in the Modern World." Where did this interest in world religions come from in Lonergan's considerations? Crowe thinks that Lonergan was inspired by the Second Vatican Council in his search "toward a common language of dialogue among the religions."[138]

After explaining the way in which genuinely religious people who have never heard Christ proclaimed can be called "anonymous Spiritans," Crowe finishes the lecture with the question of evangelization. He sees two steps in God's approach. He thinks "of God sending the Son in a second step following on the hidden gift of the Spirit."[139] While the gift of the Spirit unites us to non-Christians, "nevertheless," Crowe writes, "our confession of faith in Christ the Lord sets us apart with a difference of likewise divine proportions. We have a treasure that others do not possess; it is a treasure, however, given to be shared."[140] He finds support in Paul's experience of having to preach the Gospel (1 Corinthians 9:16). Crowe sees a parallel for the Christian's obligation to give Christ to others in Christ's own handing on to us of his divine nature (Philippians 2:6). He is also moved by the mandate of Mark 16:15: "Go forth to every part of the world, and proclaim the Good News to the whole creation."

Building on Augustine's and Aquinas's idea of the Holy Spirit as God's gift, Crowe writes: "It is possible to do now what Augustine and Aquinas did not do, and probably could not do in their time, that is, make the gift universally applicable throughout the world, and so come to a theology of the Spirit's worldwide presence among us, a presence from the beginning of human time and to the ends of human space."[141] Crucial to Crowe's thinking is the Catholic Church's teaching about the universal *offer* of salvation.[142] The fact that God offers sufficient grace to all is Crowe's reason, following Lonergan, for seeing a universal offer of the Holy Spirit. If all human beings, at all times, have been offered the grace of salvation, and such grace is the consequence of the gift of the Spirit, then that gift of the Spirit stretches back to the beginning of human history. "Such is Lonergan's theology, as I understand it," Crowe writes, "of God's first step in the divine self-communication; a step not taken in the fullness of time but at the very beginning of time; a word, but one spoken in its own way, not outwardly through seer and prophet, but inwardly in the heart, and so a word to all God's people, Jew and Gentile, Christian and non-Christian."[143] In 1975 Crowe had written about a distinct and necessary step, and in 1978 he spoke about two steps. Now, in 1984, he speaks of the Holy Spirit as God's first step towards us. The Son is God's second step.

Lonergan's analogy of human love provides Crowe with a way of understanding the unity of the divine missions from God's perspective: "God, it seems needs both the Spirit and Son to achieve the fullness of the divine being-in-love with us."[144] Notice how Crowe mentions first the Spirit and then the Son. In light of Lonergan's analogy of human love, "God really and truly falls in love with us, where the 'falling' is the gift of Love, the sending of the Spirit."[145] This real sending of the person of the Holy Spirit, according to Crowe, produces in us the gift of God's love. "But," he adds, "for reasons we must ponder long and deeply, God does not declare this Love from the beginning. There is the prolonged silence of the ages when God loves secretly, when the Spirit is present among us incognito, when in an almost human manner God holds back from a declaration of love."[146] If God wills all human beings to be saved, at all times, then there was this incognito sending of the Spirit from the beginning. But from the beginning of human history God had not sent his Son in the flesh. "Then at last," Crowe writes, "in this the final age, and in the most eloquent manner possible, the avowal is made; God's Love is declared, and the one and only Son is sent to be our savior."[147]

Under the influence of Lonergan's early-1970s analogy of human love, Crowe emphasizes the Spirit's mission in a new way. The Spirit is God's first step towards us. This gift is not seen as primarily a stepping stone towards the mission of the Son; it is a distinct step. It calls out for and demands another step. That other step is the gift of the Son. The Son's mission is seen as completing what God began with the gift of the Spirit. In 1984 Crowe speaks of a "partial moment" and a "completion."[148] The gift of the Spirit is the partial moment. That partial work is completed by meeting the Son in faith.

In a 1971 letter to a student Crowe expressed his view of the complementarity of the missions, modifying something that he had said in class: "I think now I would qualify my phrase of God speaking 'twice.' Maybe I would put it this way: as God sent first his Son and then his Spirit, so he uttered his one Word (all history, with Christ as its centre and its meaning) and enables us at the same time to hear it with the one gift of his Spirit (to prophet, evangelist, believer, etc.)."[149] At that time Crowe had not yet reversed his way of thinking about the order and context of the missions, but he connected all of history with the sending of his Son.[150] If God's historical word is some kind of mission of the Word, Crowe never separated the two divine missions from each other. The universal offer of God's grace is the fundamental inner gift, bestowed through the sending of the Holy Spirit. That first step has its counterpart in God's outer word spoken in history, "with Christ as its centre and its meaning."[151] At every moment in history, therefore, God the Father, in a mysterious way, sends his Spirit and his Son.

Building on Augustine and Aquinas, Crowe came to think that Pentecost was the moment in history that the Holy Spirit was manifested as a divine person.[152] He explained the great significance of Pentecost "through a distinction between presence and manifest presence."[153] Before Pentecost, the Holy Spirit was really present in human hearts, but not fully known to us as a divine person. The Incarnation and Pentecost disclosed the already present Holy Spirit to us.

If the manifest presence of the Spirit follows upon the mission of Christ, Crowe has not *totally* rejected the idea of the Holy Spirit's mission taking place on account of the Son's mission. As a man and woman may fall in love more after they avow their love, so Crowe thinks that there is a way in which God falls in love with us more, that is, more fully bestows the Holy Spirit, after the declaration of divine love in the Son.

This dependence of the Spirit's mission on the Son's is confirmed by Crowe's idea of "the *epoché* of the Spirit."[154] Crowe is "borrowing the word from philosophy, where it means, in particular, suspension of judgment, or, more generally, a check on one's natural activity."[155] He proposes that an *epoché* of the Spirit, analogous to the *kenosis* in the Son, "must be affirmed."[156] This check on the Spirit's activity must be affirmed because, Crowe writes, "the Spirit in our hearts still allows us to form the most preposterous ideas, to commit the most abominable deeds."[157] He sees "this self-restraint as being exercised in different degrees, as being removed step by step in the stages of history."[158] Crowe distinguishes three stages to the self-restraint of the Spirit and refers to two releases of the Spirit's activity. The Spirit's *epoché* "would be at its greatest degree of severity when the Spirit dwelt anonymously for long ages in our hearts. There would be a great release from self-restraint at Pentecost, after God's avowal of the divine Love in the only Son. There will be a complete release in our final state, when we will know as we are known (1 Cor 13:12) and enjoy the full reign of the Spirit over all our conduct."[159] Pentecost was a great release into the world of the Holy Spirit's activity. What explains the first great release of the Holy Spirit's self-restraint? It followed upon the "avowal of divine Love in the only Son." The avowal of the Son refers to his voluntarily laying down of his life, together with his Resurrection and Ascension. His paschal mystery releases the Holy Spirit into the world as never before in history. In other words, the fullness of the Spirit's mission within history depends on the Son's completion of his mission.[160]

Conclusion

On Reformation Sunday, 27 October 1968, Crowe was asked by St Luke's Lutheran Church to preach to its congregation.[161] The title of his homily was "Son and Spirit in the Church."[162] In it, he refuses to think that the "Son and Spirit can themselves be in conflict. The Spirit proceeds from the Son and works *in the context of the Son*."[163] By 1984 Crowe was convinced that there was another possibility for understanding the context of the two missions. He came to think that the Holy Spirit's mission also provided, in some ways, the context, the rationale, the special reason, for the Son's mission.

Bernard Lonergan's Latin theological works prior to 1965 provided the framework for Crowe to think about the order of the divine missions in the first stage of his pneumatology (1953–68). As he interacted with the later Lonergan's theology of love, Crowe came to think, in the second stage of his theology of the Holy Spirit (1969–84), that Lonergan had changed his mind on *the order* of the missions. The Spirit, Crowe began to suspect, was the first divine person communicated to us. He adopted this position between 1969 and 1972, even before he had begun to appreciate in earnest the analogy of human love.

As soon as Crowe began to appropriate this analogy for the roles of the Three in the world (the Holy Spirit as God's falling in love with us, the Son as declaring love, and the Father as love consummated), he also began, around 1974–5, to rethink in an obscure way *the context* of the two missions. The analogy of human love seems to provide a unified way of understanding the two missions in a single divine plan in which the Holy Spirit is sent first. Hints of this unified plan appear in his 1978 book *Theology of the Christian Word.* Through accepting this analogy of human love as explanatory for the ways in which God sends the Spirit and the Son, Crowe finds the whole question of reversing the contexts of the mission emerging in his thinking.

Crowe accepted the reversal of the contexts of the missions at first as a "hypothesis only."[164] As he grasped more deeply Lonergan's new analogy of human love, Crowe's hypothesis of the reversal of the missions became his "thesis." With the cessation of Lonergan's intellectual output, he brought his ideas on the reversal of the order and the context of the missions into the spotlight in 1983 and 1984.

While Crowe had earlier stressed that the Spirit was sent *on account of* the Son's incarnate mission, and then he later explained how the Son was sent *on account of* the Spirit, I do not think that Crowe intended these to be mutually exclusive understandings of the missions. It is true, however, that he never explicitly stated that his two ways of thinking about the contexts were complementary. Nevertheless, his understanding of Pentecost shows that Crowe never fully abandoned his earlier understanding of the context of the missions.

But why did Crowe care so much about this question of the relation of the missions? Was it purely the internal demands of trying to keep pace with the mind of Lonergan? The answer to this question leads us into the broader context of Crowe's theology, the other main factor in Crowe's change of mind. His concern for the Church's life was a major factor in his concern for the relation of the divine missions. His tensions with Church authority in this second stage convinced him of the danger of overemphasizing the mission of the Son. That struggle also convinced him to prioritize the Spirit's mission.

5 Arguing with Church Authorities as Helping to Reverse the Missions

The Son represents the institutional, but an institutional open to the full range of the human as God conceived it. The Spirit represents the charismatic, but works without disorder in the context provided by the Son. The Father awaits us in the eschatological hope.

Frederick Crowe, A Time of Change

In the year 1968 Pope Paul VI had published *Humanae vitae*,[1] and during the aftermath of the dissent over this encyclical Crowe faced a crisis over authority. In 1976 the pope approved a statement restricting priestly ordination to men.[2] Crowe faced a second crisis concerning the magisterium. He came to think that many of the leaders in the Catholic Church had an unbalanced understanding of the relationship between the institutional and charismatic dimensions of the Church. According to Crowe's later thinking, the proper context for the institutional aspects of the Church was provided by the charismatic side of the Church.[3]

Even in 1968 Crowe thought that certain problems, for instance at the time of the Protestant Reformation, were based on a misunderstanding of the relation of the two missions.[4] Catholics largely emphasized the prolongation of the mission of the incarnate Son in their focus on the institutional dimensions of Christianity, he suggested. In reaction, Protestants, he added, implicitly focused more on the prolongation of the Spirit's mission in the innovating, charismatic, and renewing aspects of the Church. There was a general failure to grasp the relation between these two necessary aspects of the Church. As the Church needed to reverse its way of thinking of the institutional and the charismatic, so it also needed, Crowe eventually thought, to reverse the order in which it thought of the mission of the Son and the mission of the Spirit. I maintain in this chapter that by at least 1983–4 he had come to think the reversal of the missions was a necessary doctrine for guiding the future life of the Church.

The first half of this chapter lays out Crowe's main struggles with Church authority in the years after the Second Vatican Council. His struggles with the magisterium's teaching on artificial birth control (section 1) and women's ordination (section 2) revealed what he thought was wrong with the mode of living in the Church. The trouble was the Roman curia's mode of dominating the learning process within the Church by an unbalanced reliance on tradition. The second half of this chapter discusses Crowe's deeper penetration into the remedy: overcoming the Church's neglect of the Holy Spirit.

Crowe's Struggle with the Magisterium

Aftermath of Humanae vitae

Pope Paul VI's encyclical, *Humanae vitae*, published on 25 July 1968, reaffirmed, contrary to the hopes of many, that all sexual acts in marriage must be open to life, and thus it rejected the use of the hormonal birth control pill. Crowe was *not* one of the eighty-seven theologians who signed a famous statement of dissent, but he agreed with their judgment of the non-binding, non-infallible character of the encyclical's teaching. He was unsettled, however, by this rupture between the pope and a great portion of the Church.[5] One does not have to agree with his quiet dissent to admit that he was asking a real and important question: what is the meaning of this widespread dissent among so many otherwise faithful Catholics? By June 1969, in his lecture "Responsibility of the Theologian, and the Learning Church," Crowe could say: "To my mind we are in a new situation; we are not the Church we were a year ago; there is a new spirit at work; we have a new awareness of our co-responsibility; God has taught us new ways of living as his people; he has sanctioned a new respect for pluralism, and brought more clearly to our attention the legitimacy of dissent within the Church. All of this I assume as fact, and I consider it the responsibility of a theologian to try to explain that fact."[6]

Crowe considered himself neither an exegete, nor a historian, but a theologian. He understood his work as one of understanding, of trying to explain, of giving reasons for religious facts. "Our responsibility [as theologians]," he adds, "is to go to the heart of the matter, to what was really involved in the chapter of history just concluded, to teach the deeper truths that will guide the long-range development of the Church's life. It is a matter of analyzing the new situation and of trying to indicate a style of life, a *modus vivendi*, principles of conduct, that suit our new assumption of responsibility."[7] What does Crowe mean by a chapter of history being concluded? It is the chapter of history, he explained a few years later, that began with the reaction of the early modern period to medieval Catholicism. He thought that certain structures in medieval Europe involved a "domination of all areas by the Church."[8] The "grave defect" of medieval Catholicism was the failure to recognize fully "the legitimate autonomy of the human, the natural, the whole range of human institutions."[9] By *legitimate autonomy of the human*, Crowe means that human and natural things have "a value in themselves."[10]

In the first place, having a value in themselves means that "human achievements are not merely means to a higher end."[11] Crowe then gives some examples, namely the arts and the study of languages and philosophy. "The arts," he writes, "do not exist simply to decorate sacred functions. The study of languages and philosophy is not undertaken solely for the exposition of scripture."[12] There is some sense in which art and human studies have their own proper end and worth. They would be valuable even if they were not used for sacred tasks by the Church.

Secondly, the fact that the human dimension has its own value means that the human or natural aspects of the world have a limited measure of autonomy. "That is to say," Crowe writes, "the multiplication table is independent of the decrees of an ecumenical council; the problems of astronomy are not solved by looking up the Bible."[13] When this limited freedom of the laws of the sciences is not recognized by theologians, we have what Crowe calls "theological imperialism."[14] He acknowledges that such imperialism may be paternal, but still "it does not correspond to the mind and will of God for his creation."[15] In other words, God created a natural world that has its own proper laws.

The trouble with such imperialism, according to Crowe, is that it "leads inevitably to rebellion."[16] In the humanistic rebellion of the early modern period that followed, there was a reaction, he maintains, against everything "the Church stood for."[17] Crowe thinks that the inner dynamism of the human, stifled by a theological imperialism, burst forth after the Middle Ages. "Philosophy refused," he writes, "to be any longer simply the handmaid of theology; the arts asserted their independence of sacred functions, to develop rather according to their own inner dynamic; nations repudiated the hegemony of a sacred rule in Rome."[18] In a word, it was "a rebellion of the whole phalanx of this world's values."[19] Crowe is not talking primarily about the Protestant Reformation; he sees this movement as a related phenomenon. But there was a more fundamental rebellion from within the culture of the Middle Ages. He sees this reaction to imperialism as a "long and sad story" spanning the last "five or six centuries of the modern era."[20] This chapter in the Church's history ends with it learning the lesson of human autonomy.

Crowe thought that this lesson was officially accepted by the Catholic Church in the Second Vatican Council's document *The Pastoral Constitution on the Church in the Modern World*. He speaks of this document as "the longest, the most unexpected, and to my mind, the most important document of that Council."[21] In it the Church "turned back to the world and took a tentative step towards it."[22] In so doing, the document "liberated us from an undue attachment to a way that is now gone."[23] The old ecclesiastical imperialism over the human, in Crowe's mind, was finished in theory.

But what would take its place? Crowe was not sure, but he was committed to developing the ideas that the Church would need in order to co-operate with the legitimate autonomy of the human world. He saw this recognition of the autonomy of the world and the need to co-operate with it as the end of a chapter in history. The human elements had been rebelling, sometimes wrongly, for centuries. Finally, with the Second Vatican Council's *Pastoral Constitution on the Church in the Modern World*, this legitimate autonomy was recognized.

Crowe also thought, however, that the Church in the late 1960s was in a more complicated situation than it had been in a generation earlier. One used to be able to say that "in those days France got the ideas, and Rome judged their orthodoxy."[24] Crowe felt that there was "real validity in the arrangement. However, that was an era when the truth was more in our possession; we had not yet begun the great migration in the world of ideas."[25] He really thought that something new was happening at the time of his lecture "Responsibility of the Theologian, and the Learning Church." "The situation today," he writes, "is not one in which we study new ideas as possible conclusions from fixed starting-points in traditional premises."[26] In other words, in the older arrangement the pope had the responsibility of speaking authoritatively in certain situations. In the new situation, Crowe is saying, the pope himself can no longer form these judgments without wider input from the Church. We are in less possession of the truth because the amount of data about the judgments that have to be made has so increased. Answers to these new questions cannot simply be deduced from premises found in the older doctrinal teachings of the Church.

Crowe is not, however, a revolutionary or a Protestant advocating discontinuity with the past: "Surely our new ideas must not contradict the ancient faith – in extreme radical eyes this will put me squarely with the conservatives – but today's ideas are so new that confrontation with the ancient faith is not the primary question – and that perhaps in conservative eyes will put me among the radicals."[27] The key words here are *today's ideas are so new*. Crowe thinks that the Church's magisterium, consisting of the pope and the bishops in union with him, is not able to pass judgment on these new ideas without a long process of learning. From this process emerges the co-responsibility of theologians and informed lay people.

Crowe considered that God was, in general, giving the Church more responsibility. "God wants us to take over more and more of the government of the world, according to our degree of maturity. As St. Thomas would say, the progressive actuation of our potencies calls for a corresponding exercise."[28] In other words, Crowe seems to think that this new role of the laity in helping the Church to learn is part of a larger growth within the Church. As God entrusted new powers to the Church, the Church needs to act accordingly. Teenagers cannot act in school as little children do, for example. Their new powers of maturity call for corresponding exercises of responsibility.

All this seems to be a bit vague. We have to remember, however, that Crowe was trying to understand what was happening. For him, understanding was about arriving at ideas that may or may not be right. His idea for explaining the validity of the widespread dissent was this: "When one man speaks for God, divine intervention must in the nature of the case occur continually; when the people speak, God can trust them a little more."[29] The "one man" he is referring to is the pope to whom God would continually be giving help to teach the truth in faith and morals. As God entrusted this role, of speaking on his behalf, to a wider number of people, the guidance would be less continual, thought Crowe. Many people in the long run, working together in a Spirit-inspired, self-correcting process of learning, can be trusted to find the truth, he is saying. The pope and Roman curia, he felt, did not seem to realize what God was doing in the Church.

Crowe was looking for what would guide the Church after it shed theological imperialism. He was clearly concerned about the life of the Church, wanting to understand what was happening and to formulate principles for the "long range development of the Church's life."[30] He eventually arrives at the principle of the reversal of the two missions and sees the priority of the Spirit's mission as fundamental to the life of the Church because the Spirit provides the grace by which the required learning can take place. Such a principle is very general and abstract, but this is the kind of analysis Crowe thought that Lonergan promoted.[31] We have to arrive at the ultimate and most general principle that will guide the Church's life.

What was ailing the Church was a neglect of learning. The required research and discernment that was needed to enable the Church to learn properly and therefore teach authentically was being overlooked. Instead there was an over-reliance on what the institutional Church had already understood and judged about Christ's revelation in his mission on earth. The most general problem that I think Crowe came to recognize was the over-emphasis on the mission of the Son to the neglect of the mission of the Holy Spirit.

Struggle over Women's Ordination

Crowe's next great struggle against the magisterium also confirmed his sense of what the Church required to guide its life. By the mid-1970s a debate over women's ordination was snowballing. Catholics and non-Catholics alike were debating the question. Finally, the pope asked the Congregation for the Doctrine of the Faith (CDF) to issue a statement.

On the feast of St Teresa of Avila, 15 October 1976, Paul VI approved the CDF's *Declaration on the Question of the Admission of Women to the Ministerial Priesthood* (*Inter insigniores*). Towards the end of its introduction the document states: "In execution of a mandate received from the Holy Father and echoing the declaration he himself made in his letter of November 30, 1975, the Sacred Congregation for the Doctrine of the Faith judges it necessary to recall that the Church, in fidelity to the example of the Lord, does not consider herself authorized to admit women to priestly ordination."[32] Despite various statements by Pope Paul VI and this statement by the CDF, Crowe was unconvinced by all the arguments against ordaining women.

Even before the release of this document the Catholic Theological Society of America had commissioned a task force of theologians in the summer of 1975 "not to perform new research, but to conduct a theological review and critique of the work that has been done by various committees and conferences under Roman Catholic and other Christian sponsorship."[33] Crowe was a part of this five-person task force, which met four times over the next two years. Together with the other members of the task force, Crowe acknowledged a global apprehension of the "relevance and irrelevance for our time of practices followed or decisions taken in the past; there is as well the possibility of discerning an emerging mentality and consensus on the signs of the times and stirring of the Holy Spirit among us."[34] Distinguishing a focus on decisions in the past from what was happening in the present, he called for a "mindset that we call open" in which "the focus is on God as operating in the eternal now and therefore still exercising a sovereign freedom with a range of possibilities open; ... [the focus] is on the Holy Spirit as the Creator Spirit leading us into an ever-new future; it is on the human race as responding to the Creator Spirit by determining the needs of our time and freely creating the means that will, under God's initiative and with God's help, provide for them."[35]

Crowe acknowledges that women have never been ordained to the pastoral ministry, but he does not think that this ends the discussion. Past decisions were made in past situations. "Women's ordination," he writes, "is a question never before addressed to the church in a comparable set of circumstances. It demands a new effort at self-understanding, and an openness to new practice under the guidance of the Creator Spirit."[36] Part of the new set of circumstances was the decision made by other Christians to admit "women to pastoral office."[37] Considering these Christians as somehow part of the Church, Crowe feels that this decision should have significance for Roman Catholic considerations of the question. The other important factor was that Catholics had allowed women in some parts of the world to carry out pastoral ministries where there was a shortage of priests. Crowe thought that input was coming to the Catholic Church on this question not so much from the past as from the present.

Behind the CDF's opposition to women's ordination Crowe feels that there is a different mindset or mentality. This "closed" mindset focuses "on the past, the already determined, the formulations and institutions already handed down to us."[38] In general, this closed mentality disregards "the competent research of dedicated Christian scholars and believers."[39] In place of such research, it tends to substitute "a decree on what the documents of faith mean."[40] In other words, women's ordination is ruled out by an appeal to the example of Christ, what Christ decided in the past. Once that decision has been made, no place is given to present-day data from modern research. Crowe adds that such decrees on what the Scriptures mean are bolstered by "an exaggerated reliance on teaching authority."[41] All the elements of this closed mindset seem to be aimed at the CDF's document on women's ordination.

In line with this distinction between an open and a closed mindset, Crowe summarizes his basic trouble with many of the arguments that oppose women's ordination. These arguments are "based on an unwarranted (because, in fact, fundamentally untraditional) adherence to past formulations and institutions as the unchanging norm for all time."[42] In other words, the basic trouble is the mentality, the presuppositions, behind the arguments. This mentality decides ahead of time what will count for evidence. Crowe, by contrast, together with the task force, recommends "the full and free investigation of the question with the readiness to form the judgments and take the decisions toward which the Holy Spirit is leading us."[43]

The issue over women's ordination can be seen as part of the larger question in Crowe's mind over authority and freedom. In this case, Crowe's reservations about the magisterium's teachings on restricting ordination to men are rooted in his conviction that human and historical data were not sufficiently considered by those in authority. The Church needed to allow the conclusions of the human sciences to be expressed freely. The data of sociology, psychology, and biology, in other words, were not being given due freedom by the magisterium as evidence in the arguments over women's ordination.

The response to this objection from the side of the magisterium of the Church, however, boils down to this: "the human sciences, however valuable their contribution in their own domain cannot suffice here, for they cannot grasp the realities of faith: the properly supernatural content of these realities is beyond their competence."[44] But the question for Crowe is whether most of the arguments used by the magisterium rely too heavily on presuppositions regarding the nature of men and women, their attributes, Jesus's attitude towards women, and the roles of men and women – presuppositions that the human sciences have called into question.[45] Unless we want a double-truth theory (in which faith teaches one thing about men and women, and the human sciences teach something else to the contrary), Crowe seems to be suggesting that the magisterium must engage more with the arguments coming from the present research.[46]

As we consider his attitude towards the human sciences of psychology, biology, and sociology, we have to understand Crowe's more critical understanding of the historicity of the Scriptures to grasp his position on women's ordination. Crowe was never a fundamentalist, and his course notes from 1965–6 show awareness of historical-critical scholarship. But by 1972 he could make a remarkable concession in his acceptance of modern criticism and mentality: "I accept the fact that the gospels are not biographies, that we really do not know exactly what Jesus said and did in the way we would like to know. I accept as quite probable the view that Jesus did not claim to be the Messiah or Son of God, that possibly he did not even claim to be Son of Man, that he did not particularly concern himself with the features of the true Messiah or with purifying the Jewish idea of the Messiah."[47] This view of Crowe's presupposes that the gospel writers attributed much to Christ that he never said. If we do not really know what Christ said, then it is difficult to draw conclusions about Christ's mindset. Such a position needs to be compared with criticisms made in *A Report on the Status of Women in Church and Society*: "It must be noted that the argument based on the praxis of Jesus rests on the confidence that we are able to say with certainty what the practical mindset of Jesus of Nazareth was. Any theological awareness of the 'Quest for the Historical Jesus' debate would shatter this confidence."[48] This passage, co-authored by Crowe, highlights how historical-critical biblical scholarship had undermined for Crowe one traditional basis against women's ordination. His own confidence in being able to draw conclusions about what Christ said and did had been seriously damaged. His trust in using the fact that Christ only chose men for the Twelve, as an argument against women's ordination, was also shattered. Crowe thought that the Roman curia, however, still relied on older notions of the historicity of the Scriptures and still held an unwarranted reliance on past formulations and institutions.

In the first half of this chapter I discussed two crises that Crowe experienced regarding the institutional Church. He was critical of the positions of the magisterium on artificial birth control and women's ordination. In addition, he was critical of the mode of operation used by the magisterium in making its decisions on these disputed questions. Crowe thought that the magisterium was neglecting data provided by the present experience of Catholics and the human sciences. He believed that the medieval ecclesiastical imperialism had not completely disappeared. Since these questions of birth control and women's ordination had always been answered negatively by the tradition, a crisis was emerging in the "relation between tradition and theology."[49] Theologians were pushing for certain new things while the magisterium claimed to be clinging to its understanding of the tradition. On the one side there was the authority of the Church's hierarchy, and on the other the freedom of theologians to investigate questions. But what could be done to find a way through this impasse between the magisterium and theologians?

Rethinking the Role of the Spirit in Relation to the Son's Mission

In 1983 Crowe saw a wonderful fittingness in the way that God communicates himself to us according to both what he is and what a human being is. Corresponding to our "orientation to the outer and objective," God sends the Word, "the one who is already God's objectified understanding."[50] The Word's character as eternal, objectified understanding continues in time within humanity's objective world. In this way, the eternal Word becomes, "in a 'natural' prolongation, the outer Word the human race needs."[51] God communicates himself to us in the data of sense through his Son, but how will he communicate himself to us according to the needs of our subjectivity, our interiority, the data of consciousness? He sends the Holy Spirit, "the one who is divine subjectivity surging up in the infinite Love that responds to the infinite Word."[52] The Holy Spirit is sent into our hearts, flooding them "with the love that makes us spiritual."[53] And so our inner focus in our relationship with God is on the Spirit. The outer focus of our Christian lives is on the Son.

1983 Lonergan Workshop Lecture

Crowe titled his 1983 Lonergan Workshop Lecture "Son and Spirit: Tension in the Divine Missions?" The word *tension* immediately suggests the earlier crises that we have examined. There the tension in the Church was between the institutional hierarchy and what the Spirit was thought to be saying through other dimensions.[54] But Crowe had come to see a more fundamental tension within the Church: "a tension for us between the role of the Son and that of the Spirit."[55] As we will see, he does not think that such a tension is intrinsic to the two distinct missions. The tension that has developed is "due, not to the Father's purpose, but to our failure to keep the two foci as clearly distinct as the Son and Spirit are themselves distinct."[56]

In the talk Crowe's basic image for helping us to understand the importance of the two missions, with their inner and outer complementary words, is that of an ellipse. In the ellipse there are two foci. Crowe contrasts the ellipse and its two foci with the single centre of a circle: "A circle, as you know, is a special form of an ellipse, one in which the two foci coincide."[57] In the past Crowe had thought that a Christocentric religious attitude had neglected the role of the Spirit. Instead of focusing on both the Son and the Spirit, the elliptical nature of our Christian life had collapsed into a circle with Christ alone at the centre. "Of course," Crowe now quickly adds, "our God is triune, and eventually we must find a place for the Father, but at least we have a first approximation on the way to a complete integration of the three persons in the work of our redemption."[58] Without mentioning Trinification, Crowe wants to find the way in which all three persons are involved in our redemption. But his special concern is the role of the Holy Spirit.

Fr Kilian McDonnell, OSB, never mentions Crowe by name in his 1985 article "A Trinitarian Theology of the Holy Spirit?,"[59] but it seems likely from internal evidence that he is reacting at least indirectly to Crowe's 1983 lecture "Son and Spirit."[60] In the middle of his article McDonnell writes, "While insisting on the 'real' distinction between the two missions of Word and Spirit, there is a danger of conceiving of them as two foci at the ends of an elongated circle."[61] He even inserts a drawing of the elongated circle, an image not found in Crowe's article (see figure 5).

McDonnell then comments: "While possibly not heretical, such a conception would be dangerous and might lead to a kind of economic tritheism."[62] His main positive rejoinder is that the Holy Spirit's function or role is to put us into contact with Christ. McDonnell believes that the two missions are better thought of as two circles superimposed on one another. There is always one focus: the incarnate Word. The Holy Spirit is *how* we are able to know him.

Noting the need to keep the two missions "in balance and fruitful tension,"[63] McDonnell does not deny the reality of the two missions or the importance of distinct roles for each divine person. He does not deny the equality of the two missions. He just thinks that they are both "at the center, but in different ways: Christ as the 'what' and the Spirit as the 'how.'"[64]

According to Michael Vertin, a friend of both Fr Kilian McDonnell and Fr Crowe, Crowe was bothered by reading the suggestion that he might be heretical. As far as I know, however, Crowe never responded to this critique. While I have not found Crowe ever repeating this idea of an ellipse, Fr Kilian repeated his warning almost twenty years later.[65]

Fr Kilian's fear is that the two foci, the Son and the Spirit, become two separate and unrelated sources of guidance for the Christian life. Given the ellipse as imagined or as drawn, the two clearly separated foci can give this impression. But what if Crowe was thinking of the ellipse not as imagined but as intelligible, according to the definition of an ellipse? An ellipse can be given various mathematical definitions, but the following seems relevant to Crowe's discussion: "An ellipse ... is the locus of points from which the sum of their distances from two fixed points (the foci) is constant."[66] Accordingly, every point on the ellipse is determined by its distance from both foci. When the ellipse is simply imagined, one does not necessarily consider every point as always

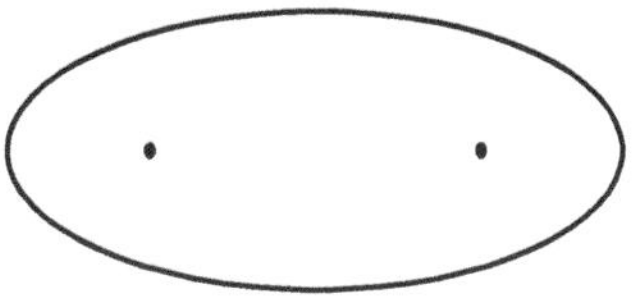

Figure 5 Kilian McDonnell's elliptical depiction of the two divine roles

related to both foci. When one thinks of the ellipse as defined, the two foci provide an analogy for the two missions, in which each is always in relation to the other. Instead of thinking of the Son and the Holy Spirit as two separate foci of attention, the ellipse *as defined* enables us to think of distinct missions, always in relation to each other.

Given Crowe's undergraduate engineering background, he must have been familiar with a definition of an ellipse. Moreover, he could not have used this analogy without having in the back of his mind Lonergan's famous passage about the definition of a circle in the opening chapter of *Insight*: "a circle is a locus of coplanar points equidistant from a centre."[67] Lonergan went on to distinguish the image of the circle from the definition of a circle. Crowe's own analogy of an ellipse *as defined* illustrates how the Spirit's mission, while distinct, is always related to the Son's; and the Son's mission, while distinct, is always related to the Spirit's.

Crowe develops the analogy of the ellipse because its two focal points reflect how the "Son and Spirit are distinct and complementary."[68] And he thinks that "the *kairos* has come for a shift from the Christocentric to the elliptical with the two foci of Son and Spirit."[69] Crowe compares this shift to the Copernican revolution in philosophy that is associated especially with Immanuel Kant. Copernicus had shifted the focus, the centre of the universe, from the earth to the sun. In a similar way, Crowe thought that Kant had shifted the focus of philosophy from the object to the subject. But he did not believe that this was a sufficient answer to the question of the importance of subjectivity. What we need is a philosophy like Lonergan's that focuses on the subject without losing the object. For this reason, Crowe thinks that the kairos has come for a shift in theology. "Our ancestors," he writes, "did not have a philosophy that would enable them to relate the roles of Son and Spirit in the fundamental way it is possible for us."[70] The philosophy that he refers to is Lonergan's philosophy of interiority.

Lonergan's philosophy, according to Crowe, is perfectly designed to help us understand better the distinct roles of the Son and the Holy Spirit in our sanctification. "Paul, Luke, and John," Crowe writes of the New Testament authors, "each contributed something to the solution of the problem."[71] He then mentions Augustine and Thomas Aquinas as helping to organize "things a bit with their doctrine of visible and invisible missions."[72] In other words, Augustine and Aquinas provided a theoretical framework, by their distinction between visible and invisible missions, for understanding the New Testament accounts of the mission or sending of the Son and Spirit. "But," Crowe adds, "it is only with the turn to the subject, with the emergence of a philosophy of interiority, with the replacement of causality by meaning as a basic category, that we have the conceptual system we need for an integrated theology of the roles of Son and Spirit in the world."[73] According to Crowe, Lonergan developed this philosophy of interiority in dialogue with thinkers after Aquinas. At the same time, however, Crowe thought that Lonergan's philosophy transposed Aquinas's theoretical distinctions without destroying them.[74]

Besides the turn to the subject, and the comprehensive theory of interiority that eventually emerges from this turn, Crowe feels that we need the replacement of causality with meaning as the basic category in theology if we want to solve the difficulty of relating the roles of Son and Spirit in a systematic way. The main problem historically is understanding the role of the Holy Spirit. But Crowe is alive to the way in which a certain theory of causality has made this problem even more difficult. No Christian theologian denies that the Son died on the Cross. This is proper to him and not just appropriated. The Son assumed a human nature in which he could die. Crowe points out, however, how it seems to many that "the Spirit, having no nature but the divine, can exercise no activity in the world that is proper to himself but only that which is common to the three persons."[75] Crowe then quotes the Council of Florence: "Pater et filius et spiritus sanctus non tria principia creaturae, sed unum principium."[76] In other words, we call the Father the Creator, but he alone is not the creator. According to a single divine operation, the Son and Holy Spirit also create the world. We appropriate this title of Creator to the Father because he is the source of all Trinitarian life. In a similar way, should we not simply see the activities attributed to the Holy Spirit as appropriations that are not uniquely his but are said for some kind of fittingness?

Crowe thinks that the replacement of causality by meaning helps to put the teaching of the Council of Florence in a new context. The metaphysical principle of Florence "becomes secondary, even marginal, in a universe where meaning, value, intentionality analysis, are basic."[77] He is not rejecting the metaphysical principle of efficient causality, which answers certain theoretical questions about the Trinity and creation that must be answered. He is not denying that there is one divine power possessed by all three divine persons. But the question is whether a perspective other than that of efficient causality can help us understand the relationship of the Trinity and the work of salvation. In this case, Crowe looks to the notion of meaning and exemplar causality for help.

In general, Crowe thought that Lonergan helped to introduce the notion of meaning into Catholic theology.[78] And he was especially moved by Lonergan's notion of "incarnate meaning."[79] In *Method in Theology*

Lonergan introduces this idea with a quotation from Newman: "Cor ad cor loquitur"[80] (heart speaks to heart). "Incarnate meaning," Lonergan continues, "combines all or at least many of the other carriers of meaning. It can be at once intersubjective, artistic, symbolic, linguistic. It is the meaning of a person, of his way of life, of his words, or of his deeds."[81] The different kinds of meaning in Lonergan are not essential for this chapter, but his connection of incarnate meaning with a "person" is significant.

The Son of God assumed a human and historical life. The incarnate meaning of his human life expressed the meaning of a divine person. This meaning, in other words, was communicated to us in history by virtue of his human life and ministry. But how can the person of the Holy Spirit have an incarnate meaning that is communicated in history when he did not incarnate?

If every person has a distinct meaning, Crowe argues, and if the Holy Spirit is a person, then the Holy Spirit has meaning in himself. Crowe claims that the "Holy Spirit has his distinct meaning, else he would not be himself."[82] The Holy Spirit "brings his own meaning into the world with him."[83] Since meaning, as Lonergan taught Crowe, is "constitutive of human and transcendent reality, so the world is affected by [the Holy Spirit's] presence."[84]

What is the meaning of the person of the Holy Spirit? His meaning is based on his unique personal property. The Holy Spirit, in Crowe's theology, proceeds from the Father and the Son as Love. What it means to be the Holy Spirit, therefore, is to be proceeding Love. The Holy Spirit has this distinct meaning within God. And Crowe thinks of this proceeding Love in two ways.

The Holy Spirit's eternal identity, as Crowe came to realize in his *Doctrine of the Most Holy Trinity*, is both proceeding Complacency and Concern. Created complacency and concern both find their exemplar in the Holy Spirit; both kinds of love provide analogies for the Holy Spirit. The Holy Spirit as proceeding Complacency is eternal loving acceptance in God of what is. The Holy Spirit, as eternal proceeding Concern, is eternal openness to change and newness. Since 1965 Crowe has been thinking of the Holy Spirit as this eternal, energetic, overflowing impulse towards those on whom God can bestow love.

The notion of incarnate meaning helps Crowe to start thinking about how the Holy Spirit can have a unique and proper role in the world without assuming a created nature like the Son did. He is the eternal exemplar for an inner religious word, a meaning that God speaks to our hearts. This created, complacent, and concerned love that God speaks to us both modifies our interiority and is patterned after the exemplar, the Holy Spirit. All three divine persons efficiently cause this love in us, but it is uniquely a created participation in the Holy Spirit's eternal identity as proceeding Love.

The fact that the Spirit did not assume a human and historical life does not mean, for Crowe, that his being sent is not real and without manifestations. Crowe thinks that there are interior manifestations of the Holy Spirit's presence: "When we are born again in the Spirit, we have an interior presence that is just as real and just as much a presence of the divine (more so, one could argue) as the presence of Jesus in the Holy Land; but we do not know how to handle it. We do not even know how to study our human interiority, as a step toward study of the interior presence of the Holy Spirit."[85] Crowe's emphasis on the reality of the presence of the Holy Spirit echoes the earlier words of Anscar Vonier, OSB. In his essay "The Coming of the Spirit" Vonier writes, "The Spirit is invisible; but this does not mean that the Spirit is not manifest."[86] Vonier even adds, "Since the Ascension of Our Lord the presence of the Spirit is *more manifest* among men than the presence of the Word Incarnate."[87]

Anticipating what Crowe will point out in his *Doctrine of the Most Holy Trinity*,[88] Vonier compares the narration of the coming of the Son as depicted in Luke 1 with the coming of the Spirit in Acts 2. He then writes: "It is as theologically accurate to say that the Holy Spirit came at the first Pentecost as it is to say that the Son of God came on the first Christmas night: the external forms were different, but there was no difference in the completeness and realism of the advents. The Son takes unto Himself a human nature, our flesh; the Spirit uses signs and wonders."[89] Vonier purposely employs the word *use* in the present tense "because the sign remains as much as Christ's humanity remains."[90] For Vonier, the Church in her visibility is the continued sign of the Spirit's presence. At the end of the essay he writes: "The Spirit will never be more manifest than he is. Substantially, the Spirit is as much with us now as He will be for all eternity."[91] What Vonier teaches about the manifest presence of the Spirit anticipates Crowe's teaching. Crowe's emphasis, however, is on the inner manifestations of the Spirit's presence in those who are born again in the Spirit.

It seems to me that, rather than talking exclusively about manifestations of the Spirit in religious conversion, Crowe could make a stronger case for an incarnate meaning of the Holy Spirit by connecting these inner manifestations especially with the sacrament of Confirmation. In his 1971 document approving a new rite of Confirmation, Pope Paul VI explained: "From that time on the apostles, in fulfillment of Christ's will, imparted to the newly baptized by the laying on of hands the gift of the Spirit that completes the grace of Baptism. For this reason in the Letter to the Hebrews the doctrine concerning Baptism and the laying on of hands is listed among the first elements of Christian instruction. The imposition of hands is rightly recognized by the Catholic tradition as the origin of the sacrament of Confirmation, *which in a certain way perpetuates the grace of Pentecost in the Church.*"[92] Part of the grace of the first Pentecost was the manifestation of the Holy Spirit as a divine person. The Holy Spirit "was not yet given," the Gospel of John says, "because Christ had not yet been glorified" (John 7:39). At Pentecost, after long centuries of hidden work, the Holy Spirit was finally given and welcomed as a divine person.[93] If Confirmation "in a certain way perpetuates the grace of Pentecost in the Church," then one could argue that Confirmation's inner effects continue to manifest the Holy Spirit to us as a divine person with an incarnate meaning.

For Crowe, the notion of incarnate meaning not only helps to explain how the Holy Spirit can have a unique role in our salvation but also helps to overcome a problem arising out of Christology. According to Crowe, the more scholars become aware of the historicity of the human life of Jesus of Nazareth, the more difficult it seems to some to apply his words and deeds to all times and places. The particularity of the Son's human and historical life causes problems for the discovery of what the followers of Christ should do in much different historical situations. He was made "man in a particular time and place, under the particular conditions that human historicity makes inevitable."[94] This historicity "automatically prevent[s] his becoming an immediate model for the whole human race in all its variety."[95]

In the context of thinking about the Holy Spirit's distinct meaning, Crowe claims that "there should be no insuperable difficulty, then, in conceiving him as the principle of indefinite adaptability which the historicity of man requires and the particularity of the God-man does not readily furnish."[96] He speaks here of the Holy Spirit as the principle of infinite adaptability. This is connected with seeing the Holy Spirit as concerned Love, open to what is not yet and what can be. The Church is in need of adapting to changing circumstances. The God-man gave us certain ways of living that we used to think were unchanging, but we now realize that they were historically conditioned. Thus, Crowe maintains, the incarnate Word is not the principle of infinite adaptation that we need for changing situations. He is urging us to think more of the distinct meaning of the Holy Spirit, instead of looking always to the incarnate Word for our model of change.

In terms of the distinct missions of the Son and the Spirit, Crowe's "own question" is this: what is the "relation between the roles of the

Son and Spirit"?[97] Crowe finds confidence in his attempt to deepen the Church's answer to this question by the trajectory of thought that he finds in the New Testament. The progress is from obscurity (in Paul), to almost asking the question (in Luke), to asking the question (in John). Crowe did not see the impossibility of "further understanding, and so of prolonging the trajectory into post-biblical times."[98]

Crowe thinks that the question of the relation of Son and Spirit is "on the verge of being articulated in St. Paul's letters."[99] He especially likes Galatians 4:4–6. God sends his Son to make adoption as sons of God possible, and then he sends the Spirit so that we might know that we are children of God. Crowe believes that Luke took a further step towards making the question thematic. He interprets Luke's gospel as focused on the Son's mission, and Luke's Acts of the Apostles as focused on the Spirit's mission. This two-volume approach comes close to asking the question directly. The Gospel of Luke recounts what Jesus did for us. In Acts, Luke presents "the power of the Spirit to witness to what happened (Acts 1:8; see Luke 24:48–9)."[100] What is remote in Paul and clearer in Luke becomes John's own question. John presents the Spirit as depending on the work of the Son (John 16:12–15). "But," Crowe writes, "it is clear that the Spirit is sent in some sense to *replace* the Son: the disciples are not to be left orphans, they will receive *another* Advocate (John 14:15–18)."[101] John's gospel even records our Lord's words that it is better that he goes away: "If I do not go away, the Advocate will not come to you; but if I go, I will send him to you" (NRSV John 16:7).

In these biblical texts "from Paul through Luke to John,"[102] Crowe sees a progress of understanding within the New Testament. He also sees a constant refusal throughout the history of the Church "to accept responsibility" for furthering the work of understanding the relation between the Son and the Spirit in our redemption.[103] What is worse, Crowe thinks, is that there has even been "a sort of suppression of the religious experience that fills the New Testament."[104] He brings up as evidence two facts. First, he contrasts the way in which the Holy Spirit guided the Church in the Acts of the Apostles and "the merely 'negative assistance' that theologians would allow him [the Holy Spirit] to exercise at ecumenical councils."[105] The second and more fundamental fact, according to Crowe, is that "we tacitly downgrade the reality of his presence among us."[106] He attributes this downgrading to an in-built tendency in human beings to consider as real only what they can sense. Since the Son was sent into the world of sense, we seem to think his mission is more real. "It is as if we took over," Crowe writes, "and gratefully applied the behaviorism of positivist psychology."[107] In so doing, he is saying, we ignore the real interior mission of the Holy Spirit.

Consequently, the ellipse of the Christian life becomes the circle with the single focus on Christ. "We allow," Crowe writes about the Holy Spirit, "the focus which should be distinctly his in the ellipse of the divine missions to vanish, to merge with that of the Son in a Christocentric religion, and so lose its proper identity."[108] Thus we distort the Christian life. The result, he is saying, is that we end up putting too much emphasis on the Son's role. We try to make him become the principal guide for all we need. The trouble is that we need the Holy Spirit's interior guidance.

Part of the reason, Crowe suggests, for the collapse of the ellipse into the circle is the subtlety with which the Spirit speaks. "Of course," he writes, "it *is* difficult to determine what the Spirit is saying. Diggings in Palestine, dictionaries of Aramaic, the comforting feeling of a holy book – all the data that make the mission of the Son so really real – they tell us nothing of what the Spirit is saying to us here and now."[109] Notice how Crowe is distinguishing what God said in the past through the Son and what he is saying now by the Spirit. The Son's message is contained in monuments from the past. Crowe's way of speaking of outer religious words in the past is parallel to his critique of the Church authorities of his day. For example, in their decision about women's ordination the authorities relied too heavily on the things that make the Son's mission so real. In a sense, they were requiring "of Jesus what the *kenosis* of human historicity leaves him unable to provide."[110] Crowe was not applying these last words explicitly to the Church leaders, but they match closely his earlier critique. He came to understand, maybe without formulating it, that the Church had too long required of the mission of the Son and its prolongation what that mission and its prolongation could not provide. "At the same time," Crowe writes, we "fail to draw on those resources which the Father gave us for precisely the need we experience, namely, the real, the really real, presence of the Holy Spirit within us."[111]

Thus, there is an implicit parallel between the institutional Church's approach critiqued by Crowe and the more general failing of the Church to balance the two missions. As the Church's magisterium failed to draw on what was provided for its guidance in the questions of birth control and women's ordination, namely the input of certain groups of people, so the Church generally failed to draw on the interior presence of the Holy Spirit. As it relied too heavily on the magisterium to answer all the questions, so the Church depended too much on the data of the Son's mission.

In the conclusion of his paper "Son and Spirit: Tension in the Divine Missions?" Crowe admits the dangers of his thesis about the need for a distinct focus on the Holy Spirit. First, he shows fear of "disloyalty to him [Jesus Christ] 'who loved me and sacrificed himself for me' (Gal. 2:20)."[112] Second, as a Jesuit, he fears "diminishing the power of that meditation on the words and deeds of Jesus which has nourished thousands of saints and millions of sinners, notably through the *Spiritual Exercises* of my own Ignatius of Loyola."[113] Third, Crowe fears "belittling the present role of Jesus, as he reigns in heaven, 'able to save absolutely those who approach God through him ... always living to plead on their behalf' (Heb. 7:25)."[114]

After expressing these three fears in relation to the Son, Crowe immediately mentions the institutional Church: "I fear doing injustice to the institutional Church, whose authorities are sinful human beings like me but *do* represent the mother who gave me my Catholic parents, the mass, the sacraments, the scriptures, my tradition, the saints whom I admire from far off."[115] The institutional Church includes the pope and the bishops in union with him, but it also includes all the other outer things he mentions: parents, the sacraments, the scripture, tradition, and the saints. Crowe is not trying to get rid of these aspects of the Church; he is afraid of doing injustice to them. What he especially wants is a reform of the way in which the institutional Church exercises its authority.

"We have laid so much stress," Crowe will later say, "on the teaching Church – and this not as a function related to and integrated with the learning function, but as an office belonging to certain people – that we have not attended to the learning function."[116] He insists that there is a good reason to distinguish the teaching Church and the learning Church as groups. Christ entrusted some members with a unique charism of truth, but Crowe insists that there is also a more basic division of functions. The whole Church, even the teaching Church, must learn before it can teach. The learning function, he explains, "is primary in regard to the Church as a whole and in relation to the totality of our cognitional procedures."[117] We have neglected this function because we have neglected the role of the Holy Spirit who "guides us into all truth" (John 16:13).

Crowe thought that the Church was like a biologist friend of his who had almost lost the use of one of his eyes because he was always looking into his microscope with the other eye. As the Church relied too much on the teaching function without using the learning function, it was also in danger of losing that function altogether. Crowe recognized, however, that the Church could not "correct that imbalance overnight."[118]

Instead of seeing the entirety of the Church's life in the context of the teaching of the institutional Church, Crowe wanted there to be a double focus in the Church: on learning and teaching. He also wanted another double focus: on the Spirit and on the Son. But Crowe clearly put priority on the Spirit's mission in his 1983 lecture "Son and Spirit: Tension in the Divine Missions?"[119] Before God discloses his love in the mission of the Son through the witness of the Church, God bestows the Holy Spirit on those who are being saved. The Spirit brings to us a share in what he eternally is, concerned Love. The Holy Spirit and the created charity he brings into our hearts enables us to learn what God wants of us (here and now) in fidelity to what God said to us in the Son. The learning Church requires both the mission of the Son and the mission of the Spirit.

1984 Chancellor's Lecture at Regis College

The second important discussion for the reversal of the divine missions is Crowe's 1984 lecture "Son of God, Holy Spirit, and World Religions." In that lecture for Regis College's convocation Crowe's "thesis" was this: "We have simply to reverse the order in which we commonly think of the Son and Spirit in the world. Commonly we think of God first sending the Son, and of the Spirit being sent in that context, to bring to completion the work of the Son."[120] Later in the lecture Crowe restates his thesis in this way: "God first sent the Spirit, and then sent the Son *in the context of the Spirit's mission*, to bring to completion – perhaps not precisely the work of the Spirit, but the work which God conceived as one work to be executed in the two steps of the twofold mission of first the Spirit and then the Son."[121] Crowe thinks that a corollary of his thesis is that it provides Christians a new way of relating to the sincere followers of the various world religions.

Crowe introduces his distinction – drawn from Lonergan, Aquinas, and Aristotle – between what is first for us (*quoad nos*) and what is first in itself (*quoad se*).[122] He does not want people to think that he is totally reworking Christianity. In God's plan what is first in itself is the gift of the Spirit, Crowe maintains, but in our experience of distinct divine persons, what is first for us is the incarnate Son. The already present person of the Spirit is made known to us through Christ's words and his manifest presence at Pentecost.

At the end of the lecture, however, Crowe addresses his real audience: the Church. He challenges the Church to be the kind of reality that other people would want to investigate. As people examined the Church, they would be led to enquire about the long-ago actions of the Lord. In other words, the whole question of rethinking the order of the missions of Son and Spirit has very practical consequences for the Church. Crowe thinks that the Church needs to re-examine "our own attitude" towards the religious people of the world.[123]

Crowe compares the religious situation of the Church in the 1980s to the situation of the people of Israel in the time of Paul, the Apostle. He explains how Paul in Romans 9–11 "has to face and accept and explain the fact that his own people, the chosen race, had stumbled and fallen from God's favour."[124] The Hebrew people "had refused to accept the gift on God's conditions, and by that refusal had lost, not only the newly offered gift but also the position that was uniquely theirs in regard to the ancient promise itself."[125] Despite all the prior graces, Paul's people had not accepted the merciful plan of God in Jesus of Nazareth to unite all nations.

As the Hebrew people failed to accept God's conditions, so, Crowe thought, the Church in the late twentieth century was in danger of failing to accept the extent of God's merciful plan. It is one thing to rejoice in the sending of the Son in the flesh, and another to rejoice in God's offering of the Holy Spirit to all people. "We too," Crowe writes, "have to beware lest, by refusing to acknowledge the breadth and depth and height of the divine mercy, we become unfaithful stewards of the very privilege that we do in fact possess, and turn into avatars of the people so broken-heartedly lamented in Romans 9–11."[126] Behind this comparison with the time of St Paul is Crowe's confidence that God offers sufficient grace for all men to be saved.

Following what he thinks is the teaching of Augustine, Aquinas, and Lonergan, Crowe links the grace of salvation with the Holy Spirit. God offers the grace, sufficient for all to be saved, Crowe maintains, when he blesses us with "the first and foundational gift of God, the divine Love in the person of the Holy Spirit."[127] Crowe did not believe that Aquinas and Augustine taught such a *universal* offer of salvation, but he thought that they did teach that those being saved were given grace through the gift of the Holy Spirit. Therefore, in the last two centuries, building on the teaching of Pope Pius IX and continuing with the subsequent teaching by the magisterium, we can posit a universal offer of the Holy Spirit to all people at some point in their lives.

Crowe did not think that this universal offer of salvation meant that the offer would be universally accepted, but that we needed to rethink our relationship to authentically religious people. He maintains, with Lonergan, that this gift of the Holy Spirit, when accepted, brings about a conversion, a new orientation "towards the mystery of love and awe."[128]

As we saw in chapter 4, Crowe argues for two steps in God's unified plan of salvation: the sending of the Spirit and the sending of the Son. The basis for his understanding of these two missions is Lonergan's "own beautiful and, I think, quite distinctive analogy: that of a man and a woman in love and of the two stages by which they achieve the fullness of being in love."[129] The declaration of love in an outward way by a man to a woman or vice versa is like the Father's sending of the Son. What is important for our purposes is how Crowe links this public proclamation of love with "the outer word of doctrine and the sacraments deriving from the Son."[130] What God declared in all history, and above all in the life of Christ, continues to be declared by the outer doctrine of the Church and its sacraments. We have a need for such outer communications in order to make a decision to serve God.

Crowe speaks of the Church as becoming practically "binitarian."[131] Instead of having room for a trinity of persons, we make room only for the Father and the Son. We practically leave out the role of the Holy Spirit. "The reason," Crowe writes, "is simple: we are all ingrained behaviorists, behaviorists by nature and by original sin."[132] The other word that Crowe uses to describe this condition of humanity is *extrovert*. "We are born extroverts, extroverts from the first moment we grope for mother's breast."[133] This natural tendency manifests throughout our lives, Crowe explains, and in our philosophy and our society. In addition, this tendency to extroversion is "the natural bent of our religion and religious institutions: our institutions always seem far more substantial than our charisms, and so the institutional Church naturally inclines to behaviorism, and naturally distrusts any movements that claim to come from the Spirit."[134] Crowe speaks here of mistrust. Earlier he spoke of the mistrust by the magisterium of contemporary evidence from the human sciences and Christian experience.

Clinging to the elements that derive from the Son's mission, the institutional Church, Crowe thinks, has missed what the Spirit is saying presently within the hearts of the people in the Church. The institutional Church is following the natural bent of the human being. In other words, practical binitarians only have one divine mission on which they tend to focus: the Son's. And thus we have developed an imbalanced "Christocentric mentality."[135]

Conclusion

In the second stage of his Trinitarian pneumatology Crowe came to rethink *the order* and *the context* of the two divine missions. He saw the institutional and charismatic sides of the Church as respective prolongations of the mission of the Son and the mission of the Spirit. He is right to argue that the Church's mission prolongs the divine missions, but there is a danger if aspects of the Church's life are exclusively linked with *only* one divine mission. Crowe, for example, treats "the outer word of doctrine and the sacraments" as "deriving from the Son."[136]

Yet the formulation of the Church's doctrines and the administration of the sacraments always involve also the work of the Holy Spirit.[137] Just as Christ's whole earthly life was carried out in and with the Holy Spirit,[138] so pastors of the Church also prolong the Son's mission in and with the Holy Spirit. There is thus a danger in Crowe's formulations of the missions of treating the Son's historical life as though it were not a kind of joint mission with the Spirit. Christ is the anointed one, anointed with the Spirit. All that Christ did was done with the help of the Holy Spirit. What the Holy Spirit brings into our hearts is, in fact, a sharing in what was already in the heart of the incarnate Lord. When we turn to the Holy Spirit for guidance, he does not speak of himself but opens us to hear and to follow the Father's Word. The Spirit disposes us to find in the incarnate Son's life the meaning that the Spirit intended his life to have for us. These reservations are not meant to undermine the value of Crowe's writings on the order of the two missions. Such reflections are precisely what Crowe's writings are meant to foster in theologians.

In the second stage of his pneumatology Crowe was not trying to provide a systematic theology of the missions; he was leaving that work to others. His main objective was to show that work needed to be done on the mission of the Spirit. One does not have to agree with his positions on artificial contraception and women's ordination to see that these tensions influenced his thinking about the relation of the divine missions. One does not have to agree with all his formulations regarding the two missions to be grateful for the challenge he has posed.

"As we become more spiritual," Crowe wrote, as far back as 1961, "we should become more aware of the Holy Spirit and his work in us; not as if we ever out-grow the Son (a recurrent heresy takes that position)."[139] This idea of the Church as spiritually maturing is at the heart of the second stage of Crowe's pneumatology. The Church after the Second Vatican Council, he thought, was being asked by God to depend more and more on the continuous guidance of the Holy Spirit. The Church must open itself to the primacy of love. As long as it neglects to listen to the Spirit, Crowe is telling us, it will neglect to learn as it should. Without the Spirit, we cannot discern the signs of the times.[140] Through the Spirit, the Church is "guided into all truth" (John 16:13).

The Holy Spirit as the First Person in the Trinity

6 Intentionality Analysis

Paving the Way for Rethinking Trinitarian Order

His trinitarian theology is tied in with the whole range of his thinking.
Frederick Crowe, *Developing the Lonergan Legacy*

What Crowe said about Bernard Lonergan's Trinitarian theology applies equally to his own. In the second stage of his Trinitarian pneumatology Crowe began to think of the Holy Spirit as the first divine person given to us in the economy of salvation. In the third stage he proposed a way of thinking of the Holy Spirit as the first person in the immanent or essential Trinity. These two positions are related, but Crowe's question in the third stage did not immediately arise from his reversal of the order of the missions. In response to an imagined objection to his position on the priority of the Holy Spirit's mission Crowe wrote in 1984: "Again it might be asked how our position accords with the tradition on trinitarian relations and processions, and the answer would be the Thomist answer that a divine person is sent into the world in virtue of the same relation and procession that belongs to that person within the Trinity: the Spirit given to all peoples is given therefore by the first and second persons of the Trinity."[1] Once Crowe had reversed the order and context of the missions, he was still thinking of the eternal order of the Trinitarian persons as Father, Son, and Holy Spirit. How did he come to ask this new question about a complementary ordering of the persons in the Trinity?

My main argument in this chapter is that Crowe asked his new question because he came to think more deeply about the implications of what Lonergan called "intentionality analysis."[2] This analysis involves a move away from understanding our knowing and loving through a theory of faculties of the soul (intellect and will) in favour of a phenomenological description of four distinct and interrelated levels of consciousness: experience, understanding, judging, and deciding. By the early 1980s Crowe had interpreted Lonergan as teaching that the four levels of consciousness possessed, according to a metaphor, two ways of development: from below upward and from above downward.

With his deeper understanding of Lonergan's two ways of development, Crowe recognized, besides the dynamic disinterested desire to know,[3] a second dynamism within human development: intersubjective love. On the basis of this dynamic operator Crowe thought that a triad emerged in consciousness: intersubjective love, truth, and "experienced orientation to mystery."[4] By 1989 he had begun to wonder whether this trio and its order could also be applied to the Trinity. As Crowe used an intellectually dynamic divine nature to explain why in God there was a Speaker, a Word, and Love, so the dynamism of intersubjective love now offered (potentially) another way of thinking about why there were three in God.

The goal of this chapter is not to evaluate the coherence or validity of Crowe's proposal of rethinking the Trinity but to answer the question of how Crowe arrived at this consideration. The first section focuses on his anticipations of it in his earlier ways of explaining the psychological analogy in terms of movement within levels of consciousness. In the second section we turn to the emergence of this reordering of the divine persons "as a separate concern."[5] Our attention will be on Crowe's 1989 article "Rethinking God-with-Us."

Crowe's Early Explanations of the Psychological Analogy

When Crowe taught his students about the eternal procession of the Son, he used various diagrams. His 1965–6 diagram is reproduced here as figure 6. At that time, following Lonergan's 1957 *Insight*, Crowe recognized three levels in the human cognitional structure: experience; understanding; and reflection.[6] Together, these three levels constitute full human knowing. He grafted the two intelligible emanations of Aquinas – the emanation of a concept and the emanation of a judgment – onto Lonergan's second and third cognitional levels.

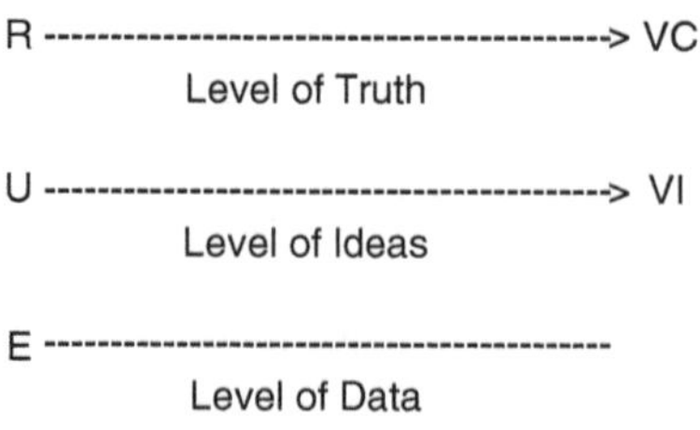

Figure 6 Crowe's own diagram for intelligible emanations

Note: R, reflection; U, understanding; E, experience; VI, verbum incomplexum, or concept; VC, verbum complexum, or judgment. Source: Frederick Crowe, *The Doctrine of the Most Holy Trinity*, 145.

Crowe explains that, in the diagram, "the arrows indicate the *emanatio intelligibilis* [intelligible emanation] that is the analogy for the processions of the divine Word."[7] *R*, *U*, and *E* represent the three levels in the Lonerganian framework of consciousness, as set forth in *Insight*. Within the second and the third levels from the bottom, understanding (*U*) and reflection (*R*), there is an analogy for the procession of the eternal Word. The Word, the Son, proceeds from the Father, as a concept or a judgment proceeds respectively from a direct insight or a reflective insight (act of understanding) uttering that inner word.

In 1965 Crowe was clear that the analogy for the procession of the eternal Word was the procession of an inner word taking place *within* a given level of consciousness. "It is a procession," Crowe writes, "not from level to level, but within a level, either within the level of understanding or within that of reflection, when a concept proceeds from understanding or a judgment from reflection."[8] His point can be illustrated in a slightly different way by figure 7.

In short, there is an intellectual dynamism within us, the unrestricted desire to know. This desire is expressed in questions, questions that move us from level to level in the process of knowing. In trying to answer these questions, our acts of direct and reflective understanding are the respective grounds for conceptualization and affirmation. These concepts and judgments of existence provide two analogies for what is one in God, the eternal procession of the Word.

These analogies for the procession of the Word come directly from the respective acts of understanding that ground them. The judgment *that something is*, for example, is not the immediate expression of the act of understanding that grasps what something is. The judgment, the unconditional assent, proceeds from a conscious reflection on the sufficiency of the evidence for answering the question "Is it so?" (*an sit?*). The reflective act of understanding that grasps the sufficiency of the evidence and from which the judgment issues is the analogue for the Father.[9]

In the three levels highlighted in 1965–6 (experience, understanding, reflection) Crowe already recognizes two kinds of movements. There is a vertical, upward movement between levels as one asks and answers

Is it so?	**3rd level**	Reflection ---------------------> Inner word of a judgment
What is it?	**2nd level**	Understanding -------------> Inner word of a concept or definition
Desire to know	**1st level**	Experience

Figure 7 Reworking of Crowe's diagram of inner words

new questions. There is also a horizontal movement within a level as concepts and judgments are formed. In 1965 he rejected the vertical movement between levels as the proper analogy for the procession of the Son.[10]

What was not clear in Crowe's 1965–6 analysis was where the acts of love fit into this diagram. Do the levels of cognitional process leave room for affective responses to the cognitional operations? Are the affections to be thought of as taking place on another level or within these same levels?[11] If acts of love were to be thought of as taking place *within* the levels, one would have a trio in the second and third levels that would act as a psychological analogy for the three persons (understanding, inner word, love). But if one thinks of love as located exclusively in another level, some kind of vertical movement will be needed to think of the procession of the Holy Spirit.

In his 1959 articles titled "Complacency and Concern in the Thought of St Thomas,"[12] Crowe has a Lonergan-inspired diagram to show that in the psychological analogy, the act of the will corresponding to the Holy Spirit is the will's act of love itself, as following upon an intellectual inner word.[13] The basic act of the will, the will's act of love itself, as following upon an intellectual inner word, is the analogy for the Holy Spirit.

In figure 8, *A* stands for an intellectual act of understanding as speaking; *B* stands for the word that is spoken; and *C* stands for the act of love itself. The vertical dotted line marks the distinction of the faculties of intellect and will. *I* stands for intellectual consciousness. Figure 8 combines the acts of intellect and will within a single level of intellectual consciousness.

In "Complacency and Concern in the Thought of St Thomas," Crowe wrote that complacent love was the basic act of the will, the affective response to a judgment of existence. Therefore, in some ways, complacent love should be placed *within* the third cognitional level as the complement to the inner word of judgment. But Crowe never said this explicitly. He knew, however, what Lonergan had said in *Insight*: "The goodness of being comes to light only by considering the extension of

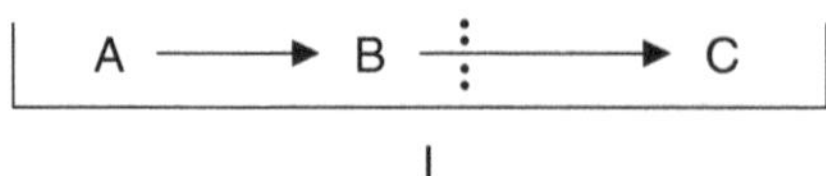

Figure 8 Crowe's diagram for the procession of love in the will
Source: Crowe, *The Doctrine of the Most Holy Trinity*, 147.

intellectual activity that we name deliberation and decision, choice and will."[14] Even in 1974 Crowe would look back on *Insight* and say that in that book "deliberation, decision, and the like, do not constitute a new and distinct level, but a continuation or extension of cognitional activity."[15] If love is also an extension of intellectual activity and not located within a distinct level, then it could be an extension of the cognitional activities especially on the third level.

Nevertheless, Crowe had already published an article in 1965 in which he seemed to suggest that love might be on a fourth level: "The foregoing account was limited to the three levels of cognitional activity. If we add now the very essential further element of the *affective* and *voluntary*, we have four levels of human consciousness and activity: the empirical (experience), the intellectual (understanding), the rational (reflection), and the moral (*voluntary*)."[16] Crowe uses the words "if we add." There is a sense of hesitation, but he does speak of "the affective and voluntary." The affective would include the affection of love. At the end of this quotation Crowe mentions the fourth level of consciousness as "the moral (voluntary)." Since he linked the affective and voluntary earlier in the paragraph, Crowe seemed to be aware in 1965 that the fourth level of consciousness might also be the level in which one experienced love.

In the late 1950s Crowe had worked out his idea of complacency and concern in the context of faculty psychology but with an eye to Lonergan's three levels of thought in *Insight*. Then in the 1960s he not only adopted as his own Lonergan's three cognitional levels but also recognized Lonergan's talking and writing about a fourth level of consciousness in which affectivity could be located. In other words, it was not easy for Crowe at that time to connect his doctrine of complacent and concerned love with Lonergan's developing levels of consciousness.

During Crowe's second stage (1969–84), there is an additional complication. Crowe begins to think of love in a radically new way. He accepts Lonergan's teaching that religious love can precede faith. We saw this in an essay from 1969: "the faith by which a believer says, 'God is my Savior,' is the spontaneous result of his falling in love with God."[17] In that same essay Crowe has the rudiments of a psychological analogy that begins with love, moves to faith, and ends with theological understanding.[18]

The trio (love, act of faith, and understanding, in that order) aligns almost exactly with the way in which Crowe later characterized the fourth, third, and second levels of consciousness. In 1969 he implicitly anticipated his psychological analogy that would be based on a downward movement between the levels of consciousness. Crowe, however, did not integrate this aspect of religious life with the four levels of consciousness until sometime after 1985. All through the 1970s and early 1980s he basically held in his mind two *un*integrated ideas: Lonergan's dynamically related levels of consciousness (adding Lonergan's fourth level in a definitive way between 1972 and 1974)[19] and one exception to the structure that occurs through falling in love with God.

Once Crowe has mastered what he calls "one of the last of [Lonergan's] great general ideas"[20] – the two paths of development – he is poised to think about the Trinity, and especially the Holy Spirit, in new ways. Crowe was especially struck by the following passage from Lonergan's 1977 lecture "Natural Right and Historical Mindedness":

> Development may be described, if a spatial metaphor is permitted, as "from below upwards": it begins from experience, is enriched with full understanding, is accepted by sound judgment, is directed not to satisfactions but values ... Again ... development ... works from above downwards: it begins in the affectivity of the infant, the child, the son, the pupil, the follower. On affectivity rests the apprehension of values. On the apprehension of values rests belief. On belief follows the growth in understanding of one who has found a genuine teacher and has been initiated into the study of the masters of the past. Then to confirm one's growth in understanding comes experience made mature and perceptive by one's developed understanding.[21]

As one moves up from experience, one comes to understand. The level of understanding leads to new questions, and we reach the level of reflection and judgment and, later, of loving decisions. A similar pattern appears in children especially, but in the reverse order. Lonergan mentions affectivity first. This affectivity leads to apprehension of values, which leads to beliefs (judgments), then to growth in understanding, and to experience made mature and perceptive. Crowe provided a table of these two paths (figure 9). As in 1965–6, but with the addition of a fourth level, he uses E for the level of experience, U for understanding, and R for the level of reflection and judgment; he uses V for the level of values and love. The two arrows "indicate the main dynamics of development."[22]

Crowe calls these two four-level paths *the way of achievement* (upward path) and *the way of heritage* (downward path). He is clear that "love is fourth-level ... activity."[23] Love, however, has a different place in the two movements: "Love, then, as it was the original gift in the way of heritage, is also the crowning element in the way of achievement."[24]

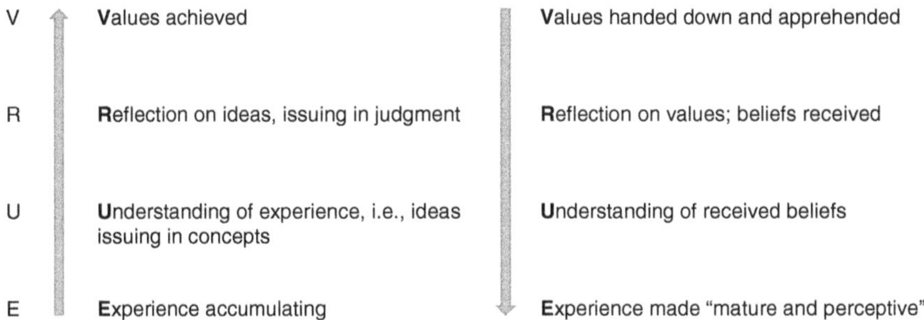

Figure 9 Crowe's own diagram for the two ways
Source: Frederick Crowe, *Old Things and New: A Strategy for Education*, 14.

On the one hand, the love that crowns the way of achievement is a kind of serenity or complacency with what is and with those around one. On the other hand, in the way of heritage, "values and judgments are communicated in an atmosphere of love and trust."[25]

Crowe admits, however, that this "diagram is simplified" because he has left out the "horizontal dynamic"[26] within each "level of thought."[27] For example, he writes, "in the left-hand column values issue in decisions, reflection issues in judgments, understanding in concepts, experience in the vast and various world of images that is the mind's treasury."[28] Without going into details, he adds that similar horizontal movements take place in the way of heritage. In short, Crowe still recognizes the very analogies that he had used earlier for the procession of the Son, but his attention is on "the movement from one level of consciousness to another."[29]

The dynamism that accounts for the movement from one level to another is represented by the arrows in Crowe's graph. "The dynamism of the upward movement," Crowe explains, "is the eros of the human spirit: it is the subject, the subject as operator. But in the new downward direction, the dynamism is not simply subjective; it is intersubjective, it is the intersubjective in its full range from spontaneous intersubjectivity to persons in community. We are 'we' before we are 'you' and 'I' and this makes operative a dynamism of love that is quite distinct and different from the eros of *Insight*."[30] In using the word *intersubjective* and the distinction between a prior *we* and a subsequent recognition of *you* and *I*, Crowe is drawing on Lonergan's *Method in Theology*. The first section, "Intersubjectivity," of its chapter on meaning begins: "Prior to the 'we' that results from the mutual love of an 'I' and a 'thou,' there is the earlier 'we' that precedes the distinction of subjects and survives its oblivion. This prior 'we' is vital and functional. Just as one spontaneously raises one's arm to ward off a blow from one's head, so with the same spontaneity one reaches out to save another from falling ... It is as if 'we' were members of one another prior to our distinctions of each from the others."[31]

Crowe thinks that he is using the word *intersubjective* in a slightly broader fashion than Lonergan is using it. "I use the word 'intersubjectivity,'" Crowe writes, "to refer here to the full range of relations between subjects; this is not, I think, the particular use Lonergan sometimes makes of the term, as when he refers to the intersubjectivity that is vital and functional, and intersubjectivity of 'action and feeling.'"[32] But the point is that, from our relations with other subjects in a community, a love exists in each person that can spontaneously act as an operator for our personal human development.

As we have seen, Crowe explicitly distinguishes the desire to know from this operator of intersubjective love. He goes on to describe in a basic way "the great difference in modes of operation as the two dynamisms move us in opposite directions from level to level."[33] Crowe starts with an example from the top two levels: "It is one thing to move up from judgments of facts and values to a responsible decision (third level to fourth); it is quite another for a mother to ponder in love what is best for her child (fourth level to third). In the former we may well speak of duty, and think of it as the 'Stern Daughter of the Voice of God,' but surely not in the latter."[34] Crowe then gives a description of the movements between the bottom two levels in both the upward and the downward direction. His special interest is the relationship between insight (second level) and image (first level). "It is one thing to struggle for the upward emergence from the image [to] insight into the image (first level to second), and quite another to evoke images in illustration of an insight we already possess (second level to first). In the former case, as Lonergan said years ago, 'we are at the mercy of fortune, the sub-conscious, or a teacher's skill ... in the ferment of trying to grasp we know not what,' but in the latter 'we can operate on our own, marshalling images to a habitually known end.'"[35] In short, images precede the insights in the upward movement. In the downward movement our insights enable us to produce new images as ways of evoking that same insight, as teachers do when they are trying to help their students understand. Crowe has not applied his rethinking of intentionality analysis to the Trinity, but the tools that he will use later to do so were in place by 1985.

As Crowe came to recognize and adopt Lonergan's two ways of development, he accepted that the downward path of development had intersubjective love as its dynamic operator. At the beginning of his third stage of reflecting on the Holy Spirit (1985–2000), Crowe had in place a robust image of human consciousness operating in two directions. This twofold path of development lay behind the emergence of Crowe's question about whether the Holy Spirit could be thought of as the first person in the Trinity.

Emergence of the Question of the Holy Spirit's Firstness

After Crowe gave his 1984 lecture "Son of God, Holy Spirit, and World Religions," there was a small buzz of excitement surrounding it in Jesuit circles. The lecture was published in 1985, together with the homily delivered by Crowe at Bernard Lonergan's funeral mass. Over the next few years, Crowe received letters of encouragement and gratitude from Jesuit theologians such as Jacques Dupuis and Francis X. Clooney. Dupuis wrote that Crowe's idea on the mission of the Spirit "goes much in the same line of my own thinking on the subject."[36]

On 9 December 1986, Crowe wrote to Francis Clooney, SJ, a professor at Boston College: "One reason that I asked for your comments is that I want to incorporate this idea into a larger work on the dynamics of the Three in the world. I hope to get started on this after Christmas and I will be pondering then what you had to say on the lecture."[37] This letter shows that Crowe wanted to continue thinking about the economic Trinity, the Three in the world. Unfortunately, his proposed book never appeared, and no record of it has yet been found in the Crowe Archive at the Lonergan Research Institute in Toronto.

What did appear was an article in 1989 called "Rethinking God-with-Us: Categories from Lonergan."[38] It includes a distillation and clarification of the ideas we saw in Crowe's 1983 and 1984 lectures on the Holy Spirit. The focus is on the economic Trinity, the God of our experience, and not the immanent Trinitarian life. This 1989 article, however, indicates a new question in Crowe's mind about the eternal life of the Trinity. By 1989 Crowe thought that a new psychological analogy might be applicable to the inner life of the Trinity, in which the Holy Spirit is thought of as the first person.[39]

In the first stage of Crowe's pneumatology (1953–68) the distinctive role of the Father was set within the beatific vision in the next life. But was it possible to think of a place for the Father in our experience during this life? By 1989 Crowe was able to write, "Like the long obscurity of the Spirit while the focus was on the Son, there has been an obscuring of the personal role of the Father, both in the final state of eternal life and in the present temporary state of the Father's absence."[40] The newness here is on a role for the Father in the present temporary state.

As Crowe reflected on the role of the Father in our present state, he came to think of the Father as present in our experience by our consciousness of a lack, a need. "There is," Crowe writes, "a sense of our potential infinity, and therefore of an infinite emptiness. There is an experience of the dark night of the senses and of the human spirit. It is the absence, the lack, the need, the hunger, the emptiness, the longing, the abandonment, experienced in our human condition as long as we are separated from the presence of the Father in our world."[41] Crowe thinks that the Father's absence is "the absence, as experienced absence, of God as 'fons divinitatis' [fount of divinity], the absence of God the Father, originating person in the sending of the Son and Spirit, God our eschatological hope."[42]

Crowe notes that in traditional theological language the absence that he is describing is our lack of a beatific vision, but he is talking about this absence from the side of the subject. The absence of God "is understood experientially now."[43] Crowe has an idea about our outer experience of the Son and our inner experience of the Holy Spirit. He has come to see that "ordinarily (I do not wish to pronounce on the extraordinary experience of the mystics) there is in this world no experience of God (the Father), but there is experience of the mystery of mysteries – experience, so to speak, of the absence of experience."[44]

In 1989 Crowe tried to develop this role of the Father's absence. In "Rethinking God-with-Us" he begins on the philosophical level, referring to various passages in Lonergan where he speaks of the question of God as being more important than the way in which we answer that question. He then moves quickly to the notion of a Trinitarian spirituality. Philosophical questioning about God is "only the pale philosophic copy of the desire of Trinitarian spirituality, once we have learned of the sending of the Son and Spirit, to glimpse the mystery of mysteries, the originating divinity who is principle of the presence of the Spirit and Son among us in our exile."[45]

Crowe notes that "there is never an answer" when "we call out to the Father for understanding of the mystery of evil, for assurance of the divine truth we have received, for communion with dear ones who have gone from among us."[46] Crowe develops this silence in relation to the dear ones who have died. They too are silent. "No word comes back from those who have gone before us."[47] He is speaking not only of his beloved brother who died so young, and his sister who died in her early thirties, but also about the whole mystical body of Christ: "Not from our dear ones, not from our brothers or sisters in religion, not from Mary, the mother of the Lord, not from Jesus himself. They have gone into the presence of the originating divinity and seem to have forgotten us."[48] Crowe admits that there may be authentic apparitions (e.g., at Lourdes), but "this seems only to deepen the longing for the revelation and presence of the Father. All this, I suggest, belongs to the Trinitarian spirituality of our relation to the Father."[49]

Behind this way of speaking of the Father is a passage in Lonergan: "An orientation to transcendent mystery is basic to systematic theology. It provides the primary and fundamental meaning of the name, God."[50] Crowe has taken this orientation to transcendent mystery and applied it to our orientation to God the Father. Slowly, he begins to prefer *Mystery* as the way to speak of the Father.[51]

Why does the Father, the Mystery of mysteries, not enter our present world except by our experience of his absence? Over the years Crowe always sought an answer to the ways of God in the world by looking for fittingness arguments based on the eternal characteristics of the Three according to the Thomistic psychological analogy. In terms of the fittingness for the Father's presence as last, Crowe answers this question by reviewing Lonergan's Thomistic 1964 theology of the immanent Trinity. "The Father," Crowe writes, "is the *Intelligere Dicens* [the Act of Understanding as Speaking] in the Trinity, the source of all divinity, the Understanding that issues in Truth, and in such Truth as will issue in infinite Love. Therefore, since the Father is the hidden, original, abysmal Source of the other persons in God and of their mission to us, it is fitting that the Father remain hidden in this life and be instead the final revelation, the One who becomes present to us through our understanding, in the light of the beatific vision."[52] Lonergan offered a basis for seeing the fittingness of the Father entering our world only in this hidden way. As we saw in stage two, this Thomistic account of the Trinitarian presence in the world provided by the psychological analogy was not sufficient for Crowe in accounting for the order and context of the missions. He deployed Lonergan's analogy of human lovers (falling in love, declaring love, consummating love) to supplement the psychological analogy in explaining God's ways in the world.

In 1989 a slightly different issue emerged as Crowe tried to find the fittingness of the Father's absence. He notes that "rather late in life Lonergan began to change his way of explaining the psychological analogy."[53] The key change introduced by Lonergan, according to Crowe, was a rethinking of the analogue of the Father. Instead of being thought of by the analogy of an act of understanding speaking a word, the first person is "now conceived as originating love expressing itself in a judgement of value."[54] Crowe quotes a 1975 passage of Lonergan: "In God the origin is the Father ... identified with *agape* ... such love expresses itself in its Word, its Logos, its *verbum spirans amorem* [word spirating love], which is a judgment of value. The judgment of value is sincere, and so grounds the proceeding love that is identified with the Holy Spirit."[55] Lonergan adds a bit later that each of the divine persons "in his own distinct manner is subject of the infinite act that God is, the Father as originating love, the Son as judgment of value expressing that love, and the Spirit as originated loving."[56] Table 6 combines these two passages of Lonergan's 1975 analogy.

By 1989 Crowe thought that there was a problem using this analogy (as it stood) to understand the presence of the Three in the world. The problem was that Lonergan's thinking was on the move. Lonergan had expressed the 1975 analogy, Crowe explains, in the midst of trying to think out "one of the last of his great general ideas before he turned, in the final years of his active life, to the specific field of economics."[57] This late, great general idea was the idea of two ways of human development.

According to Crowe, Lonergan did not leave us with a fully worked-out and revised psychological analogy. "It seems to me," Crowe writes, "speaking now from the viewpoint of 1977, that what he was after in 1975, in the first step of the psychological analogy, was the knowledge born of love that he took from Pascal but did not fully develop in *Method*."[58] In other words, Lonergan in 1975 had not yet considered the downward path of development as an ordinary part of human life. Nevertheless, in his psychological analogy at that time, in speaking of the first divine person as originating love, Lonergan was implicitly referring to a downward path of human development. "If that is the case," Crowe adds, "then the Three and their processions should 'logically' have been conceived now on the analogy of the way down, in the full sequence of the movement from love to knowledge rather than from knowledge to love."[59] In addition, Crowe writes: "In the 'logic' of the sequence there are some options; but using the scheme of 'Natural Right and Historical Mindedness' I would tend to think of Father, Son, and Spirit in terms respectively of love, knowledge born of love, and experience made mature and perceptive."[60] Following is a chart that depicts Crowe's first approximation at using the downward development as an analogy for the immanent Trinity (figure 10).

Table 6 Summary of Lonergan's 1975 psychological analogy

(Originating) love	Judgment of value (expressing that love)	(Originated) proceeding love
Father	Word	Holy Spirit

Level	Main activity in that level	Corresponding divine person
4	Loving ↓	Father
3	[Judging] **"KNOWLEDGE BORN OF LOVE"**	Son
2	[Understanding] ↓	
1	Mature experiencing	Holy Spirit

Figure 10 My interpretation of Crowe's first proposal for a psychological analogy from above downwards
Note: In the second and third levels, I have placed brackets around *Judging* and *Understanding* because Crowe combines these two levels of cognition in his first proposal for a psychological analogy from above downwards. The activities of judging truth and understanding the truth are combined here to form "knowledge born of love."

Crowe combines levels two and three, applies them as an analogy for the eternal Son, and calls them "knowledge born of love." He situates "originating love" on the fourth level, and "the judgment of value"[61] on the third level, now called "knowledge born of religious love." Crowe admits that Lonergan never explicitly connected experience with the Holy Spirit. "Would he have taken the step of using experience for an analogy of the Holy Spirit? Maybe yes, in some quite eminent sense of experience; but maybe no. I have not found an answer to this historical question in the record he left us."[62] Crowe is picking up on a shift in Lonergan's conception of the psychological "analogy found in the creature,"[63] but he interprets Lonergan in light of the downward path of development.

Was this interpretation necessary? In 1975 Lonergan provided three analogues for the three divine persons: "the dynamic state of being in love ... judgments of value ... decisions that are acts of loving."[64] The judgment of value as a manifestation or expression of the gift of God's love is like the Son of God. The judgment of value then is the ground for an act of loving that is like the Holy Spirit. Since a judgment of value, for Lonergan, has to do with affirming that something is worthwhile to do and requires an apprehension of value "given of feelings,"[65] one could easily interpret Lonergan's triad as a horizontal movement *within* the fourth level, not a vertical movement.[66] Within the fourth level of consciousness, in other words, we have a psychological analogy: the dynamic state of being in love represents the Father, the judgment of value issuing forth from that state of love represents the Son, and the decisions that are acts of loving represent the Holy Spirit.

We have to remember Crowe's earlier (1965) claim about the analogy for the procession of the Word: "it is a procession, not from level to level, but *within* a level."[67] Crowe interpreted Lonergan's psychological analogies for the procession of the Son as occurring within a level of intentionality. By 1989 Crowe was no longer thinking of the psychological analogy as being explained exclusively from within levels of consciousness. He writes: "the Three and their processions should 'logically' have been conceived now on the analogy of the way down, in the full sequence of the movement from love to knowledge rather than from knowledge to love."[68]

Crowe speaks of two sequences. The first one goes *from knowledge to love* (figure 11). This must be the path of development from below upwards. From the data of our experience we come to know through acts of understanding and judgment. This knowing leads to questions of what is worthwhile to do and (hopefully) to subsequent responsible decisions, that is, acts of love. The implication is that this upward sequence between levels provides the analogy for the Trinity in which the Father is conceived of as the Understanding speaking a Word,[69] and the Son as that Word breathing forth the Love that is the Holy Spirit. From the second level we move to the third and then the fourth.

The other sequence mentioned by Crowe is from *love to knowledge*. He is explicit that this sequence has some options in terms of application

Level	Levels of consciousness on the way up	Corresponding divine persons
4	Loving decisions	Holy Spirit
3	Judging	Word
2	Understanding	Father
1	Experiencing	

Figure 11 "From Knowledge to Love" – Crowe's analogy for the Trinity to the divine persons. On the basis of Lonergan's 1977 writings, Crowe says that he "would tend to think of Father, Son, and Holy Spirit in terms respectively of love, knowledge born of love, and experience made mature and perceptive."[70] In the analogy of the way up, the Father is the first person and corresponds to the second level, the level of understanding. In the analogy of the way down, the Father is still, according to Lonergan, the first person but now corresponds to the level of love.

Even though Crowe says that he tends to think of the Father as corresponding to the fourth level, he says this as an interpretation of Lonergan. Crowe himself says that there are various options for the analogy on the way down. What are the other, unspecified options? The most obvious option would be to make understanding, instead of experience, the analogy for the Holy Spirit. But is it possible that Crowe is also thinking of more radical options?

He goes on to say that there are two questions concerning the use of the "downward movement for Trinitarian analogy."[71] The first is how to interpret Lonergan. The second is the objective question itself, that is, whether the downward movement can even be used as a psychological analogy. In terms of answering the objective question, Crowe thinks "it likely that we will get Lonergan's answer only by carrying his idea beyond the point he himself had reached in 1975."[72] This quotation needs to be read in conjunction with Crowe's suggestion that there are various options for the downward movement when applied to the Trinity. In 1975 Lonergan still was thinking of the Holy Spirit as proceeding Love; the Son was still "a Word breathing forth Love."[73] The only change in Lonergan's 1975 analogy, according to Crowe, was the conception of the first person, the Father. To move beyond the point that Lonergan reached in 1975 could mean rethinking the other two persons as well, the Son and the Holy Spirit.

What if we think of the Holy Spirit not so much as proceeding Love but by the analogy of intersubjective or interpersonal love? As far back as the summer of 1972 Crowe had written: "Most of Lonergan's work in Christology was prior to 1965 when he spoke in terms of intellect and will and saw understanding in the mind of Christ as prior to love in the heart of Christ. But most of his work on values is subsequent to 1965; he does not now speak of intellect and will but of levels of consciousness and when he applies this to our human condition on earth he sees falling in love with God as prior to faith in the traditional sense."[74] But Crowe also added: "The general principle operative here is that the relationship between mind and heart is the *opposite* in our religious experience and faith life of what it is in the blessed and what it is conceived to be in God. That is, the order in God is Father, Son, and

Holy Spirit; or, in the Thomist transformation of these biblical names, the order is Understanding, Word, and Love. And this I take to be the natural order of the rationally conscious universe."[75]

For decades Crowe taught that the order in God is Father, Son, and Holy Spirit.[76] This ordering of the persons, accepted in faith, was understood in theology through an analogous order of operations that obtains in the blessed and in our natural order of conscious operations from below upwards: understanding, truth, love. Since the early 1970s Crowe was convinced that another order obtained in our graced life of faith: love, true beliefs, understanding (theology). These graced operations occur in an "inverse order"[77] to what Crowe then considered our natural order of conscious operations. The inverse order of love, truth, and understanding corresponds to their exemplars: Holy Spirit, Son, and Father. This ordering is implicitly connected with a downward version of the psychological analogy as laid out in figure 11, in which the Holy Spirit is placed in the fourth level.

Conclusion

In the second stage of his pneumatology (1969–84) Crowe was already thinking of love as coming before faith and the understanding of theology. While he did not apply that triad (love, faith, understanding) to the downward movement of consciousness (Crowe was not yet aware of such a movement as a normal aspect of human conscious operations),[78] his idea of the priority of love is easily mapped onto the downward movement. Was Crowe thinking about love in the downward movement as an analogy for the Holy Spirit when he said that we need to move beyond the point reached by Lonergan in 1975? I believe so. Crowe began to consider that the downward movement could be best applied to the Trinity if the first person was not the Father but rather the Holy Spirit.

In 1989 Crowe did not say this explicitly. He simply added, "Meanwhile, we remain with his very Thomist analogy of 1964, modifying it only in the conception of the first person as originating Love uttering a Word."[79] Crowe was looking for "an integral view of God-with-us."[80] In other words, he wanted an analogy that would help us understand the presence of the Three in a unified manner, *per modum unius*. He had been thinking about "relating levels of thinking to one another"[81] and had expressed hopes that a downward-moving analogy between levels might provide this unified view. Crowe will carry Lonergan's idea further in 1995, but what we see here is the emergence of a question. Can we think of another eternal ordering of the persons that better explains our new understanding of their presence in the world?

7 Hiding His Goal

Crowe's Reordering of the Three Persons

To elaborate a Lonerganian theology of the divine economy working in human history would therefore be a long and difficult task, and I do not know whether in the end enough data would be found for a comprehensive view ... What I feel is the fascination of the question, ... the hope that someone may yet be able to undertake the study.

Frederick Crowe, "Lonergan's Universalist View of Religion"

By the mid-1990s it seemed that Frederick Crowe had finished his work on the Trinity. He was still captivated by questions of the presence of the Trinity in the world, but his long-desired book on the economic Trinity would have to be left to someone else to write.[1] Then a young Jesuit theology student asked him for a directed reading course on the Trinity. "I was fascinated by his Trinity notes from the 1960s," Gilles Mongeau said.[2] And so Mongeau approached Crowe about supervising a course based on those notes together with other Trinitarian texts. Crowe agreed, and he oversaw the course in the fall of 1994 (October–December). Crowe's syllabus and handwritten notes are in the Crowe Archive.[3]

As Crowe prepared the course, he reread Basil, Augustine, Aquinas, Lonergan, and Rahner. Out of that course came the confidence to publish his last major article on the Trinity: "Rethinking the Trinity: Taking Seriously the *Homoousios*."[4] In it Crowe revisited many questions from his earlier Trinitarian theology, but the most radical new question was his willingness to think of an eternal order in the Trinity with the Holy Spirit as the first person.

The article begins in section 1 with an account of what it means for the three divine persons to be *homoousios*.[5] Crowe especially liked the interpretation of *consubstantial* offered by George Prestige: "that the Son is God in the same sense as the Father is God."[6] In section 2 Crowe lays out a theological trajectory that takes seriously the equality of the three persons. The trajectory starts with the Council of Nicaea's doctrine of *homoousios* and the Athanasian Creed's teaching about there being no priority among the persons. The arc moves towards the thought of Aquinas and his many interpreters, especially Bernard Lonergan, to show how Thomist teaching on divine eternal processions and relations rules out any priority among the divine persons.[7] Section 3 asks about trying to develop this theological tradition in terms of the order of the divine persons. Is Father, Son, Holy Spirit the only way to think of the order of the persons in the immanent Trinity? Crowe does not deny the traditional belief in that ordering but proposes the order Spirit, Son, Father as a complementary way of thinking about the persons. Section 4 takes us into a few questions of theological method that are evoked by Crowe's rethinking of the Trinity.

In a crucial sentence in the final section Crowe summarizes the purpose of his essay as working for a "true advance in theology that takes seriously not only the *homoousios* but also the Thomist view of Trinitarian relations."[8] His reference to relation at the end of the essay tells us what his essay is really about: Trinitarian relations. The reordering of the divine persons is an effort to help us take seriously the doctrine of mutual and simultaneous Trinitarian relations.

Crowe's decision to speak about real relations in the economic Trinity also indicates where the deep interest of this essay lies. He asks: "Are we dealing with a real relation that pertains to the person of the Spirit – that is, a Trinitarian relation to the Son and Father – or are we dealing with only a sequence of created events in our human return to God?"[9] Crowe then asks, "What does this real relation reveal to us about the inner life of God?"[10] Later on he repeats this idea: "But if the church agrees that real Trinitarian relations of the Spirit are involved in the Spirit's task of revealing the Son, and agrees that such real relations in the economic Trinity lead us into the immanent Trinity, then perhaps the conceptual system Lonergan has provided will be of some use in understanding this new development."[11] Crowe, as we will see, does not think that sufficient attention has been paid to the way in which each Trinitarian relation conditions the other term of that relation. He proposes a different ordering of the persons because he thinks that it brings out the eternal "characterization" of the Father and Son by the Holy Spirit – not in terms of origin but in terms of implication.

People do not seem to understand, Crowe is telling us, what it truly means for the Holy Spirit to be fully God *as a relation*. The traditional ordering (Father, Son, Spirit) is still valid and important, but, by providing sets of concepts for thinking of the three persons in another order, with the Spirit placed first, Crowe enables the reader to make diagrams or phantasms of the two orderings. Making these two diagrams helps one to grasp more fully what it means for the Holy Spirit to be a Trinitarian relation.

At the very end of his third stage of development (1985–2000) Crowe wrote an essay called "'Stare at a Triangle ...': A Note on How to Get an Insight and How Not To,"[12] in which he proposed "the shuffling of the data"[13] as a key to getting an insight. We need to have the free images or phantasms in the right arrangement for the insight to emerge.[14] This is precisely what I think Crowe is doing in this essay. He is trying to guide the production of the appropriate phantasm by shuffling the data about the ordering of the persons. The goal is to elicit the appropriate insight into the Holy Spirit as a Trinitarian relation. In short, he wants us to grasp that the Son and the Father, in some way, "depend on" or are characterized by the Holy Spirit in eternity. To ignore this aspect of the Holy Spirit is not to take seriously the Spirit's equality with the Father and the Son. The key to unlocking the rhetorical strategy of the essay is Crowe's stated desire at the end of the article, namely, "of gaining further insight into the infinite mystery that God is."[15] How do we gain insights? We need appropriate phantasms. Diagrams or phantasms depicting the Holy Spirit as the first person help theological insight to emerge.

Crowe's Stated Reasons for Rethinking the Order of the Divine Persons

Crowe offers two explicit reasons for his new ordering of the divine persons. The first is that he is trying to determine whether people really think that the Holy Spirit is God in the same sense as they think that the Father and the Son are God. He wonders whether "we include in our unexamined concept of the Father's 'firstness' a character or trait or aspect or property (in the sense of an absolute property) or excellence or glory or quality or virtue or possession or rank or grade or role or distinction (in the sense of honor) – a 'dignitas' in Latin, an 'axioma' in Greek – that prevents the Son or Spirit from being God in the same sense as the Father is God."[16] Crowe wants to expel such a "contradiction"[17] within the theological community of the Church. The contradiction is found in those who hold that the three persons are consubstantial, *homoousioi*, but who treat "the Son and Spirit as if they were somewhat less than the Father."[18] By conceiving a real order in the Trinity that starts with the Spirit, we make "the Spirit fully the equal of the Father" and thus "advance one more step in the task of taking seriously the *homoousios*."[19]

The second reason for Crowe's proposed new ordering is that such an ordering *might* be necessary depending on the Church's judgment regarding the role of the Holy Spirit in revealing the Son to us. Is a real relation involved in that task of the Holy Spirit? If so, does this real relation in the economic order lead us back to an aspect of the "immanent Trinity"?[20] Early in "Rethinking the Trinity" Crowe briefly examines the tradition for evidence of an ordering of the divine persons that begins with the Holy Spirit. He looks at the Scriptures, at the Fathers, and among theologians.

In terms of the New Testament, Crowe especially mentions the way the Spirit reveals or directs us to the Son: "No one can say 'Jesus is Lord' except by the Holy Spirit" (1 Corinthians 12:3). He also cites the passage in which it is said that the Holy Spirit "did not allow" Paul and Timothy to enter Bithynia (Acts 16:7). He refers us to the ways that the Holy Spirit directs "even the Lord Jesus" after his baptism, according to Matthew 4:1, Mark 1:12, Luke 4:1–2, 14.[21] Crowe especially likes St Paul's phrase "for through him [Christ] we both have access in one Spirit to the Father" (Ephesians 4:28). In short, Crowe thinks that the Scriptures suggest a "general context of our return, through the Son and in the Spirit, to the God who made us."[22]

According to Crowe, St Basil explicitly formulates what the Scriptures teach: "Thus the way to the knowledge of God is from one Spirit, through the one Son, to the one Father."[23] As in his first stage, Crowe tries in this third stage to follow in St Basil's footsteps. He notes how "immediately after the passage" just quoted, "he [Basil] has the following: 'conversely, the natural goodness and the natural power to sanctify, and the royal dignity, pass from the Father through the Only-begotten, to reach the Spirit.'"[24] Crowe's point is that "Basil has the two orders side by side."[25]

It is true that Basil is setting what we could call the economic order side by side with the immanent order of the persons. What Crowe is trying to do, however, is to ask whether two *eternal* orderings of the persons can be thought of as side by side. He proposes that an eternal ordering that starts with the Spirit "would simply add to the traditional belief in the hope of gaining further insight into the infinite mystery that God is."[26]

After referring to St Basil and the Scriptures, Crowe says, "These few soundings I leave for biblical and patristic theologians to develop further or reject, as it seems best to them."[27] He then mentions one piece of evidence "from the side of theological systematics ... namely, the view that the Spirit is the nexus of Father and Son."[28] He highlights the work of François Bourassa, SJ,[29] "who wrote frequently on the topic in the pages of *Sciences ecclésiastiques*, its successor, *Science et Esprit*, and

Gregorianum."[30] Crowe thought that the growing appreciation of the idea of the Holy Spirit as nexus supported the inverse ordering of the divine persons.

In the first and third stages of his pneumatology Crowe was uneasy with the idea of the Holy Spirit as the "nexus," bond, or link of Father and Son.[31] He knew that the idea was in Aquinas, but he preferred the idea of proceeding love to the idea of nexus to understand the identity of the Spirit.[32] Crowe wrote, "The nexus concept fits uneasily in the order Father, Son, and Spirit, in which Father and Son have to be already united, in order to be the one principle of the Holy Spirit."[33] In other words, the doctrine of the Father and Son as a single principle of spiration requires that they be united for there to be one principle of spiration. If they are "already" united and "then" breathe forth the Spirit, how is the Spirit their nexus? Yet, when one begins to think about the order of the persons as Spirit, Son, and Father, Crowe thinks, the idea of nexus works much better, "and, I would say, more coherently."[34] How is this so?

In the order Spirit, Son, and Father, "the Spirit is first conceived in relation to the Father and Son as they are one in the Spirit's love, a love that as it were unites them in that one relation before they are distinguished."[35] "In this conception," Crowe goes on to say, "the infinite Love that is the Spirit finds its 'object' and 'partner' first in the Word and Mystery as one, as united in the nexus of the Spirit's love, and then as distinguished from one another, as the 'You' of the Word and the 'You' of the Mystery of whom the Word is the expression."[36] In the more traditional order, the nexus follows upon the distinction of Father and Son, Crowe maintains. In his proposed order that begins with the Holy Spirit, the nexus "has a role in the distinction of Father and Son, again of course in our thought process."[37]

His essay is not trying to prove the validity of this new ordering. Crowe is simply trying to provide a few reasons for thinking that the Spirit could be thought first and then to investigate what he calls the "intellectual equipment" needed to understand such an ordering. If the Church were to conclude that the Spirit is in some way first in the immanent Trinity, how could such an order be made intelligible to us?

We must return for a moment to his earlier ideas about relations. Crowe's argument for there being eternal relations in God was based on the divine missions:

> The Father really sends the Son into the world, and a real sending means a real mutual relation between sender and sent. On the part of the Father, this real relation has to be eternal, since he has not human nature to ground a temporal relation. On the part of the Son, it has to be eternal,

first, because it is mutual, and if it is eternal in the Father it is eternal in
the Son too; secondly, because the "sending" and "being sent" are prior
by nature to his "being in the world" with a human nature, and therefore
have their basis in his eternal being.[38]

After deducing the eternal mutual relations of Father and Son from the
sending of the Son by the Father, Crowe makes a similar argument for
thinking of the Holy Spirit as a real relation: "He too is really sent by
the Father, and since neither of them assumes a created nature, the real
relation implied must be eternal; he is really sent by the Son, and the
real relation implied here must likewise be eternal; eternal in the Spirit
who has no ground for a temporal relation, and eternal in the Son, both
because it is mutual, and because he cannot as Man send the Spirit,
it is as God that he sends him."[39] Crowe's argument rests on the idea
that the real sending of a divine person implies or "involves" a relation
between the one sent and the one sending.[40] A relation, for Crowe and
Lonergan, means the "order of one thing to another."[41] The Son is eternally related to the Father as being from him. The Father is the one from
whom the Son is. The Spirit is from the Father and the Son. Knowledge
of these eternal relations is based on the way the Son and the Spirit are
in the world as from another.

Whether Crowe's argument is sound is not the point for now.[42] The
point is to see how Crowe thought of relations. He was convinced that
a divine mission implied a real relation. In other words, he moved from
the economic order to the immanent life of Trinity.

In light of scriptural passages that imply a sending of the Son by the
Spirit or suggest that the Spirit is the first person sent to those being
saved, Crowe thinks there are basically two questions that the Church
will eventually have to answer. The first is this: "In this aspect of the tradition [scriptural witness to an order that starts with the Spirit], are we
dealing with a real relation that pertains to the Spirit – that is, a Trinitarian
relation to the Son and Father – or are we only dealing with a sequence of
created events in our return to God?"[43] In light of his earlier theology, he
is asking whether the Son is ever shown to be sent or led by the Spirit.[44]

If the answer is that the Spirit's role in the mission of the Son involves
a real relation, then Crowe thinks that another question will have to be
answered: "If there is some reason to maintain such a Trinitarian relation in the economy of salvation, what does this real relation reveal to
us about the inner life of God?"[45] From the missions and real relations
in the divine carrying out of the plan of salvation, Crowe is saying, we
learn about the inner life of God. And so he tries to lay a conceptual
framework "for thinking of an aspect of intra-Trinitarian life that starts
with the Spirit."[46]

Crowe is not overturning the doctrine of relations of origin. He is not denying that the Father brings forth the Son, and the Spirit proceeds from the Father and the Son. But he has become interested in another aspect of the Trinitarian life. From his earlier years as a seminary professor, "another question haunt[ed]" him. Crowe wrote: "How can we show that there are only three in God? that no one proceeds from the Holy Spirit?"[47] In other words, why do the Father and the Son require the existence of a third person, the Holy Spirit, and no more? In 1995 Crowe was still thinking about the way in which the Holy Spirit was necessary in God. Thinking of the Holy Spirit as the first person is a way of bringing out how any one divine person mutually implies the other two. Crowe wants to carry theology "forward another step in our time."[48]

In this way he was earnest in his desire to supply a way of thinking of the Spirit as the first person. The essay is not simply about providing appropriate phantasms to provoke insights. We know that Crowe was convinced that the Holy Spirit's mission, in some ways, was prior and provided the context for the Son's mission. The priority of the Spirit's mission gives a basis in revelation for thinking that this temporal relationship of the Spirit to Christ points towards an eternal ordering. As theologians move from the sending of the Spirit by the Father and the Son to the procession of the Spirit from the Father and the Son, so Crowe wants to move in an analogous way from the role of the Spirit in time to his identity in eternity.

Following Augustine, Aquinas, and Lonergan, Crowe, in his first stage, found an analogy for the distinction of the Son and the Spirit in God in the knowing and loving acts of human beings. The procession of a word and the procession of love offered analogies for the processions of the Son and the Spirit. In a similar manner Crowe looked to Lonergan's downward development as an analogy for a new ordering of the Three that began with the Holy Spirit and complemented the traditional ordering of Father, Son, and Holy Spirit.

Trying to Win a Hearing: First Set of Concepts

Crowe says that there are two sets of "concepts in Lonergan" that he uses to try to win "a hearing for [his] proposal."[49] The first set is Lonergan's notion of "love consciously oriented to a beloved."[50] The second is the two paths of development: the way of achievement and the way of heritage.

In his 1995 essay "Rethinking the Trinity" Crowe distinguishes proceeding love from an interpersonal or intersubjective love that is "consciously oriented to a beloved."[51] The love that is found in the summit of the way of achievement is a proceeding love. It is the end of a process. The love that is found in the fourth level in the way of heritage (especially the gift of God's love) is the beginning of a new process of development. Crowe writes: "But now this gift is not taken as the end of a process (as is the procession of the Spirit in the usual order); it is taken rather as a beginning, as a first in our return to God."[52] He uses both kinds of love as analogies for the Holy Spirit: "We start with the Holy Spirit as love: not as proceeding love – though as I keep repeating, that concept retains its validity – but as love consciously oriented to a beloved, as love in intersubjective relationship, not simply love of infinite goodness, but love for which the other is a 'you.'"[53] This notion of the Holy Spirit as proceeding Love stayed constant in Crowe from the beginning of his life as a theologian, but he added to it the idea of the Holy Spirit as interpersonal or intersubjective Love.

One might object, however, that Crowe has misunderstood Lonergan on this point of interpersonal or intersubjective love and has applied this love too widely. In answering a question in 1972, Lonergan said: "The religious experience of the Christian is specifically distinct from religious experience in general. It is intersubjective. It is not only this gift of God's love, but it has an objective manifestation of God's love in Christ Jesus. That intersubjective component creates a difference."[54] In Christianity the one we are in love with has already been found: Jesus of Nazareth. This is why Lonergan says that Christian religious experience is intersubjective. Two days earlier he had said: "There is an intersubjective element to love that is present in Christianity, where God is expressing his love in Christ as well as giving you the grace in your heart; and this element is missing when you haven't got a Christian revelation."[55] The love that God gives to those outside Christianity, general religious experience, is not, according to Lonergan, intersubjective. If Lonergan was so clear about the Christian basis for religious love being intersubjective, why would Crowe use the idea of intersubjective love more broadly?

Crowe is puzzled by another passage in those lectures in which religious love seems to be oriented towards God. Lonergan claims that the gift of God's love is what leads people

> to seek knowledge of God. God's gift of his love is God's free and gratuitous gift. It does not suppose that we know God. It does not proceed from our knowledge of God. On the contrary, I have suggested that the gift occurs with indeed a determinate content but without an intellectually apprehended object. Religious experience at its root is experience of an unconditioned and unrestricted being in love. But what we are in love with remains something that we must find out. When we find it out in the

context of a philosophy, there results a philosophy of God. When we find it out in the context of a functionally differentiated theology, there results a functional specialty, systematics. So it turns out that one and the same God has unknowingly been found and is differently being sought by both philosopher and theologian.[56]

What Crowe notes is the way this religious love leads us to seek and find knowledge of God. His point is that "love has cognitional consequences."[57] In Lonergan's own words, the cognitional consequences are a philosophy or theology of God.

Crowe applies this idea of our love of God having cognitional consequences to the inner life of God. He compares such love and knowledge of God to the Spirit and Son by saying: "And in God there 'results' the Word as determinate 'object' of the Spirit's love, and as a conscious subject consciously returning that love in a mutual relationship. Hence the Spirit is a love for which the Word is not just an object but a 'you,' and a love that has the Word responding as to a 'you.'"[58] Notice how the Word is responding to the Spirit and not the Father, as "you," in Crowe's analysis. In this analogy the Word is understood to depend on the Spirit.

Having spoken of the mutual relationship of the Spirit and the Son, Crowe then turns to the emergence of a third divine person. "Further," he writes, "love desires to know more and more about the beloved. Consequently, in human love of God, which 'knows' with the heart 'that' God is but does not know with the head 'what' God is, philosophy and theology keep striving forever to penetrate more deeply into the what."[59] It might seem that Crowe is playing fast and loose now with Lonergan's thought. Lonergan had two analogues: a love of God and a resulting philosophy or theology of God. Crowe is turning these two into analogues for three persons.

Without being explicit about his sources, Crowe is probably drawing on Aquinas's treatment of God in the *Summa Theologiae*. First, Aquinas asks *whether* God is (part I, q. 2). When this has been answered, he takes up the questions about *what* God is (part I, qq. 3–13). On this basis Crowe can distinguish two general moments in a philosophy or theology of God. There is the discovery *that* he is and *what* he is. The latter moment is a "penetrating more deeply into 'what,'"[60] that is, a moment of human understanding. In the end, however, this understanding is more about penetrating deeply into what God is not, rather than into what God is.[61] And so Crowe cleverly applies this latter moment to the Father, whom he calls "Mystery." "Analogously, the divine love the Spirit has for the Son reaches beyond the Son to the ultimate, the infinite Mystery of the One uttering the Word."[62]

Crowe knows that Lonergan did not use directly these concepts of the emergence of a philosophy and theology of God for God's inner life. He thinks, however, that this set of concepts "seems applicable to God."[63] In setting up this analogy between Lonergan's doctrine of the origin of a philosophy of God grounded in religious love, and the inner Trinitarian life, Crowe does not totally leave aside differences between the human and the divine side of the analogy. The human side involves not knowing and then seeking and finding, "while on the divine side there is no stage of unknowing, no seeking, but eternally full and conscious intersubjective communion of Love Word, and Mystery."[64] At the same time, Crowe notes that such cautions are also required "in the order Father, Son, and Spirit."[65] In the traditional order "there is no stage of un-being, no priority of Communicator over those receiving the communication, when the Father communicates the divine being to Son and Spirit."[66]

Crowe has not forgotten his earlier suggestion of the Holy Spirit as the nexus of love. "If we wish," he adds in parentheses, "to retain the idea of the Spirit as nexus, we would introduce an intermediate step: the Spirit oriented to 'what' the Spirit loves, with 'what' the Spirit loves then being differentiated into the two persons who are Word and Mystery."[67] This intermediate step seems more in keeping with Lonergan's account of the love of God, in a general religious experience, as not having an intellectually determinate object. The recognition of a divine "you" seems to be discovered later.

Winning a Proposal: Second Set of Concepts

After discussing the first set of concepts to help win a hearing for his proposal regarding the inner Trinitarian order of persons, Crowe takes up the second set of concepts found in Lonergan. Crowe's discussion is very brief, but this is only because the first set of concepts (intersubjective love, knowing the one loved, understanding mystery) is intimately tied to the second set. The second set comprises a twofold ordering of human knowing "that has come to be known as 'the way up' and 'the way down,' though the spatial metaphor is only a handy mnemonic."[68]

We looked at these two orderings of human development earlier, in chapter 6. The way up is the way that begins with experiencing data and then moves by means of questions to an understanding of those data, a judgment on that understanding, and a decision about what the responsible response is. The ordering on "the way down" reverses the relations of the levels. We begin with the level of values and love, then come judgments, then understanding of those truths, and finally more perceptive experience of the world.[69] Crowe thinks that the relevance of this twofold ordering is that each ordering can be applied respectively to the two orderings of the divine persons he has been discussing. The traditional ordering, for Crowe, aligns with the development from below upwards (see figure 12), and his proposed new ordering with the downward development (see figure 13).

Crowe thinks that both of these analogies can help us understand different aspects of the mystery of God. At first glance this proposal has something to it. In both phantasms Crowe keeps the fairly traditional triad (understanding, inner word, and love) as analogous to the Father, Son, and Holy Spirit. He preserves what he considers to be the eternal characteristics of the divine persons, while making room for a psychological development from above.

Levels	Levels of intentionality on the way up	Corresponding divine persons
4	Loving decisions	Holy Spirit
3	Judging ⬆	Word ⬆
2	Understanding ⬆	Father ⬆
1	Experiencing	

Figure 12 Summary of Crowe's psychological analogy "From Below Upwards"

Levels	Levels of intentionality on the way down	Corresponding divine persons
4	Loving ⬇	Holy Spirit or Love ⬇
3	Believing a word ⬇	Son or Word ⬇
2	Understanding	Father or Mystery
1	Experiencing	

Figure 13 Phantasm for Crowe's psychological analogy "From Above Downwards"

There are drawbacks, however, to this use of analogies between levels of consciousness. In making the Son analogous to the judging on the third level, and the Father analogous to the understanding on the second level, Crowe has chosen analogues from human activity that do not immediately relate to or depend on one another. The understanding on the second level helps to answer the question, "What is this that I am experiencing?" A (direct) act of insight gives rise to an inner word, a hypothesis, a concept, a definition, a formulation. The judgment that corresponds to the Son takes place only through another kind of insight or act of understanding. Once the person has asked the question, "But is it so?" about that hypothesis, concept, or formulation, a grasp of the sufficiency of the evidence can take place. Evidence is gathered and weighed. The (reflective) insight emerges, for example, that this formulation cannot be otherwise. And on the basis of that reflective insight, the judgment, the yes, can emerge. By contrast, Crowe's analogues among our conscious acts seem to be related only indirectly to one another. He relates the judgment of fact to the act of understanding of what something is to help us understand the relation of Son and Father. When Crowe decides to use this vertical movement for a Trinitarian psychological analogy, it could be objected that he is weakening his ability to explain why the Son and the Spirit proceed.

Crowe's response could be that he is not dealing with analogies of acts any more. His psychological analogies are based on the levels themselves. The level of understanding itself is like the Father. The level of judgment is like the Son. The level of loving decision is like the Holy Spirit.[70] Every analogy limps, he might say. An analogy between levels – like so many analogies (shamrock, three matches, etc.) – can be useful in some way, but it is less illuminating for the processions than is the analogy within a level of consciousness.

Why would Crowe make these theological sacrifices? Was he allowing his imagination to get the better of him? Was he misled by what people call the shorthand way in which Lonergan referred to the levels of consciousness by one act? Or did Crowe know what he was doing?

Pedagogical Purpose of the Two Sets of Concepts

Looking back on his own growth, Crowe admitted in 2007, "I am grateful to have focused first on intelligible emanation and to have come later to an appreciation of interpersonal relations."[71] This reference to interpersonal relations gives us a clue about Crowe's strategy and should be read in conjunction with several remarks about relations in his "Rethinking the Trinity: Taking Seriously the *Homoousios*." Speaking about Thomist Trinitarian theology, Crowe says: "The crowning step in this development, however, is still to come. It is found in the doctrine of the Trinitarian relations, which we conceive as mutual, inclusive of one another, equally 'productive' of one another and totally simultaneous."[72] By calling it the crowning step, Crowe is indicating his greater appreciation of this idea of relations in the Trinity. His great interest in 1995 was in the Trinitarian relations. Looking back, he later admitted that "the potentialities of the psychological triad had one drawback: they kept me from attending sufficiently to the riches of interpersonal relations."[73] He acknowledged that he found these riches in Lonergan's *Divinarum Personarum*, especially chapters 5 and 6. "Even after those chapters came out in print," Crowe added, "and I was teaching them, I was still for some years a particular fan of the *emanatio intelligibilis* [intelligible emanation]."[74]

When Crowe was teaching the Trinity in the first stage of his pneumatology, he was dedicated to explaining Aquinas's understanding of intelligible emanations, especially as it applied to the procession of love. In his 1995 article he characterizes the Thomist understanding of relations as follows: "Divine Utterance is as 'dependent' on the divine Word as the divine Word is dependent on the divine Utterance – neither more nor less. The Father-Son relationship, considered as relation, is no more due to the Father's initiative and activity than it is to the Son's: it emerges simultaneously and without priority in the two terms."[75] Crowe speaks, in a loose manner, of the Father-Son relation in the singular, instead of speaking of two mutually opposed relations. The point he wants to make, I think, is this: the Father is the Father precisely because he brings forth the Son. The Father *is* in so far as he is towards the Son. The Son *is* in so far as he is from the Father. Crowe then speaks in a similar fashion about the Holy Spirit: "Similarly, the relation, considered as a relation, between the Spirit and the spirating Principle is conceived as mutual and simultaneous, without any one-sided initiative attributed to either term: as relation it emerges simultaneously and without priority in both terms at once."[76]

Finally, Crowe addresses the Thomistic doctrine of the connection between relations and processions: "Furthermore, the relations 'emerge' from the processions, and the processions are intrinsic to the divine being. From that viewpoint there is no first person, no second person, no third person, but all Three are coeternal and coequal, as declared in the *Quicumque*; and all three together offer a new insight into what God is by nature."[77] One could comment on many things in Crowe's summary of Thomist Trinitarian theology, but the main point is his emphasis and characterization of the terms of the relations as mutually dependent on each other. He finishes this section of his essay thus: "we reach the furthest point yet achieved in this trajectory ["established by Augustine, the *Quicumque*, and Thomas Aquinas"][78] with the Thomist doctrine of relations, which are mutual, simultaneous, and without priority on either side."[79]

By the time of his third stage Crowe had sought a psychological analogy that more clearly grounded a doctrine of Trinitarian relations "as mutual and simultaneous, without any one-sided initiative attributed to either term."[80] How can one think, for example, of a way to express the point that the Son proceeds from the Father, but the Father is also dependent on the Son? In the two paths of development taken together Crowe can depict the dependence of the persons on one another (see figure 14).

Towards the end of "Rethinking the Trinity," Frederick Crowe says: "The traditional order of understanding, word, and love follows the upward course, while the order I propose follows the downward course; and since the two are equally part of ordinary life, they serve to support the two ways of thinking of Trinitarian order."[81]

In the upward course, Crowe provides an appropriate phantasm for thinking of the Son, analogous to the third level, as proceeding from the Father, who is analogous to the second level. Likewise, the path from below upwards, by placing the Spirit on the fourth level, expresses the truth of the Filioque.[82] The Spirit proceeds from the Father and the Son or through the Son.

In the downward course, the Father, as equivalent to the second level, is implied by the Son, the Word that is born of Love. In placing the Spirit

Analogy from Below	Levels of Intentionality	Analogy from Above
Holy Spirit	**4. Decision/Love**	Holy Spirit
Word	**3. Judgment**	Word
Father	**2. Understanding**	Mystery or Father
	1. Experiencing	

Figure 14 Upwards and downwards analogies taken together

on the fourth level, Crowe highlights how the spirating Principle, the Father-Son, is simultaneous with the One spirated. For this reason he says that we can think of the Spirit "oriented to 'what' the Spirit loves, with what the Spirit loves being differentiated into the two persons who are Word and Mystery."[83] On the way down, the analogy helps to grasp how the Father and Son as one spirator "depend" on the other relation as well. In short, the vertical analogy between levels is less useful for grasping Aquinas's doctrine of intellectual emanation, but the two sides of the analogy are more useful, Crowe proposes, in understanding the richness of the interpersonal relations.

Conclusion

Crowe's desire to gain insight into the Holy Spirit as a real relation is similar to one of the desires of the Pontifical Council for Promoting Christian Unity in its 1995 clarification, "The Greek and Latin Traditions Regarding the Procession of the Holy Spirit."[84] The document deals with the question of whether the Father and the Son are eternally characterized in reference to the Spirit. Towards the end of the document we find these words: "This role of the Spirit in the innermost human existence of the Son of God made man derives from an eternal Trinitarian relationship through which the Spirit, in his mystery as Gift of Love, characterizes the relation between the Father, as source of love, and his beloved Son."[85] I have found no evidence that Crowe had this document in mind in writing his essay. Pope John Paul II seems to have requested the clarification only in June 1995, and Crowe had finished a first draft of his essay in December 1994.[86] What this document of the pontifical council shows, however, is that the problem addressed by Crowe in his 1995 essay was in the theological air. His interest was not an isolated one.

Crowe brought to that essay all his theological learning, as well as his rhetorical skills. He disguises his purposes. In asking us to make the sign of the Cross backwards, in providing two sets of concepts, Crowe acts as the teacher. He provides phantasms to promote insights. We have his earlier writings that provide phantasms for intelligible emanations. This pneumatological work seeks to open up "the riches of interpersonal relations."[87]

Conclusion

Crowe's Contribution as a Trinitarian Pneumatologist

Frederick Crowe was inspired by the writings of Lonergan to explore complacency in Thomas Aquinas.[1] He adopted the analogy of human lovers from Lonergan. He learned about the idea of interpersonal love from Lonergan. Lonergan introduced Crowe to these various ideas of love, but Crowe developed and applied them in new ways to the Holy Spirit.

Lonergan taught Crowe that the Holy Spirit was best understood, even scripturally, as Love.[2] Lonergan, however, never focused on complacency as an analogue for the eternal procession of the Holy Spirit; he never explicitly used his idea of falling in love to reverse the order and the context of the two divine missions; and he never tried to use intersubjective love to understand the eternal ordering of the Trinitarian persons. At each of the three main stages of his own development Crowe creatively expanded and developed what he had learned from Lonergan and applied these ideas to the Holy Spirit in ways that went beyond Lonergan.

If it is objected that these three creative refinements of the pneumatology of Lonergan do not constitute Crowe as a pneumatologist in his own right, I would distinguish. In his doctrine of complacency Crowe shows a significant independence from Lonergan. He maintained his teaching on *complacentia boni* despite Lonergan's silence about the significance of Crowe's work on the subject. Whether or not Lonergan approved, Crowe stuck to his own ideas about the first act of love. And these ideas, as I will explain, shaped the rest of Crowe's distinctive pneumatology.

If we mean, by a pneumatologist in his own right, a theologian whose pneumatology can be separated from Lonergan's, then Crowe is not a theologian of the Holy Spirit in his own right. This book has consistently used Lonergan to understand Crowe. Crowe's thought has originality, but its originality is largely in the use he makes of Lonergan's own thought. There is no way to begin to understand Crowe's pneumatology apart from Lonergan's. Crowe wanted to refine and to clarify Lonergan's achievement.

Charles Hefling recently was asked how he would characterize Crowe's influence on himself as a theologian. He responded: "If I had to characterize it, perhaps I would say that FEC knew better than anyone else what *theologians* could do with Lonergan – what he was 'good for' – how to adopt, adapt, and apply his work."[3] This quotation fits, I think, with Crowe's own pneumatology.

Crowe's writings were meant to help us get over "a few hurdles" *in adopting* Lonergan's own Trinitarian pneumatology. His writings were meant to help teachers *to adapt* Lonergan's pneumatology to each new generation. In addition, his writings with their modest expansions were meant to show us how *to apply* Lonergan's theology of the Holy Spirit to new cultural and ecclesiastical problems.

Neil Ormerod was also recently asked whether Crowe had influenced him. Ormerod mentioned having read Crowe's major works, but he did not think there was much direct intellectual influence. He largely considered Crowe's work as so subsumed into the Lonergan horizon that there was not much distinctiveness left. But Ormerod then referred to a personal influence: "at a personal level it was [Crowe's] visit to Australia ... that made me take Lonergan's work seriously."[4] When pressed to say more, he explained:

> Fred was giving a number of public lectures around Australia and a friend of mine who knew a little bit about Lonergan suggested we go ... I found it very interesting (I was just getting into some theological studies after completing my PhD in maths). We were living in a student house at the time and there was a copy of *Insight* there. So I picked it up and read the preface and introduction and thought to myself, either this guy is crazy or I have to read the whole book. So I set to reading it; took me 6 months but it changed everything. Never looked back. And all because I went to Fred's talk and got the bug.[5]

This personal testimony is one illustration of how Crowe in no way wanted to take us away from Lonergan. He wanted the opposite: to lead people to Lonergan.

For this reason it is fitting to have a picture of Lonergan on the cover of this book about Crowe's own intellectual development. In this image, which hangs in the Lonergan Research Institute, Lonergan is kneeling before the three angels who appeared to Abraham as human beings

(Genesis 18:1–19; Hebrews 13:2). Those three angels who spoke to Abraham are referred to sometimes in the plural (Genesis 18:2, 16) and sometimes as *Lord*, in the singular (Genesis 18:3, 13, 17, 19).[6] Theologians and artists have seen the three visitors as prefiguring the mystery of the Trinity, three distinct persons who are perfectly one in being. Lonergan thus kneels before the Most Holy Trinity and is being drawn by one of the persons into a participation in the eternal processions.

As Crowe's own theology points us to Lonergan, so I hope this book on Crowe points us back to Lonergan, the theologian of the Trinity. As Lonergan's own books helped Crowe contemplate more deeply and share more fully the inner life of the Trinity, so Lonergan's works can continue to help those who will take up his books and read. I hope that this work on the three stages of Crowe's theology of the Holy Spirit may revive interest in Lonergan's Trinitarian theology. In the painting on the cover of this book Lonergan's work lies open before us.

In this study I have argued that Crowe's pneumatology goes through three stages with two main transition points. Are these three stages unified in any way? Do they have importance for the life of the Church? Can Crowe's thought be developed at all? In the rest of the conclusion I will attempt to answer these three questions.

The Root and Unity of the Three Stages

What unites the three stages of Crowe's developing pneumatology, beyond his concern for the life of the Church, is the fact that his pneumatological questions are rooted in his theory of human love. In the first part of this book, after discussing Crowe's interpretation of Aquinas's *complacentia boni*, I asked the question raised by Michael Sherwin's critique of Crowe: Are the two loves (complacency and concern) really distinct?[7] Crowe thought they were. Complacent love primarily follows a judgment of existence. Another judgment is required for the act of concern to emerge, a judgment of what could be and was not.[8] Both restful and restless love "proceed." The Holy Spirit relates to the Father and the Son, as an act of proceeding love relates to the act of understanding and to the judgment that is spoken on the basis of the understanding. In stage one Crowe used this dual conception of love as restful and restless to understand the role of the Holy Spirit in the world. His book *The Doctrine of the Most Holy Trinity* explained the presence of the Three in the world by means of the characteristics of the three divine persons according to the psychological analogy.

Crowe's way of distinguishing complacency and concern as the end of one process and the beginning of another maps onto his distinction between proceeding love and interpersonal or intersubjective love. His acceptance of the analogy of human lovers, with Lonergan's description of falling in love, marks the transition from Crowe's distinction of two kinds of love in stage one to the two kinds of love (proceeding and intersubjective) in stage three. The falling in love is both the beginning of a process and a kind of interpersonal love for someone as the object of the love. The notion of a human falling in love (stage two) is an anticipation of Crowe's idea of intersubjective love (stage three).

In stage three, as he embraced the two paths of human development, Crowe clearly distinguishes proceeding love from intersubjective love. Why was Crowe so open to this distinction? He thinks that he finds it in Lonergan. But Crowe's interpretation of this distinction is deeply rooted in his earlier distinction between complacent and concerned love.

Crowe's notion of "concerned love" is not exactly identical to his later notion of intersubjective love. Concerned love was still a love proceeding from a judgment. Intersubjective love was not a proceeding love for Crowe. Yet Crowe transposed his distinction between the two kinds of love from the context of faculty psychology to the context of intentionality analysis.

Stage One (1953–1968): Crowe's Doctrine of Complacency

Within a few years of the publication of Crowe's "Complacency and Concern" articles, two young Lonergan scholars had published articles recognizing their importance. David Burrell referred to them as a "profound study of the structure of love."[9] The following year Philip McShane referred approvingly to Crowe's historical work on complacency and the Holy Spirit as a "further refinement in the question of the will and of the second procession."[10] Thirty-five years later, another former Lonergan student, David Tracy, spoke at the twenty-third annual Lonergan Workshop, *The Structure and Rhythms of Love*, which "celebrated the life and work of Frederick E. Crowe, SJ."[11] According to Fred Lawrence, "David Tracy's tribute to Fred was a *tour de force* on the idea of love in the history of Western philosophy and theology."[12]

At that same Lonergan Workshop, Robert Doran claimed that the distinction between complacency and concern was pertinent to his attempt to transpose some of Lonergan's more metaphysically based teachings on sanctifying grace into categories "derived more directly or proximately from interiorly and religiously differentiated consciousness."[13] Towards the end of his 2004 article "The Two Modes of Human Love: Thomas Aquinas as Interpreted by Frederick Crowe,"[14] Michael Vertin explores some theological, philosophical, and cultural implications of

Crowe's findings on the reality of complacent willing. "If Crowe's contention is correct," Vertin writes, "what is primary in psycho-spiritual well-being is delight in what one has already been given."[15] Crowe's work on complacent love, in other words, continues to have a modest influence on Lonergan scholarship, but with vast implications.

Crowe himself spoke at the 1997 Lonergan Workshop on the subject of complacency.[16] He admitted that over the past forty years he had moved on to other intellectual interests but that his work on complacency had left a lasting mark. Crowe never abandoned his first great idea and the root of his later developments.

If *complacentia boni* lies at the root of all his reflections on love, and if his reflections on love underlie all his pneumatological developments, then some kind of evaluation of Crowe's understanding of complacency is necessary. If Crowe is wrong about this kind of love, then the ship of his theological thought was off course early on. As a ship that begins to be off course at the start ends up far from its intended destination, so a mistake about complacency might explain why so few scholars have found Crowe's work worthwhile to study. If, however, Crowe is right about complacency, if he is on to something fundamental in human life and Christian spirituality, then this insight of his might spark more interest in his other writings on the Holy Spirit.

As we discussed in chapter 2, Crowe's articles "Complacency and Concern in the Thought of St Thomas" illustrated his interpretation of complacency by appealing above all to the notion of *abandon* in the spiritual classic *Self-Abandonment to Divine Providence*.[17] But Crowe also referred to St Francis de Sales's *Treatise on the Love of God*.[18] Crowe claimed that St Francis de Sales's famous distinction between affective and effective love was relevant for his own distinction between complacency and concern.[19] "St. Francis de Sales," Crowe writes, "includes both complacency and desires in affective love, and puts obedience to God's commands and acceptance of his decrees together under effective love."[20] Crowe then remarks, "Our division would put desires under concern, acceptance under complacency (a later essay will exploit this more fully)."[21] In other words, Crowe seems to think that there could be affective complacency and affective concern, but also effective complacency and effective concern.

If one wanted to keep St Francis de Sales's division and to defend Crowe's division of complacency and concern as more basic, the division of our love for God would look like figure 15.

Like Crowe, St Francis was a Thomist heavily influenced by the Jesuits. He was "educated at the Jesuit college at Clermont (later Lycée Louis-le Grand) in Paris ... He lived under Jesuit direction from his school days

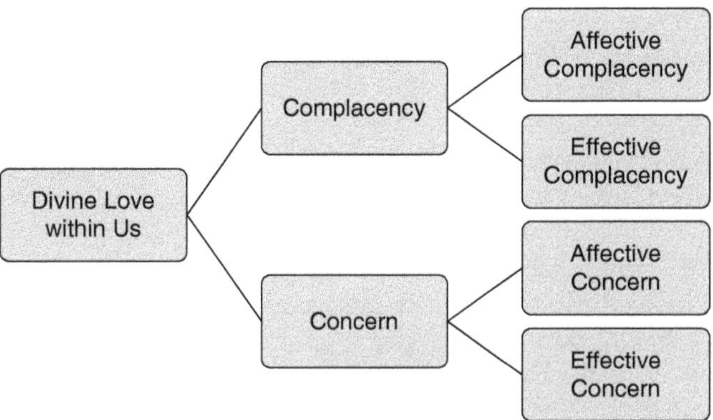

Figure 15 Crowe's way of dividing St Francis de Sales's distinction

onward, he made the Spiritual Exercises annually at a private retreat."[22] In the *Treatise on the Love of God*, St Francis offers a Thomistically inspired account of love that has been nourished by the Ignatian turn towards subjectivity.[23] De Sales's *Treatise*, moreover, returns over and over again to the idea of complacent love from different angles.[24]

It is also not an accident that Crowe connected his view of complacency with both St Francis de Sales and Jean-Pierre de Caussade. De Caussade had connections with the Visitation nuns, founded by St Francis de Sales; he was their chaplain in Nancy from 1728 to 1731 and from 1733 to 1739.[25] Many of his letters about abandonment to divine providence were written to these nuns. In addition, their own founder's treatment of this subject in "the whole of book IX" of the *Treatise* is considered to be foundational for later writers. Although "the spiritual literature on l'abandon is considerable," Marcel Viller, SJ, adds, "[St Francis de Sales] is able to be considered as the doctor of l'abandon."[26] So, it is here in the school of de Sales and de Caussade, with their emphasis on complacency and *l'abandon*, that we can best locate Crowe's own reflections on the notion of complacency. It would take us too far afield to trace St Francis's teaching on complacency and compare it with Crowe's and Aquinas's. Nevertheless, Crowe's teaching on complacency has a strong tradition behind it.

In short, I find St Francis de Sales compelling on the distinction *in this life* between complacency and a second moment of love. If there is a distinct act of complacency, if it is a kind of love, and if the Holy Spirit is to be thought of as love, then *why can this complacent love not be used as an analogy for the Holy Spirit?* Crowe saw this question more clearly than others did. Even if one wanted to disagree with an aspect of his account of complacency, the question remains: can such a love help us to understand the distinctive eternal identity of the Holy Spirit and his role in our spiritual lives?

Stage Two (1969–1984): Evaluation of Crowe's Reversing of the Missions

In the first volume of his book *Trinity and History: A Theology of the Divine Missions*, Robert Doran makes a remarkable claim: "I follow Frederick E. Crowe's great paper, 'Son of God, Holy Spirit, and World Religions,' which I think should ground the work of Lonergan scholars in systematic theology well into the twenty-first century. If Crowe is right, his thesis changes the parameters of systematic theology."[27] Doran is referring to Crowe's lecture at the Regis College convocation held on 26 November 1984, which he attended. Doran had been teaching at Regis College and working at the Lonergan Research Institute in Toronto since 1979. He stated, "The lecture 'Son of God, Holy Spirit, and World Religions' has been one of the most important theological writings in my own development."[28] For many years after that lecture he followed "without qualification the theological doctrine of Frederick Crowe" regarding the priority of the Spirit's mission.[29] More recently, Doran has qualified his praise of Crowe's achievement: "The order of the divine missions must be that of the divine processions, since the missions are the processions joined to a created external term. Thus, the mission of the Holy Spirit cannot precede the mission of the Son unless further qualifications are added. Crowe has set us on a right path, but more must be said to fill out his basic hunch."[30] To put Crowe's position on the right path, Doran insists that "for the divine missions ... there is never Spirit without Word or Word without Spirit, whether the mission be 'visible' or 'invisible.'"[31] Does Crowe actually think that the Spirit can be in the world without the Word?

In stage two Crowe appropriated Lonergan's analogy of humans who fall in love, avow their love, and consummate their love. The giving of the Spirit is analogous to the falling in love. Crowe even thought that this analogy could be used to explain the reasonableness of the Incarnation. Why would God send his Son as a man? The Incarnation is like a wedding ceremony in which a formal declaration of love is given. In this way one can even think of the universal gift of the Holy Spirit as providing the context for the Son's mission. The divine plan can be looked at through this analogy of human lovers.

As we have seen in chapters 4 and 5, however, there are at least three reasons for thinking that Crowe did not believe this analogy to be the exclusive way to understand the relations of the two missions. First of all, since he thinks of "history [as] the primary word of God,"[32] there is always an outer word of God that corresponds to the inner word of the Holy Spirit. According to Crowe, "the real word of God, his primary word, consists simply in the events of his four-dimensional space-time universe with the incarnate Son at its center."[33] Second of all, Crowe uses an ellipse for an analogy of the two missions with its two interrelated foci. Every point on the perimeter of the ellipse is always related to both foci. There is never a moment when someone is related to only the Holy Spirit and not the Son. There is never a moment when someone is in relation to the Son without the Holy Spirit. Third of all, Crowe thinks that the fullness of the mission of the Holy Spirit at Pentecost depended on the Son's fidelity to his mission to give his life on the Cross. The Spirit was sent in his fullness on account of the Son's paschal mystery. The Holy Spirit, in other words, was sent in the context of the Son's mission.

Without ever separating the two missions, Crowe rightly points to a widespread neglect of how the Spirit leads us to the Son. We need to reverse, he is saying, how we commonly think of the relation of the missions. Crowe is not saying that this reversal, the prioritizing of the Spirit's mission, is the exclusive way to think of the missions. Our common way of thinking is not the only way to think of the missions.

A proper Trinitarian theology of the Holy Spirit holds both orderings of the two missions. The Spirit leads us to the Son, and the Son gives us the Holy Spirit. In different ways both of these claims are true.[34] The mission of the Holy Spirit is, at times, prior to the mission of the Son. The Son's mission, in some ways, is prior to the Spirit's. Crowe had both of these orders in mind, even if he seemed to emphasize the priority of the Spirit's mission. If Crowe had not had both temporal orderings in mind, he never would have proposed his later idea of two ways of thinking of the eternal ordering of the divine persons.

Stage Three (1985–2000): Evaluating Crowe's Methodological Contribution

In his book *God One and Triune: Retrievals and Explorations*, Jean-Marc Laporte, SJ, speaks of a "fine progression" in Crowe's work from 1982 to 1995.[35] Crowe moves, Laporte writes, "towards a more explicit inclusion of the Father in the economic Trinity in which the usual order of Son before Spirit is reversed, and raising the question of implications of this move for the imminent Trinity."[36] Is Crowe's 1995 article part of a fine progression, or is it a kind of theological regression that neglects the eternal processions? Neither, I think. It is a pedagogical tool.

D. Juvenal Merriell has pointed out the often-overlooked, but central, place that concern for the Holy Spirit has in the whole of Augustine's

De Trinitate.[37] The question of how the Holy Spirit is to be distinguished within the Trinity is one of the two central questions of the book.[38] Something similar can be said, *mutatis mutandis*, about the focus of Frederick Crowe's 1995 essay "Rethinking the Trinity." One of the special problems of that essay is "how to conceive" the real relation of the Holy Spirit to the Son "in the inner life of God."[39] In asking about whether there can be two complementary orderings of the divine persons, Father-Son-Spirit and Spirit-Son-Father, Crowe is largely seeking a way to understand better how the Holy Spirit is both truly God and a relation within the Trinity.

His answer was to think of the Holy Spirit according to the analogies of both proceeding love and intersubjective or interpersonal love. The analogy of proceeding love on the way up slightly modifies the more traditional Augustinian analogy as interpreted by Aquinas and Lonergan. The analogy on the way down, with intersubjective love being the analogue for the Holy Spirit as the first person, was Crowe's own invention (though inspired by Lonergan's later thought).[40] What is true of Crowe's 1995 essay is also true of his entire Trinitarian pneumatology. He was carrying on, in his own small way, the Augustinian project. Like St Augustine in the *De Trinitate*, Crowe sought to understand what distinguishes the Holy Spirit from the Son by means of an analogy of love, but in his search he explicitly located this question of the *proprium* of the Spirit in relation to Basil, not Augustine.

The third stage of his Trinitarian pneumatology shows that Crowe never gave up on the psychological analogy. But how can he opt for different versions of the psychological analogy? Each acts as a "side door" for entering into the inner life of God. In the late 1940s, for example, Lonergan wrote the following about the psychological analogy:

> As long as our concepts are in development, the psychological analogy commands the situation. But once our concepts reach their term, the analogy is transcended and we are confronted with the mystery. In other words, the psychological analogy truly gives a deeper insight into what God is. Still, that insight stands upon analogy; it does not penetrate to the very core, the essence of God, in which alone trinitarian doctrine can be contemplated with in its full intelligibility; grasping properly *quid est Deus* [what God is] is the beatific vision., ... The theologian ... under the direction of divine revelation really operates in virtue of and towards an understanding that he personally in this life cannot possess.
>
> Hence it is that the psychological analogy enables one to argue that there are two and only two processions in God, that the first is "per modum intelligibilis actionis" [through the mode of intelligible action]

and a natural generation; that the second is "per modum amoris" [through the mode of love] and not a generation; that there are four real relations in God and three of them really distinct; that the names *verbum* and *imago* [*word* and *image*] are proper to the Son, while the names *amor* and *donum* [*love* and *gift*] are proper to the Holy Spirit. But do not think that Aquinas allows the psychological analogy to take the place of the divine essence as the one sufficient principle of explanation. The psychological analogy is just the side door through which we enter for an imperfect look.[41]

Lonergan wrote these words when Frederick Crowe was his student in Toronto (1947–50). Under Lonergan's influence, Crowe became fascinated by the analogy's ability to shed some partial light on the eternal processions of divine persons.

While Crowe understood each analogy to provide an imperfect look at the Trinity, he also accepted Lonergan's interpretation of the hypothetical nature of theological understanding.[42] "Thomist trinitarian theory," Lonergan writes, "on its own showing, is no more than a hypothesis which does not attempt to exclude the possibility of alternatives."[43] Crowe says the following about the hypothesis of the psychological analogy:

> A word now on the "hypothetical" and "deductive" nature of our procedures. We are saying that, *if* God is rational in the way described, *then* it will follow that there are two processions in the interior of the deity, which result in opposed relations, which relations constitute persons; and we acknowledge that the consequence is not a true "deduction." This may seem to leave the whole process up in the air. But remember that the psychological analogy is not a mere hypothesis; it has a solid basis in itself as the term of the *via analytica* [the way of analysis]. It is only as starting point of the treatise that its validity is hypothetical, and this hypothetical element diminishes with the success of the hypothesis in giving a coherent view of the Trinity, in emerging over rival analogies as the most intelligible, the most far-reaching, the most faithful to the data of revelation, etc. And remember with regard to the "make-believe" character of the deduction that we are simply ordering our ideas, not ordering realities in God; our ideas of relations can follow from our idea of processions, but in God relations do not follow from anything, they are eternal, subsistent, and identical with the divine essence.[44]

On the one hand, the psychological analogy was always a hypothesis for Crowe. On the other hand, its success in explaining the Trinity makes it more and more probable in his mind. Crowe never abandoned either of these ideas.

Crowe's earliest interests were in the eternal processions, the coming forths, of the Son and the Spirit by way of two intelligible emanations. In his later analogy on the way up, Crowe still had a basis for distinguishing the procession of the Son from the procession of the Holy Spirit. The Son proceeds as a word of truth proceeds in our minds. The Holy Spirit proceeds according to the mode of love. In the third stage of his Trinitarian pneumatology Crowe proposed various modified hypotheses about the Trinity. The most innovative was his attempt to use an analogy from above downwards. He used inter-personal or intersubjective love as an analogy for the Holy Spirit in order to help us understand better the way in which the Holy Spirit eternally characterizes the Father and the Son. At the end of his third stage Crowe had analogies on the way up and analogies on the way down, but they were all psychological analogies. They start in some way with what is closest to us. Through our own experiences within ourselves, we understand analogously something of the inner life of God.[45] Despite all the criticisms of the psychological analogy,[46] Crowe never abandoned a version of it.

According to a critique by Karl Rahner, however, the psychological analogy rests on "circular reasoning."[47] He claims that the classical model of human knowing that is used to understand the eternal procession of the Son, and the model of human loving used to understand the procession of the Holy Spirit, are postulated "from the doctrine of the Trinity."[48] Rather than the analogies being something known prior to Trinitarian theology and then used to explicate the mystery, a somewhat questionable account of knowing and loving was derived from the doctrine itself and then applied to the doctrine of the Trinity.

Crowe never answered this objection directly, but in Lonergan's and Crowe's creativeness in developing analogies we have the beginning of an answer to the charge of circularity. As we have seen in this book, Lonergan kept refining his version of the psychological analogy. He clarified in his *Verbum* articles that the inner word in Aquinas was not just the concept or definition but could also mean a judgment. There are, in other words, at least two intellectual analogies in us for the generation of the Son. Lonergan, however, was not content with these two analogies. He thought that there was an even better psychological analogy for the Son's procession, the inner word of a judgment of value, from which a loving decision proceeds. Lonergan would later modify his psychological analogy further, thinking of the Father not as infinite Understanding speaking a Word of judgment but more as originating Love. Lonergan kept searching within the human person, made to the image of God (Genesis 1:26), for a more verifiable analogy of the three divine persons. Something similar can be said of Crowe's earlier creativity in using complacency and then concern as analogies for the Spirit's eternal life, and, later, in his third stage, the two ways of human development as complementary ways of understanding the life of the three divine persons. Crowe too kept looking for better and more verifiable analogues for understanding the Church's faith in the Trinity.

It may be true that thinking about the Trinity led Augustine and Aquinas, Lonergan and Crowe, to discover aspects of the human soul that had not been emphasized before. But this does not necessarily mean that their theology of the Trinity caused them to read elements into the human mind that are not verifiable by a heightened attentiveness to our knowing and loving. In the moment of discovery, looking for these triads is influenced by our faith seeking understanding. But in the moment of proof, in the verification of the relevant judgments and acts of love, these operations of the soul are known to exist by means of our own experience of them.

This fundamental confidence in the validity of the psychological analogy is Crowe's most valuable methodological contribution to pneumatology. He helps to keep alive the role of the psychological analogy in the Church. In the freshness with which he proposes analogies, he holds up the whole question before theologians. There is more to be explored, he tells us, but we have to be creative. One does not need to agree completely with his approach or his way of explaining real relations in God to appreciate his interest in the psychological analogy. Crowe was convinced that a psychological analogy helped to disclose why there are three persons in God, what distinguishes them, and how they relate.

A Final Word

High above the tomb of St Ignatius of Loyola in Rome is a massive sculpture of the Holy Trinity.[49] Crowe would have visited this tomb of his founder in the church of the *Gesù* during his student days in Rome (1950–2) and on subsequent visits to the Eternal City. As a Jesuit, he wanted to find God in all things. But God is triune, and Crowe's special concern was to find the Father, the Son, and the Holy Spirit in all things. His concern was Trinification.

Not far from the *Gesù* is the Chiesa Nuova, the church that contains the relics of St Philip Neri. St Philip and St Ignatius, though vastly different in background, age, and temperament, became friends in mid-sixteenth-century Rome. St Ignatius reportedly called St Philip "the bell of the Society." Like the bell of a church, St Philip called men to enter the Society of Jesus, but he did not enter into the Society himself.[50] Some of the early spiritual sons of St Philip and the spiritual sons of St Ignatius were also close friends of one another.[51] As a Toronto Oratorian and a spiritual son of St Philip, I consider it a great privilege to carry on this tradition and to enter into the world of the Canadian Jesuit theologian Frederick Crowe, the spiritual son of St Ignatius.

My own view is that Crowe could have combined his idea of complacency with his notion of intersubjective love, the love in which the other is a "You." He could then have thought of the Holy Spirit, not just as the loving acceptance of what is but as the loving acceptance of the other, another person. In this way the Holy Spirit would be the loving acceptance of the Son in the Father. He would be the loving acceptance of the Father in the Son. In the Holy Spirit, in the unity of this accepting Love, the Father and the Son are one. As the Father's voice said at the waters of the Jordan, "You are my Son, the beloved; in you I have complacency within myself [*in te complacui mihi*]" (Luke 3:22).[52]

There exists in human beings this loving acceptance of the mystery of the other. Think of St Ignatius and St Philip. Such complacent love can be experienced especially with people who are different from us and with whom we are not looking forward to spending time. One can pray to the Holy Spirit in those moments.[53] The subsequent effect within may be the sudden loving acceptance of this other person as he or she is, combined with a concerned love for what this other person may become. Frederick Crowe once wrote: "His Spirit is in us, then, as *proceeding from* the Father and Son; he is in us in a way the Father and Son are not. And this presence corresponds to his eternal character in heaven, where he is *Amor* [Love]."[54]

The Holy Spirit brings into our troubled hearts what he eternally is: restful, accepting love of the other. As Gilles Emery has written, "the Holy Spirit manifests himself in the communion of love that is poured out when he dwells in the heart of believers. Through what he does, the Holy Spirit reveals who he is."[55] And Brian Daley notes that the "work of the Spirit, this manifestation of divine love, is not simply something superadded to his existence as a distinct person within the life of God; it is a living out, in temporal, created terms, of what the Holy Spirit is as a divine person."[56] Having this proceeding Love within us was Christ's final request at the Last Supper, "that the love with which thou hast loved me may be in them, and I in them" (John 17:26).

"Veni, Creator Spiritus, ... and in our hearts take up Thy rest."[57]

Notes

Abbreviations

Crowe Archive	Crowe Papers, Lonergan Research Institute, Toronto.
CWL	*Collected Works of Bernard Lonergan.*
DS	*Enchiridion symbolorum*, ed. Heinrich Joseph Dominicus Denzinger. Barcelona: Herder, 1976.
NRSV	*The Holy Bible.* New revised standard version, Catholic edition. 1989.
PG	*Patrologiae Cursus Completus.* Series Graeca, ed. Jacques-Paul Migne. Paris, 1857–66. Cited by volume, column, and section, e.g., PG 26: 1145a.
PL	*Patrologiae Cursus Completus.* Series Latina, ed. Jacques-Paul Migne. Paris, 1844–64. Cited by volume, column, and section.
RSV	*The Holy Bible.* Revised standard version, Catholic edition. Toronto: Thomas Nelson & Sons, 1966.

Epigraph

1 *"Gratia Operans*: A Study of the Speculative Development in the Writings of St Thomas Aquinas" in Bernard Lonergan, *Grace and Freedom: Operative Grace in the Thought of Thomas Aquinas*, vol. 1 of *CWL*, ed. Frederick E. Crowe and Robert M. Doran (Toronto: University of Toronto Press, 2000), 159–60.

Preface

1 John Henry Newman, "Fragment of a Life of St Philip," *Newman the Oratorian*, ed. Placid Murray, OSB (Leominster, UK: Fowler Wright Books, 1980), 267.

2 Ibid., 268–9. For the account of this event according to St Philip's first biographer, see Antonio Gallonio, *La Vita di San Filippo Neri* (Rome: Presidenza del Consiglio, 1995 [1601]), 27n58. Cf. Gallonio, *The Life of St Philip Neri*, translated by Jerome Bertram (San Francisco: Ignatius Press, 2005), 16–18.

3 Newman, *Idea of a University* (Oxford: Oxford University Press, 1976), 200. For a recent discussion of questions surrounding Philip's Pentecost experience and his subsequent ministry in Rome see Jonathan Robinson, *In No Strange Land: The Embodied Mysticism of Saint Philip Neri* (Kettering, OH: Angelico Press, 2015), 175–89.

4 Francesco Antonio Agnelli, *The Excellences of the Congregation of the Oratory of St Philip Neri*, trans. and abridged by Frederick Ignatius Antrobus of the Congregation of London (Oxford: Oxford Oratory, 2012), 196.

5 Cf. John R. Connolly and Brian W. Hughes, ed., *Newman and Life in the Spirit* (Minneapolis, MN: Fortress Publishers, 2014), 10–11, 31–2. For examples of the depths of Newman's love for the Holy Spirit see Newman, "Four Prayers to St Philip," in *Prayers, Verses, and Devotions* (San Francisco: Ignatius Press, 2000), 325–6.

6 https://w2.vatican.va/content/francesco/en/messages/pont-messages/2015/documents/papa-francesco_20150526_messaggio-v-centenario-san-filippo-neri.html, accessed 29 October 2018. For the sayings of St Philip see Philip Neri, *The Maxims and Counsels of St Philip Neri: Arranged for Each Day of the Year* (Toronto: The Toronto Oratory, 2011).

7 For a helpful and concise discussion of how adopted children of God can address the eternal Father, see Yves Congar, OP, *I Believe in the Holy Spirit*, vol. 2, trans. David Smith (New York: Crossroad, 2013), 90–2.

8 Pietro Giacomo Bacci, *The Life of St Philip Neri, Apostle of Rome*, vol. 1 (London: Thomas Richardson & Sons, 1847), 237.

9 Frederick Crowe, SJ, *The Doctrine of the Most Holy Trinity* (Willowdale, ON: Regis College, 1970 [1965]), 178.

10 T.S. Eliot, "Burnt Norton," in *Four Quartets* (London: Faber & Faber, 1970), section 2, line 72, p. 16.

11 McNichols's icon, *Holy Theologian Bernard Lonergan in the Mystery of the Trinity*, commissioned in 2002, hangs in the Lonergan Research Institute at Regis College in Toronto. McNichols dedicated the icon to Frederick Crowe and Robert Doran. For a discussion of the icon and its inspiration see John Dadosky and William Hart McNichols, *Image to Insight: The Art of William Hart McNichols* (Albuquerque, NM: University of New Mexico Press, 2018), 48–50.

12 Frederick Crowe, *Lonergan and the Level of Our Time* (Toronto: University of Toronto Press, 2010), vii–viii. See François Mauriac, *The Frontenac Mystery*, trans. Gerard Hopkins (London: Eyre and Spottiswoode, 1971).

Introduction

1 Louis Roy, OP, *Engaging the Thought of Bernard Lonergan* (Montreal and Kingston: McGill-Queen's University Press, 2016), 13–15. Born in 1942, Louis Roy taught for many years at Boston College. He was also the chief translator into French of Lonergan's *Method in Theology*.

2 Roy, *Engaging the Thought of Bernard Lonergan*, 14.

3 Bernard Lonergan, SJ, "Belief: Today's Issue," in *A Second Collection*, ed. Robert M. Doran and John D. Dadosky, vol. 13 of *Collected Works of Bernard Lonergan* (Toronto: University of Toronto Press, 2016), 85 [99] (emphasis is mine). As a rule, I will be referring to Lonergan's works in their *CWL* editions. For those who do not have convenient access to these editions, I have also included, for certain key passages, the page numbers in the older editions. The bracketed number [99], in this case, refers to the pagination in Lonergan, *A Second Collection*, ed. William F.J. Ryan and Bernard J. Tyrrell (Philadelphia, PA: Westminster Press, 1974).

4 See Frederick E. Crowe, SJ, "The Lonergan Center," *Jesuit Bulletin*, 1975, 3. The idea was suggested to Crowe in 1970 by J. Patout Burns and Gerard Fagin, and the centre's name was put forward by the late Michael Novak (cf. "The Lonergan Center," 4). In 1985 the centre received an Ontario provincial charter and became the Lonergan Research Institute (LRI). All Crowe's papers are fittingly kept in the Lonergan Research Institute at Regis College, the Jesuit school of theology at the University of Toronto and a member of the Toronto School of Theology (TST). Crowe not only founded the Lonergan Research Institute but was also instrumental in the formation of TST in 1968.

5 There have been shorter studies on aspects of his thought. In 1978 a Festschrift was published to honour Crowe. See Thomas A. Dunne and Jean-Marc Laporte, eds, *Trinification of the World* (Toronto: Regis College Press, 1978). Over the past fifteen years there have been a few articles on Crowe's theology and philosophy. See, for example, James R. Pambrun, "Revelation and Interiority: The Contribution of Frederick Crowe, S.J.," *Theological Studies* 67, no. 2 (2006): 320–44; Michael Vertin, *"The Two Modes of Human Love*: Thomas Aquinas Interpreted by Frederick Crowe," *Irish Theological Quarterly* 69 (2004): 31–45; and Eric James Morelli, "Insight and the Subject," *International Philosophical Quarterly* 51, no. 2 (2011): 137–48.

6 Frederick E. Crowe, SJ, *Theology of the Christian Word: A Study in History* (New York: Paulist Press, 1978).

7 Ibid., 107.

8 Ibid., 49.

9 Ibid., 52.

10 Cf. Frederick E. Crowe, SJ, *A Time of Change: Guidelines for the Perplexed Catholic* (Milwaukee, WI: Bruce Publishing, 1968), vii.

11 Frederick E. Crowe, SJ, "Dogma versus the Self-Correcting Process of Learning," in *Lonergan and the Level of Our Time*, ed. Michael Vertin (Toronto: University of Toronto Press, 2010), 259.

12 Ibid.

13 Lonergan, "The Future of Christianity," in *A Second Collection*, 132 [155]. This article originally appeared in *Holy Cross Quarterly* 2, no. 2 (1969): 5–10.

14 Frederick E. Crowe, SJ, "Responsibility of the Theologian, and the Learning Church," in *Appropriating the Lonergan Idea*, ed. Michael Vertin (Toronto: University of Toronto Press, 2006), 175. This paper was delivered in 1969.

15 Frederick E. Crowe, "Rethinking the Trinity: Taking Seriously the *Homoousios*," in *Lonergan and the Level of Our Time*, 404.

16 Ibid., 404–5. Crowe continued to publish articles and books well into the third Christian millennium, but there are no new major questions about the Holy Spirit that emerge after the year 2000. Crowe lived until the age of ninety-six, dying on Easter Sunday, 8 April 2012.

17 Thomas Aquinas, *Summa Theologiae* (Turin: Edizioni San Paulo, 1988), part I, q. 42, art. 3 ("oportet ibi esse ordinem secundum originem, absque prioritate").

18 Bernard Lonergan, SJ, *The Triune God: Systematics*, trans. Michael G. Shields from *De Deo Trino: Pars systematica* (1964), and ed. Robert M. Doran and H. Daniel Monsour (Toronto: University of Toronto Press, for Lonergan Research Institute of Regis College, 2007), 371–3; vol. 12 of *CWL*. In 1957 Lonergan first published his systematic Trinitarian work *Divinarum personarum conceptionem analogicam evolvit Bernardus Lonergan, S.I.* (Rome: Gregorian University Press, 1957). In 1959 Lonergan reissued *Divinarum personarum*. In the early 1960s he published a historical companion to this systematic Trinitarian theology, called *De Deo Trino: Pars analytica*, which became in 1964, in revised form, *De Deo Trino: Pars dogmatica*; it was published together with *De Deo Trino: Pars systematica*, a revised version of *Divinarum personarum* (*The Triune God: Doctrines*, xvii). This two-volume 1964 *De Deo Trino* has been republished with an English facing translation as *The Triune God: Doctrines*, vol. 11 of *CWL*, and *The Triune God: Systematics*, vol. 12 of *CWL*.

19 Lonergan, *The Triune God: Systematics*, 373.

20 Ibid.

21 Crowe, "Rethinking the Trinity: Taking Seriously the *Homoousios*," in *Level of Our Time*, 408.

22 Ibid., 396.

23 Ibid., 397.

24 Ibid.

25 Ibid., 396.

26 Ibid.

27 See Crowe, "Rethinking God-with-Us, Categories from Lonergan," in *Level of Our Time*, 332–59.

28 *Enchiridion symbolorum*, ed. Heinrich Joseph Dominicus Denzinger (Barcelona: Herder, 1976) (hereafter cited as DS), 3016. This translation is taken from vol. 12 of *CWL*, 19. For Lonergan's commentary on this teaching of *Dei Filius*, see vol. 12 of *CWL*, 10–19.

29 Anne Hunt, "The Trinity through Paschal Eyes," in *Rethinking Trinitarian Theology: Disputed Questions and Contemporary Issues in Trinitarian Theology*, ed. Robert J. Wozniak and Giulio Maspero (London: T&T Clark, 2012), 489.

30 Ibid., 488.

31 Ibid., 489.

32 Ibid., 488.

33 Matthew Levering, *Engaging the Doctrine of the Holy Spirit: Love and Gift in the Trinity and the Church* (Grand Rapids, MI: Baker Academic, 2016), 97.

34 Gilles Emery, OP, *Trinitarian Theology of Saint Thomas Aquinas*, trans. Francesca Aran Murphy (Oxford: Oxford University Press, 2011), 222n13.

35 David Coffey, *Deus Trinitas: The Doctrine of the Triune God* (Oxford: Oxford University Press, 1999), 30. For a discussion of Coffey's claims, see Matthew Levering, *Scripture and Metaphysics: Aquinas and the Renewal of Trinitarian Theology* (Malden, MA: Blackwell, 2004), 144ff.

36 Coffey, *Deus Trinitas*, 30.

37 Lonergan, *The Triune God: Doctrines*, 638–85.

38 Crowe, *The Doctrine of the Most Holy Trinity*, 120.

39 Ibid.

40 Ibid.

41 *The Holy Bible*, revised standard version, Catholic edition (Toronto: Thomas Nelson & Sons, 1966), is my default translation of the Bible in this book.

42 Lonergan, *The Triune God: Doctrines*, 685.

43 Crowe, *The Doctrine of the Most Holy Trinity*, 120–1.

44 Ibid., 121. Crowe's translation of these passage from Augustine's *De Trinitate* seems to be his own. *De Trinitate* comprises fifteen books. The references in this quotation are to the chapter and paragraph numbers from book 8 as found in the Latin version of Augustine's *De Trinitate*, in *Patrologiae Cursus Completus*, Series Latina 42, ed. J.P. Migne et al., 820–1097 (Paris, 1886) (hereafter cited as PL). For a recent translation of the *De Trinitate*, see Augustine, *The Trinity*, trans. Edmund Hill (Hyde Park, NY: New City Press, 2012). For the recent renewal of interest in Augustine's *De Trinitate*, see Rowan Williams, "The Paradoxes of Self-Knowledge in Augustine's Trinitarian Thought," and "*Sapientia*: Wisdom and the Trinitarian Relations," in *On Augustine* (London: Bloomsbury, 2016), 155–90. Attacking interpretations of Augustine as a proto-Cartesian, Williams sees Augustine's psychological analogies as "elaboration of a theological anthropology which would be the exact opposite of the infliction of an anthropological bent to theology" (Luigi

Gioia, *The Theological Epistemology of Augustine's "De Trinitate"* [Oxford: Oxford University Press, 2008], 16). For a rich discussion of the influence of Christ, original sin, and grace in the way that Augustine develops his triadic analogies for the Trinity, see Lewis Ayres, *Augustine and the Trinity* (Cambridge: Cambridge University Press, 2012). Unless otherwise noted, Latin translations into English in this book are my own.

45 Crowe, *The Doctrine of the Most Holy Trinity*, 122. Cf. Augustine, *The Trinity*, 5.14, 9.12, 15.27.

46 Crowe, *The Doctrine of the Most Holy Trinity*, 123.

47 Ibid., 124.

48 Ibid.

49 Ibid. Later on, Crowe also mentions other analogies, including Dorothy Sayers's analogy from the field of art (ibid., 143–4). See also Christine Fletcher, *The Artist and the Trinity: Dorothy Sayers' Theology of Work* (Eugene, OR: Pickwick, 2013).

50 See Crowe, *The Doctrine of the Most Holy Trinity*, 144.

51 For a very recent and vigorous defence of Lonergan's use of the psychological analogy, see Jeremy D. Wilkins, *Before Truth: Lonergan, Aquinas, and the Problem of Wisdom* (Washington, DC: Catholic University of America Press, 2018), 278–315.

52 *Collected Works of Bernard Lonergan*, ed. Frederick Crowe, SJ, and Robert Doran, SJ (Toronto: University of Toronto Press, 1988).

53 Michael Vertin, "The Writings of Frederick Crowe," in *Level of Our Time*, 455–70.

54 For the more recent reprint of this volume see Crowe, *Appropriating the Lonergan Idea*, ed. Vertin (Toronto: University of Toronto Press, 2006).

55 Frederick E. Crowe, *Three Thomist Studies*, ed. Michael Vertin, Supplementary issue of *Lonergan Workshop*, vol. 16, ed. Fred Lawrence (Boston: Lonergan Institute of Boston College, 2000).

56 This long, three-part essay first appeared in *Theological Studies* 20 (1959): 1–39, 198–230, 343–95.

57 Frederick E. Crowe, S.J., *Developing the Lonergan Legacy: Historical, Theoretical, and Existential Themes*, ed. Michael Vertin (Toronto: University of Toronto Press, 2004).

58 Editor's introduction to *Lonergan and the Level of Our Time*, ix.

59 Ibid., xi.

60 Ibid.

61 This Jesuit publication ran from 1891 to 2014.

62 Frederick E. Crowe, SJ, *The Lonergan Enterprise* (Cambridge, MA: Cowley, 1980).

63 Frederick Crowe, SJ, *Old Things and New: A Strategy for Education*, supplementary issue of the *Lonergan Workshop*, vol. 5 (Atlanta, GA: Scholars Press, 1985).

64 Frederick E. Crowe, SJ, *Lonergan* (London: Geoffrey Chapman, and Collegeville, MN: Liturgical Press, 1992).

65 Frederick E. Crowe, SJ, *Christ and History: The Christology of Bernard Lonergan from 1935 to 1982* (Toronto: University of Toronto Press, 2015).

66 See Crowe Papers, Lonergan Research Institute, Toronto (hereafter referred to as Crowe Archive), A-3-4-1; the second-to-last file contains Crowe's correspondence regarding the notes.

67 Bruce D. Marshall, "The Deep Things of God: Trinitarian Pneumatology," in *The Oxford Handbook of the Trinity*, ed. Gilles Emery, OP, and Matthew Levering (Oxford: Oxford University Press, 2011), 400.

68 Levering, *Engaging the Doctrine of the Holy Spirit*, 84.

69 Crowe, *The Doctrine of the Most Holy Trinity*, 195.

70 Ibid.

71 Thinking he was quoting St Francis de Sales, John Henry Newman took this phrase as his motto when he was named a cardinal. Sheridan Gilley, *Newman and His Age* (London: Darton, Longman, & Todd, 1990), 400.

1 Frederick Crowe, SJ

1 Crowe, *Lonergan*, 1.

2 Ibid., 2.

3 Ibid., 1.

4 Patricia Byrne, interview by the author, 26 August 2015, Sussex, NB.

5 Ibid.

6 Crowe, *Old Things and New*, 18. Crowe did not claim that this account was autobiographical, but the description aimed "at being concrete in the measure that is possible for me" (18).

7 Crowe was eleven when his eight-year-old brother Johnny died on 28 March 1927. "It almost killed her," described someone about the effect of John Vincent's death on Margaret Crowe. Cousins of Frederick Crowe, interview by author, 26 August 2015, Sussex, NB.

8 For example, see Crowe, *Old Things and New*, 87.

9 Cf. ibid., 65–74, esp. 66n3. Copies of those books are still available.

10 Cf. Cecil Jeffries, *Early Schools of Kings County, New Brunswick*, published by Kings County Retired Teachers' Association (Sussex, NB: Royal Printing, 1985), 223. Many of Crowe's female relatives were teachers.

11 Crowe, *Christ and History*, 10.

12 Frank and Olive Cogger, interview by the author, 25 August 2015, Saint John, NB. Olive, for her part, insisted that Fr Crowe was "an ordinary person, like we are. He was easy to talk to."

13 Michael Vertin, editor's introduction to *Appropriating the Lonergan Idea*, by Crowe, ix.

14 The Jesuits had some schools in the Maritimes, but not in New Brunswick.

15 Michael Swan, "Jesuits 1611–2011: 400 Years of Giving," *The Catholic Register*, 15 September 2011. The Jesuit novitiate in Guelph is about ninety miles south of the Martyr's Shrine, Midland, Ontario, near where St Jean de Brebeuf and others gave up their lives in the 1640s.

16 Crowe, "The Growing Idea," in *Appropriating the Lonergan Idea*, 3.

17 Ibid.

18 By the time that Crowe joined the Jesuits, a separate English province had been formed, in 1924. According to Jean-Marc Laporte, SJ, "Fr. Crowe was the kind of guy who would do what his superiors said. Those years of the juniorate were for studying Greek, Latin, French, English, literature, and the arts of communication. We [as Jesuits] are meant to communicate the truth to others and had to be trained how to organize our thoughts, how to think logically, and how to write. Crowe was intelligent, but he also took his commitments seriously. If his superiors told him that this was what these years were for, then he would throw himself into that work" (Jean-Marc Laporte, SJ, interview by the author, 10 November 2015, Toronto).

19 Crowe, "The Growing Idea," in *Appropriating the Lonergan Idea*, 3.

20 Crowe, *Lonergan*, 11. If Crowe was "fresh from" his juniorate, it seems that the date should have been 1940. William A. Mathews, however, puts this "preached retreat, four talks a day plus a conference, following the Ignatian format," given to "Jesuit students of philosophy," in the summer of 1941. Mathews, *Lonergan's Quest: A Study of Desire in the Authoring of "Insight"* (Toronto: University of Toronto Press, 2005), 110.

21 See *Dictionary of Jesuit Biography: Ministry to English Canada, 1842–1987* (Toronto: Canadian Institute of Jesuit Studies, 1991), xvi–xx. In 1958, in order to focus more on teaching theology, Regis College closed its faculty of philosophy, and Jesuit philosophy students were sent to St Michael's College, Gonzaga University. "Regis became a pontifical faculty with the ability to grant ecclesiastical degrees in 1956 and eventually moved to the campus of the University of Toronto in 1976." Swan, "Jesuits 1611–2011: 400 Years of Giving," *The Catholic Register*, 15 September 2011.

22 Crowe, *Lonergan*, 17.

23 Crowe Archive, A-3-4-1, file "Footnotes."

24 See Lonergan, *Verbum: Word and Idea in Aquinas*, ed. Frederick E. Crowe and Robert Doran, vol. 2 of *CWL* (Toronto: University of Toronto Press, 1997), xxiii n72. See also Mathews, *Lonergan's Quest*, 178. The course, called "The Divine Processions," was attended by five students, including Walter Principe, CSB. Principe "remembered it as his first real exposure to serious textually based historical scholarship, and initially found it overwhelming. Lonergan struck him as having a computer-like mind" (*Lonergan's Quest*, 178).

25 Crowe, *The Lonergan Enterprise*, ix.

26 Ibid.

27 According to Michael Vertin, Crowe would occasionally "brag" about this honour. For Crowe's description of Lonergan's teaching method see Mathews, *Lonergan's Quest*, 178.

28 Crowe, *Lonergan*, 43; the description comes in Crowe's discussion of Lonergan's dissertation on operative grace in Thomas Aquinas (1939) – Bernard Lonergan, "St Thomas' Thought on *Gratia Operans,*" *Theological Studies* 2 (1941): 289–324; 3 (1942): 69–88, 375–402, 533–78. Lonergan's articles, based on his dissertation, were collected into a book in 1971: Bernard J.F. Lonergan, SJ, *Grace and Freedom*, ed. J. Patout Burns, SJ, with an introduction by Frederick E. Crowe, SJ (London: Darton, Longman, & Todd, 1971). More recently, Lonergan's original dissertation and the subsequent articles were published as *Grace and Freedom: Operative Grace in the Thought of St Thomas Aquinas*, vol. 1 of *CWL*, ed. Frederick E. Crowe, and Robert M. Doran (Toronto: University of Toronto Press, 2000). For background on Lonergan's own doctoral work see Crowe, *Lonergan*, 42–8.

29 Cf. Bernard Lonergan, SJ, "The Concept of Verbum in the Writings of Thomas Aquinas," *Theological Studies* 7 (1946): 349–92; 8 (1947): 35–79, 404–44; 10 (1949): 3–40, 359–93. These articles were edited by David Burrell, CSC, and published together in 1967. See Lonergan, *Verbum: Word and Idea in Aquinas* (Notre Dame, IN: University of Notre Dame Press, 1967). Cf. *Verbum: Word and Idea in Aquinas*, vol. 2 of *CWL*.

30 Mathews, *Lonergan's Quest*, 110.

31 Crowe, preface to *Grace and Freedom* (1971), by Lonergan, x.

32 Ibid. For a recent account of Lonergan's understanding of grace, see Jeremy Wilkins, "Grace and Growth: Aquinas, Lonergan, and the Problematic of Habitual Grace," *Theological Studies* 72, no. 4 (2011): 723–49.

33 General editors' preface to *The Triune God: Systematics*, by Lonergan, xx. Crowe studied theology for four years at Regis College (1946–50).

34 It was the first time that Lonergan had taught the course in Regis College's four-year cycle of courses. In that same semester he was given the Catholic Theological Society of America's (CTSA's) Spellman Medal at a special dinner in the fall of 1949 for his articles on Aquinas. See Mathews, *Lonergan's Quest*, 202. For the minutes of the CTSA Fourth Annual Meeting in June 1949 see http://ejournals.bc.edu/ojs/index.php/ctsa/article/viewFile/2271/1865 (accessed on 11 April 2017). Lonergan was the secretary of the gathering, but also was designated as the recipient of this award.

35 "General Editors' Preface," *The Triune God: Systematics*, xx (emphasis mine).

36 In 1950 Crowe finished a licentiate in theology at Regis College. He wrote his dissertation, "The Unity of the Virtues in St Thomas Aquinas," under the supervision of Lonergan. Crowe later wrote his doctoral dissertation on Aquinas: "Conflict and Unification in Man: The Data in the Writings of

St Thomas Aquinas." He completed the doctorate in 1952 at the Gregorian University in Rome. After Crowe finished his dissertation, a fifty-two-page extract was published the following year. See Frederick E. Crowe, SJ, *Conflict and Unification in Man: The Data in the Writings of St Thomas Aquinas* (Rome: Gregorian University, 1953).

37 Crowe, *Lonergan*, 27.

38 Ibid., 71n44. A native of France, Charles Boyer (1884–1980) joined the Society of Jesus in 1907 and began teaching at the Gregorian University in 1922. He was Lonergan's dissertation director and lived at the Gregorian until his death in 1980. For information on his publications in philosophy and theology see "In Memoriam," *Augustinian Studies* 11 (1980): 3–4.

39 Bernard Lonergan, "*Insight* Revisited," in *A Second Collection*, 225–6.

40 Crowe, *Lonergan*, 71.

41 Ibid., 72.

42 Ibid., 83.

43 Ibid., 80. Cf. Jeremy Wilkins, *Before Truth: Lonergan, Aquinas, and the Problem of Wisdom* (Washington, DC: Catholic University of America, 2018). Wilkins examines Lonergan's methodology through exposure to his actual theology.

44 In 1961–2 Lonergan had taught a graduate seminar called *De Methodo Theologiae* at the Gregorian University. In the summer of 1962, from 9 to 20 July, Lonergan lectured at Regis College in English on "The Method of Theology" (Crowe, *Lonergan*, 93). Cf. Frederick Crowe, "On the Method of Theology," *Theological Studies* 23, no. 4 (1962): 637–42.

45 See Crowe's various introductions to Lonergan's works in *Early Latin Theology*, vol. 19 of *CWL* (Toronto: University of Toronto Press, 2011), 54–61, 257–62, 413–14.

46 In 1962 the Jesuits moved Regis College to a more rural setting on Bayview Avenue in Willowdale, Ontario, just outside Toronto.

47 According to Jean-Marc Laporte, SJ, this issue and the subsequent rift with Lonergan was painful for Crowe who was heavily involved in the move of Regis College (Jean-Marc Laporte, SJ, interview by the author, 10 November 2015). In leaving the large Jesuit residence in Willowdale, the Jesuits would be moving into a number of houses in downtown Toronto and would no longer be living in the same building as the Jesuit library. Part of Lonergan's objection was based on the need to live in a building with a good library for doing real scholarly work.

48 Crowe, *Theology of the Christian Word*. This book will be discussed in part 2. Louis Roy, OP, has singled it out as one of "the most impressive" books dealing with one of Lonergan's functional specialties (*Engaging the Thought of Bernard Lonergan*, 24). According to Charles Hefling, *Theology of the Christian Word* "is Crowe's best *published* work" (private correspondence, 27 October 2018).

49 These issues dealing with Crowe's attitude towards the Magisterium will
be discussed in chapters 4 and 5.

50 Crowe finished teaching the Trinity course at Regis College in 1977. In
that same year he reviewed Giovanni Sala's 1976 book, *Dogma e storia
nella dichiarazione 'Mysterium ecclesiae.'* See Frederick Crowe, SJ, "Doctrines
and Historicity in the Context of Lonergan's *Method in Theology*: A Review
Article," in *Level of Our Time*, 30. Giovanni Sala, SJ (1930–2011) had begun
publishing on Lonergan in 1965. In 1977 Crowe noted: "His doctoral
dissertation, completed at the University of Bonn, was a study of the a
priori in Kant and Lonergan. He has published studies of Lonergan in
the periodicals of Italy, Germany, France, Austria, and the United States"
("Doctrines and Historicity," in *Level of Our Time*, 30n11). Cf. Matthew
L. Lamb, "Fr. Giovanni Sala, S.J., Philosopher and Theologian," *Nova et
Vetera* (English edition) 15, no. 1 (2017): 75–88.

51 See Frederick E. Crowe, *De Verbo Dei cum hominibus communicato* (Toronto:
Regis College, 1963).

52 Crowe, *Theology of the Christian Word*, 104ff.

53 Crowe, *The Lonergan Enterprise*, ix. The inaugural St Michael's Lectures,
in December 1972, were subsequently published as *Philosophy of God, and
Theology*, by Bernard Lonergan (Philadelphia, PA: Westminster Press, 1974).

54 Crowe, *The Lonergan Enterprise*, vii.

55 Ibid.

56 Ibid.

57 Ibid., ix.

58 Ibid. The first lecture was later delivered at Marquette University in
Milwaukee and appeared "as the Père Marquette Lecture of 1980 under
the title, *Method in Theology: An Organon for Our Time*" (Crowe, *The
Lonergan Enterprise*, x).

59 Newman published this work in 1870: *An Essay in Aid of a Grammar of
Assent* (Notre Dame, IN: University of Notre Dame Press, 2008). Even
before his time as a Jesuit, Crowe was familiar with Newman's sermons. In
a 1968 book review Crowe noted: "Theologians brought up on Newman's
prose, with the cadences of *The Second Spring* and *Christ upon the Waters* still
making music in our minds, find it hard to discuss Newman technically ...
In our tradition Newman functions, I think, somewhat as he conceived the
deposit to function in the early Church. *He is our blood. His mentality guides
us implicitly, not only the positions he worked out but also the deeper notions that,
by a kind of intellectual instinct, formed his judgments* ... notions that I think
are absorbed and operative in the unformulated system *of those steeped in
Newman from their youth.*" Frederick E. Crowe, SJ, review of *Bible et tradition chez Newman: Aux origines de la théorie du développement*, by Jean Stern,
Theological Studies 29, no. 4 (1968): 777–9 (emphasis mine).

It was only, I think, later on in his theology studies that Crowe would become familiar with Newman's *Essay on the Development of Christian Doctrine* and *Essay in Aid of a Grammar of Assent* (cf. Crowe Archive, A-3-4-1, file "Footnotes"). After 1960, these two essays had a clear and explicit influence on Crowe's thinking. But the exact nature of Newman's influence is hard to delineate. For the sermon that seems most relevant to Crowe's pneumatology see John Henry Newman, "The Indwelling Spirit," in *Parochial and Plain Sermons*, vol. 2, sermon 19 (London: Longmans, Green, 1902).

60 John Henry Newman in reply, 16 March 1870, *The Letters and Diaries of John Henry Newman*, vol. 25 (Oxford: Clarendon Press, 1973), 56–7. The key passage from Dale's letter to Newman can also be found in Crowe, *The Lonergan Enterprise*, xxii.

61 Newman, *Letters and Diaries*, vol. 25, 56–7.

62 Crowe, "The Janus Problematic," in *Appropriating the Lonergan Idea*, 287. The address was on the nest of questions surrounding the relationship between our orientation to the past and to the future, to tradition and innovation.

63 Ibid.

64 Ibid.

65 Ibid.

66 Lonergan, *Verbum*, 12n2. See Ludovicus Billot, *De Deo Uno et Trino* (Rome: Gregorian University Press, 1910), 335. Billot (1846–1931) taught theology at the Gregorian University.

67 "Lonergan began his studies of the verbum," Crowe explains, "by pointing out the contrast between Billot, for whom the imagination offered as good an analogy as intellect for the procession, and St. Thomas who insisted that only in the rational part of man is there the *imago Dei* that offers such an analogy" (*The Doctrine of the Most Holy Trinity*, 144; emphasis in the original). Lonergan wrote his *Verbum* articles when Frederick Crowe was his student in Toronto (1947–50).

68 Crowe, *The Doctrine of the Most Holy Trinity*, 145 (emphasis in the original).

69 Ibid. (emphasis in the original).

70 Ibid.

71 Ibid.

72 Ibid., 146.

73 Ibid., 145.

74 Lonergan, *Verbum*, 13. See Maurílio T.-L. Penido, "Gloses sur la procession d'amour dans la Trinité," *Ephemerides Theologica Lovanienses* 14 (1937): 33–68. Maurílio Penido (1896–1970), a Brazilian-born theologian, wrote this article when he was a theology professor at the University of Freiburg. For a useful discussion of some of Penido's difficulties in using a procession of love to understand the Holy Spirit's procession, see

Kenneth M. Loyer, *God's Love through the Spirit: The Holy Spirit in Thomas Aquinas and John Wesley* (Washington, DC: Catholic University of America Press, 2014), 104–7, 127–34.

75 Crowe, "Complacency and Concern," in *Three Thomist Studies*, 87–8 (emphasis in the original). See Lonergan, *Verbum*, 109–10. Crowe's original article had three parts plus an appendix and appeared in March, June, and September in issues of *Theological Studies* 20 (1959): 1–39, 198–230, 343–82, 383–95. "Complacency and Concern" forms chapters 3–6 of *Three Thomist Studies*. Chapter 3 (pp. 73–112) is part 1 of the original article; chapter 4 (pp. 113–47) is part 2; chapter 5 (148–87) is part 3. Chapter 6 (pp. 189–203) is an important appendix dealing with the question of whether intellect and will are distinct faculties in the human soul.

76 Lonergan, *Verbum*, 198. See for example Thomas Aquinas, *Summa Theologiae*, I, q. 14, art. 4.

77 Lonergan, *Verbum*, 198–9. Cf. Thomas Aquinas, *Summa Theologiae*, I, q. 34, art. 1, ad 3; and art. 2, ad 4.

78 Lonergan, *Verbum*, 213. On the distinction between two different orders of learning, the way of teaching (*via doctrinae*) and the way of discovery (*via inventionis*), see Lonergan, "Theology and Understanding," in *Collection*, ed. Frederick E. Crowe, SJ, and Robert M. Doran, vol. 4 of *CWL* (Toronto: University of Toronto Press, 1988), 123–7.

79 Lonergan, *Verbum*, 213.

80 Lonergan, *The Triune God: Systematics*, 193.

81 Ibid., 195.

82 For an example see Frederick D. Wilhelmsen, "The Priority of Judgment over Question: Reflections on Transcendental Thomism," *International Philosophical Quarterly* 14, no. 4 (1974): 476. For contemporary negative reactions by Jesuits to the *Verbum* articles see Mathews, *Lonergan's Quest*, 182–4. At the end of the third stage of his pneumatological development Crowe took up Lonergan's notion of the rationality of the divine nature as helping us to understand why there are processions in God. Crowe, "For Inserting a New Question (26A) into the *Pars Prima*," *The Thomist* 64 (2000): 565–80. This article was reprinted in Crowe, *Developing the Lonergan Legacy*, 332–46. In a response that is fairly sympathetic to Crowe's main concern, Sebastian Walshe, OP, suggests instead that "Trinitarian theology is an extended reflection upon the happiness of God" ("*Beata Trinitas*: The Beatitude of God as Prelude to the Trinitarian Processions," *The Thomist* 76 [2012]: 189–209); for Walshe's direct discussions of Crowe's position, see 189n1, 201n32, 204n37.

83 Lonergan, *The Triune God: Systematics*, 195. "Aseity (Latin *a*, from; *se*, itself: *ens a se*) is the property by which a being exists of and from itself." George M. Sauvage, CSC, *The Catholic Encyclopedia*, vol. 1 (New York: Robert Appleton, 1907), 774.

84 Lonergan, *The Triune God: Systematics*, 197. Cf. Aristotle, *Physics* 2.1.192b.23.
85 Lonergan, *The Triune God: Systematics*, 197.
86 Ibid.
87 Thomas Aquinas, *Summa Theologiae*, I, q. 93, art. 5 (emphasis mine).
88 Ibid., art. 6. Cf. Thomas Aquinas, *Summa Theologiae*, I, q. 28, art. 3.
89 Lonergan, *The Triune God: Systematics*, 199.
90 Crowe, *The Doctrine of the Most Holy Trinity*, 119.
91 Ibid.
92 Lonergan, *Verbum*, 47.
93 Ibid.
94 Ibid.
95 Ibid., 207.
96 Crowe, *The Doctrine of the Most Holy Trinity*, 142. Crowe capitalizes *Speaker*, *Word*, and *Love* because he is using them respectively as proper names for the three persons of the Trinity: Father, Son, and Holy Spirit. Throughout this book I will follow Crowe's custom.
97 Ibid., 119.
98 Lonergan, *Verbum*, 215–16.
99 Crowe, *The Doctrine of the Holy Trinity*, 119.
100 Ibid.
101 Crowe, "The Origin and Scope of Bernard Lonergan's *Insight*," in *Appropriating the Lonergan Idea*, 13.
102 Ibid.
103 Ibid., 21.
104 Ibid. "To strengthen and complete the old by aid of the new." *Aeterni Patris*, Encyclical Letter on the Restoration of Christian Philosophy (Boston: St Paul Books and Media, 1985), 18.
105 Crowe, "The Origin and Scope of Bernard Lonergan's *Insight*," in *Appropriating the Lonergan Idea*, 21.
106 Ibid.
107 Ibid., 26.
108 Crowe, "The Origin and Scope of Bernard Lonergan's *Insight*," in *Appropriating the Lonergan Idea*, 26.
109 Ibid., 17. Cf. Bernard Lonergan, *Insight: A Study of Human Understanding*, ed. Frederick Crowe and Robert Doran, vol. 3 of *CWL* (Toronto: University of Toronto Press, 1992), 769 [748]. The bracketed number refers to the pagination in Lonergan, *Insight: A Study of Human Understanding* (New York: Philosophical Library, 1970). Since Crowe's own references are usually to the pagination of the older edition, I often include the page reference for this older edition of *Insight*.

110 Crowe, "Neither Jew Nor Greek, but One Human Nature and Operation in All," in *Appropriating the Lonergan Idea*, 36.
111 Ibid., 36–7.
112 Crowe, "The Origin and Scope of Bernard Lonergan's *Insight*," in *Appropriating the Lonergan Idea*, 28.
113 Lonergan, *Insight* (1970), 407. Cf. Crowe, "The Origin and Scope of Bernard Lonergan's *Insight*," in *Appropriating the Lonergan Idea*, 28.
114 Lonergan, *Insight* (1970), 430. Cf. Crowe, "The Origin and Scope of Bernard Lonergan's *Insight*," in *Appropriating the Lonergan Idea*, 29.
115 Crowe, "The Origin and Scope of Bernard Lonergan's *Insight*," in *Appropriating the Lonergan Idea*, 30.
116 Ibid.
117 Ibid.
118 Ibid. For a recent presentation and defence of Lonergan's position on the importance of self-appropriation for philosophy, see Wilkins, *Before Truth*, 131–79.
119 Crowe, "St Thomas and the Isomorphism of Knowing and Its Proper Object," in *Three Thomist Studies*, 207. For Lonergan's use of the word *contents* Crowe refers us to *Insight: A Study of Human Understanding* (New York: Philosophical Library, 1970), 399–400 (vol. 3 of *CWL*, 424–5). For the defence of the reality of the three metaphysical principles Crowe refers to *Insight* (1970), 499–502 (*CWL*, 522–6) as well as 432 (457). Lonergan wrote an article in 1958 on the isomorphism of Thomistic and scientific thought.
120 Crowe later nuanced his understanding of the actual history of Lonergan's thought. See Crowe, *Lonergan*, 39.
121 Lonergan, *Insight* (1970), 748. Crowe speaks of Lonergan's eleven years (1938–49) of intense work on Aquinas as Lonergan's apprenticeship to Thomas Aquinas (*Lonergan*, 39–55). Like Lonergan, Crowe never lost his own appreciation of Thomas Aquinas.
122 Crowe, "Neither Jew Nor Greek, but One Human Nature and Operation in All," in *Appropriating the Lonergan Idea*, 49.
123 Crowe's 1959 article will be the main focus of chapter 3.
124 Cf. Lonergan's mention of *complacency* in appendix 2b, "From the Image to the Eternal Exemplar," in *The Triune God: Systematics*, 674–5.
125 Frederick Crowe, "Early Jottings on Bernard Lonergan's *Method in Theology*," *Science et Esprit* 25 (1973): 121–38.
126 Ibid., 123.
127 Ibid.
128 Ibid., 131.
129 Ibid.

130 Crowe, *Lonergan*, 81ff. The chapter is titled "Experiments in Method: A Quarter-Century of Exploration."

131 Ibid., 110.

132 Ibid., 111.

133 Cf. Crowe, *The Lonergan Enterprise*, 89.

134 "It is by knowing what we are," Crowe says about theology's reflection on conversion, "that we will know what formulation of doctrines is appropriate for our time, and we are what we are by the gift of the Spirit of God" (*The Lonergan Enterprise*, 89).

135 Crowe, "The Task of Interpreting Lonergan," in *Appropriating the Lonergan Idea*, 158.

136 From a lecture given on 10 September 1976 at St Mary's University, Halifax, Nova Scotia. See Lonergan, "The Human Good," in *Philosophical and Theological Papers, 1965–1980*, ed. Robert C. Croken and Robert M. Doran, vol. 17 of *CWL* (Toronto: University of Toronto Press, 2004), 340.

137 These issues will be taken up at greater length in part 3 of this book when we discuss Lonergan's notion of "intentionality analysis." In short, Crowe links the fourth level of consciousness with both responsible decision and human love.

138 From a lecture given at the thirty-second annual convention of the Catholic Theological Society of America on 16 June 1977 in Toronto. See Lonergan, "Theology and Praxis," in *A Third Collection*, ed. Robert M. Doran and John D. Dadosky, vol. 16 of *CWL* (Toronto: University of Toronto Press, 2017), 192 [196]. The bracketed number refers to pagination in the more widely available version: Lonergan, *A Third Collection*, ed. Frederick E. Crowe (New York: Paulist Press, 1985).

139 From a paper presented at the Lonergan workshop in June 1976. See Crowe, "Dialectic and the Ignatian *Spiritual Exercises*," in *Appropriating the Lonergan Idea*, 158 (emphasis mine).

140 Crowe, *The Lonergan Enterprise*, 72–3. Nevertheless, Crowe does say that the second, downward path "has its source in gift, but the first in achievement" (72).

141 Crowe, "On Ultimate Reality and Meaning," in *Appropriating the Lonergan Idea*, 102. For the two phases see Lonergan, *Method in Theology*, chapter 5. The movements from below upwards and from above downwards will be the focus of part 3 of this book. For the place in which Crowe thinks that the distinction of two movements is almost made explicit, see *Method in Theology*, ed. Doran and Dadosky, vol. 14 of *CWL* (Toronto: University of Toronto Press, 2017), 135–6 [142]. Since the 1972 edition of *Method in Theology* is more widely available, I have included the page references to that edition in brackets.

142 Crowe, "Son and Spirit: Tensions in the Divine Missions?" in *Appropriating the Lonergan Idea*, 304.

2 Appropriating Aquinas on Love

1 "Persona Spiritus Sancti [insinuatur] in complacentia qua vidit Deus esse bonum quod factum est" (Thomas Aquinas, *Summa Theologiae*, I, q. 74, art. 3, ad 3).

2 This long, three-part study, together with an appendix, first appeared in *Theological Studies* 20 (1959): 1–39, 198–230, 343–95. "Complacency and Concern" was reprinted with two of Crowe's other essays as *Three Thomist Studies*, ed. Michael Vertin. Cf. Crowe, "Universal Norms and the Concrete *Operabile* in St Thomas Aquinas," *Sciences ecclésiastiques* (1955): 115–49, 257–91; and "St Thomas and the Isomorphism of Human Knowing and Its Proper Object," *Sciences ecclésiastiques* 13 (1961): 167–90. Since 1968 *Sciences ecclésiastiques* has been called *Science et Esprit*.

3 Michael Sherwin, OP, *By Knowledge and by Love: Charity and Knowledge in the Moral Theology of St Thomas Aquinas* (Washington, DC: Catholic University of America Press, 2005), 78n67. Sherwin is not alone in lauding Crowe's achievement in these articles. See Diana Fritz Cates, *Aquinas on the Emotions: A Religious-Ethical Inquiry* (Washington, DC: Georgetown University Press, 2009), 19n11; and *Choosing to Feel: Virtue, Friendship, and Compassion for Friends* (Notre Dame, IN: University of Notre Dame Press, 1997), 100. See also William McDonough, "Etty Hillesum's Learning to Live and Preparing to Die: *Complacentia boni* as the Beginning of Acquired and Infused Virtue," *Journal of the Society of Christian Ethics* 25, no. 2 (2005): 183–7. See as well Mark J. Doorley, "Resting Reality: Reflections on Crowe's 'Complacency and Concern,'" *Lonergan Workshop* 13 (1997): 33–56.

4 Thomas Aquinas, *Summa Theologiae* I, q. 33, art. 2.

5 Thomas Aquinas, *Summa Theologiae* I, q. 37, art. 1, ad 4. For places in which Aquinas repeats the phrase "*Amor procedens*," see *Summa Theologiae* I, q. 37, art. 2, and art. 2, ad 3.

6 Crowe, *Three Thomist Studies*, 155.

7 Ibid.

8 Ibid.

9 Ibid., 75.

10 Ibid., 78. Cf. Robert Browning, "Weiss's Doctrine of Concern," *Review of Metaphysics* 9 (1955–6): 334. For Weiss's own words within Browning's quotation, see Paul Weiss, *Nature and Man* (New York: Holt, 1947), 53.

11 Crowe, *Three Thomist Studies*, 106.

12 Ibid., 77. The second part of the *Summa Theologiae* is divided into two sections: the Prima secundae (I-II) and the Secunda secundae (II-II). The Prima secundae treats of our last end (beatitude) and, in general, the acts and causes that lead us to our last end. The Secunda secundae discusses the specific virtues, gifts, and states of life that enable us to reach eternal happiness.

13 Since Crowe was "primarily interested in the complacent aspect of willing, concern is considered mainly as clarifying by contrast" (*Three Thomist
  Studies*, 78), and he mentions only one other thinker's notion of concern,
  namely Paul Tillich's. Crowe says that Tillich's notion of concern, though
  exclusively applied to religious questions, prepares "our minds for its
  reception in systematic thought" (78). Later on, however, Crowe has a
  section entitled "Thomist Complacency and Modern *Eros*" (169ff). In that
  section he briefly discusses the way in which Eros occupied the thought
  of Arthur Schopenhauer, Friedrich Nietzsche, and various existentialists,
  including Heidegger. In that and earlier sections (*Three Thomist Studies*,
  155n9, 172–3n56) Crowe seems to suggest a connection between concern
  and Heidegger's notion of care (*Sorge*). For example, Crowe explains that,
  for existentialists, care "defines the mode of existence of the human being" and "is the structure of the phenomena" so often described by existentialists (173). "Care," he adds, is "looking to the future, self-projecting,
  in advance of itself, concerned for what is to be; care looking to the past,
  to my being already found cast into a world; care bound up with other
  beings encountered in the world, in the grip of particular preoccupa-
  tions" (173–4). After discussing various thinkers, Crowe writes, "We have
  been illustrating the modern interest in *eros*, understanding that term in
  its widest sense as human concern" (174).
14 Crowe, *Three Thomist Studies*, 76.
15 Ibid.
16 Crowe explains: "The Thomist terms are usually *complacere* and *intendere*,
  but to translate the first by 'complacency,' as I did in a series of articles
  in *Theological Studies*, vol. 20 (1959), is to sabotage what seems to me an
  important idea. 'Serenity' is better, but it suggests the somewhat helpless
  attitude adopted in adversity, as in the AA's serenity prayer. The Thomist *complacere* is a more positive joy in what is, manifested most purely, I
  think, in the spontaneous joy that a child has in people and things before
  his psychological life becomes complicated by the concerns of older realism. But 'joy' itself lacks the intellectual connotation. In fact, we have no
  word in English for the idea" ("Pull of the Future and Link with the Past:
  On the Need for Theological Method," *Continuum* 7 [1969], 41n26).
17 Crowe, *Three Thomist Studies*, 149.
18 Ibid., 113–14.
19 Ibid., 114.
20 "Et similiter coaptatio appetitus sensitivi, vel voluntatis, ad aliquod
  bonum, idest ipsa complacentia boni, dicitur amor sensitivus, vel intellec-
  tivus seu rationalis" (Thomas Aquinas, *Summa Theologiae*, I-II, q. 26 art. 1;
  emphasis mine). See Crowe, *Three Thomist Studies*, 99.

21 "Sic etiam ipsum appetibile dat appetitui, primo quidem, quandam coaptationem ad ipsum, quae est complacentia appetibilis; ex qua sequitur motus ad appetibile ... Prima ergo immutatio appetitus ab appetibili vocatur amor, qui nihil est aliud quam complacentia appetibilis" (Thomas Aquinas, *Summa Theologiae*, I-II, q. 26, art. 2; emphasis mine). See Crowe, *Three Thomist Studies*, 100, for the places from which I pieced together this translation.

22 "Ipsa autem aptitudo sive proportio appetitus ad bonum est amor, qui nihil aliud est quam complacentia boni" (Thomas Aquinas, *Summa Theologiae*, I-II, q. 25, art. 2). See Crowe, *Three Thomist Studies*, 99.

23 Vertin, "Editor's Introduction," in *Three Thomist Studies*, by Crowe, iv.

24 Crowe, *Three Thomist Studies*, 114.

25 Ibid., 114. Cf. ibid., 108.

26 See Francis de Sales, *Treatise on the Love of God*, trans. Henry Benedict Mackey, OSB (Rockford, IL: Tan Books, 1997). St Francis (1567–1622) finished the treatise with its twelve books in 1616. The volume grew out of his work with St Jane Frances de Chantal, the first superior of the Visitation nuns.

27 Crowe, *Three Thomist Studies*, 85.

28 For an outline of the twelve books, see Francis X. Clooney, SJ, *Beyond Compare: St Francis de Sales and Sri Vedanta Desika on Loving Surrender to God* (Washington, DC: Georgetown University Press, 2005), 16–18. Although Clooney principally makes use of Mackey's translation of the *Treatise on the Love of God*, he adjusts that translation at points (*Beyond Compare*, 217n39). For example, Clooney translates the French equivalent of *complacentia*, *complaisance*, as "deep pleasure" (166). He then has an extended discussion of *complaisance* (deep pleasure). Clooney stresses that "faith in the value and reliability of this instinctive deep pleasure is key to the exposition de Sales makes central to the whole *Treatise*" (170).

29 Book 1.7 of *Treatise on the Love of God* has many more references to complacency. Clooney writes, "At the end of chapter 7, de Sales concedes that love itself is a kind of deep pleasure" (*Beyond Compare*, 240n64). Books 1.16 and 2.13–15 are also full of places where de Sales contrasts love as complacency with love as a movement towards something.

30 Crowe, *Three Thomist Studies*, 77. For the translation used by Crowe see Jean-Pierre de Caussade, *Self-Abandonment to Divine Providence*, trans. A. Thorold (London: Burns & Oates, 1933). For de Caussade's connection with Francis de Sales see Elizabeth Stopp, "Francis de Sales," in Cheslyn Jones, Geoffrey Wainwright, and Edward Yarnold, SJ, eds, *The Study of Spirituality* (New York: Oxford University Press, 1986), 417. See also David Knowles's introduction to *Self-Abandonment to Divine Providence*, by Jean-Pierre de Caussade, trans. A. Thorold (Rockford, IL: TAN Books, 1987), vi–vii. I return to this connection in my final chapter.

31 Knowles, introduction to *Self-Abandonment to Divine Providence*, by de Caussade, ix.
32 De Caussade, *Self-Abandonment to Divine Providence*, 179.
33 Ibid.
34 Ibid., 120. Cf. Pierre Rousselot, *The Problem of Love in the Middle Ages: A Historical Contribution*, Marquette Studies in Philosophy 24 (Milwaukee, WI: Marquette University Press, 2002).
35 See Anders Nygren, *Eros och Agape* (Stockholm, 1966; first published 1932). The second part of Nygren's study was published in English in two volumes in 1938 and 1939. Finally, in 1953, a complete translation of Nygren's work came out in English, *Agape and Eros* (1930–6), trans. P.S. Watson (London: SPCK, 1953), to which edition Crowe refers.
36 Crowe, *Three Thomist Studies*, 73.
37 Ibid.
38 Ibid.
39 *Cursus theologicus*, ed. Solesmes, vol. 4 (Paris: Desclés, 1953), disp. 32, a. 7, N. 8: "intellectus trahit obiectum ad se … appetitus vero allicitur et trahitur ab obiecto, et sic obiectum est pondus eius." Cf. "Complacency and Concern," in *Three Thomist Studies*, 74. The more general question of the way in which the human intellect and human will relate to reality is taken up in the appendix written by Crowe for "Complacency and Concern." See "Appendix: The Realism of Intellect and Will," in *Three Thomist Studies*, 189–203.
40 Crowe, *Three Thomist Studies*, 75. Cf. Henri-Dominique Simonin, "Autour de la solution thomiste du problème de l'amour," *Archives d'histoire doctrinale et littéraire du moyen-âge* 6 (1931): 174–276.
41 Crowe, *Three Thomist Studies*, 75. Crowe will argue that this shift in language is not an abandonment of the view of love as resting, but the use of a better terminology for this passive aspect of love.
42 Crowe, *Three Thomist Studies*, 75. Cf. F.A. Blanche, review of *Autour de la solution thomiste du problème de l'amour*, by H.D. Simonin, *Bulletin Thomiste* 3 (1930–3): 523–8.
43 Crowe, *Three Thomist Studies*, 75.
44 Sherwin, *By Knowledge and by Love*, 77.
45 Ibid., 78n67.
46 Ibid.
47 Crowe, *Three Thomist Studies*, 76–7.
48 Ibid., 77.
49 Ibid.
50 Ibid., 90. The diagram is on the same page.
51 For a helpful account of this diagram, see Michael Vertin, *"The Two Modes of Human Love*: Thomas Aquinas Interpreted by Frederick Crowe," *Irish Theological Quarterly* 69 (2004): 31–45.

52 Crowe, *Three Thomist Studies*, 90. By using the words *mota et movens* (moved and moving) Crowe is referring us to Aquinas's language in *Summa Theologiae*, I-II, q. 111, art. 2, in which Aquinas explains the difference between operative and co-operative grace. Aquinas's discussion of operative and co-operative grace in *ST*, I-II, q. 111, art. 2, was the focus of Lonergan's own dissertation at the Gregorian University. The dissertation, as mentioned in chapter 1, was reworked and published in a series of articles around the time that Crowe first met Lonergan.

53 Crowe, *Three Thomist Studies*, 134. For intending the end as the ordering of the mind towards the end without any determination of means to that end, see Thomas Aquinas, *Summa Theologiae*, I-II, q. 12, art. 1, ad 3; q. 12, art. 5, sed contra; and q. 12, art. 4, ad 3.

54 Crowe, *Three Thomist Studies*, 133. See Thomas Aquinas, *Summa Theologiae*, I-II, q. 40, art. 2: "secundum diversas rationes obiecti apprehensi, subsequuntur diversi motus in vi appetitiva" (according to diverse aspects of the object apprehended, diverse changes follow in the appetitive power).

55 "I must be content to distinguish elements as clearly as possible, leaving their exploitation to another occasion" (Crowe, *Three Thomist Studies*, 134).

56 Ibid., 113.

57 Ibid.

58 "Ita ex hoc quod aliquis rem aliquam amat, provenit quaedam impressio, ut ita loquor, rei amatae in affectu amantis, secundum quam amatum dicitur esse in amante" (Thomas Aquinas, *Summa Theologiae*, I, q. 37, art. 1).

59 "Amatum continetur in amante, inquantum est impressum in affectu eius per quandam complacentia" (Thomas Aquinas, *Summa Theologiae*, I-II, q. 28, art. 2, ad 1).

60 Ibid., I, q. 36, art. 2.

61 Ibid., I, q. 27, art. 3, ad 3.

62 Ibid., I, q. 27, art. 3, ad 3.

63 Ibid., I, q. 27, art. 1.

64 Ibid., I, q. 93, art. 6. Cf. I, q. 36, art. 2.

65 Ibid., I, q. 93, art. 6.

66 Crowe, *Three Thomist Studies*, 91.

67 Thomas Aquinas, *Summa Theologiae*, I, q. 37, art. 2 (emphasis mine).

68 Ibid., I, q. 34, art. 3 ad 2.

69 Ibid., I, q. 34, art. 3.

70 Ibid., I, q. 34, art. 3, ad 4.

71 Ibid., I, q. 37, art. 2, ad 3.

72 Ibid.

73 Crowe, *Three Thomist Studies*, 164.

74 Cf. Thomas Aquinas, *Summa Contra Gentiles* (Turin: Marietti, 1961), bk. 4, chap. 19, n. 10, where Aquinas also speaks of the will and love "as inclining ... and impelling." Earlier in that same chapter love is

repeatedly spoken of as "an inclination" (nn. 2–3). Meanwhile, the object of love is described as being in the will "as the term of the motion in a proportionate motive principle" (n. 10).

75 Thomas Aquinas, *Summa Theologiae,* I, q. 27, art. 4.

76 Crowe, *Three Thomist Studies,* 140.

77 Ibid.

78 Ibid. Crowe is not always careful to distinguish the terminology of *love as tendency* from *love as the principle of movement.* Sherwin, as we have seen, wants to insist that love is the principle of tending. When Crowe speaks of love as tendency, I think he is using a kind of shorthand.

79 Crowe, *Three Thomist Studies,* 140.

80 Ibid., 163.

81 Ibid.

82 Thomas Aquinas, *Summa Theologiae,* I, q. 37, art. 2, ad 3.

83 Ibid., I, q. 34, art. 3, ad 5.

84 Ibid., I, q. 37, art. 2, ad 3.

85 Ibid.

86 In 1959 Crowe wrote a brief and more popular article with a shorter title: "Complacency and Concern," *Cross and Crown* 11 (1959): 180–90. This article is an application of his distinction between the two aspects of love to the spiritual life. In this book, "Complacency and Concern" always refers to his scholarly article that first appeared in *Theological Studies* and was later reprinted in *Three Thomist Studies.*

87 Cf. Crowe, general editors' preface to *The Triune God: Systematics,* by Lonergan, xx.

3 Basil Helps to Extend the Search into the Economy of Salvation

1 Crowe, *The Doctrine of the Most Holy Trinity,* 91 (emphasis in the original). For the text of Basil, Crowe refers the reader to "Epistola 236," in *Patrologiae Cursus Completus,* Series Graeca 32, ed. J.P. Migne et al. (Paris, 1886), 883a–b. He also refers us to M.J. Rouët de Journel, *Enchiridion Patristicum: Loci ss. patrum, doctorum, scriptorum, ecclesiasticorum; Quos in usum scholarum collegit* (Friburgi Brisgoviae: Herder, 1953), 926. The translation of Basil's principle seems to be Crowe's own. That portion of letter 236, written about the year 376 AD, is contained in Rouët de Journel, *Enchiridion Patristicum.* The letter was written after Basil's treatise *On the Holy Spirit* and, together with letters 233–5, recapitulates "the theological vision of *Against Eunomius.*" Stephen M. Hildebrand, *The Trinitarian Theology of Basil of Caesarea: A Synthesis of Greek Thought and Biblical Truth* (Washington, DC: Catholic University of America Press, 2007, 27). Born around 330 AD, St Basil died on 1 January 379 in Caesarea. His *Against*

Eunomius was written between 360 and 365. Letter 236 was written to Amphilochius, his spiritual son and student, late in Basil's life "at a time of theological and ecclesiastical maturity in his life, at a time when he had grown confident in what he wanted to say about God" (Hildebrand, *The Trinitarian Theology*, 28). Hildebrand dates *On the Holy Spirit* to 373 or 375. For recent translations see Basil the Great, *On the Holy Spirit*, trans. Stephen Hildebrand (Crestwood, NY: St Vladimir's Seminary Press, 2011), and *Against Eunomius*, trans. Mark Del Cogliano and Andrew Radde-Gallwitz (Washington, DC: Catholic University of America Press, 2011).

2 Crowe, *The Doctrine of the Most Holy Trinity*, 91.

3 Ibid.

4 Ibid.

5 Ibid., 195.

6 In the beginning of his notes Crowe writes: "The debt to Bernard Lonergan's *De Deo Trino* of almost every page of these notes on the Trinity is hereby acknowledged in general; sometimes more particular references are given, sometimes they are not. And the greater than the debt for items of objective doctrine is the one I owe for the very idea of dividing the treatise into analytic and synthetic parts and structuring them according to a fundamental principle of cognitional theory" (*The Doctrine of the Most Holy Trinity*, 4). Crowe uses Lonergan's principle of cognitional theory in his organizing of "the wealth of the deposit of faith" (ibid.).

7 Lonergan, *The Triune God: Doctrines*, 628–9. Cf. Bernardus Lonergan, *De Deo Trino, Pars analytica* (Rome: Pontificia Universitas Gregoriana, 1961), 298. Although Lonergan changed the name of his first volume in 1964 to *Pars dogmatica*, he kept this paragraph in which he describes the way of analysis.

8 Crowe, *The Doctrine of the Most Holy Trinity*, 141.

9 Ibid., 144.

10 Ibid., 143.

11 Ibid.

12 Ibid., 144.

13 Ibid.

14 Ibid., 137.

15 Ibid. Among those responsible for reviving questions on the invisible missions of the Son and Spirit was Lucien Chambat, OSB, *Presence et union: Les missions des personnes de la Trinité selon Saint Thomas Aquinas* (Abbaye Saint-Wandrille, France: Fontenelle, 1945). The main work in English in this period is Francis Cunningham's *The Indwelling of the Trinity: A Historical Study of the Theory of St Thomas Aquinas* (Dubuque, IA: Priory Press, 1955). Crowe's course notes show that he was aware of these works. At their heart is the question of the invisible mission of the Son, a mission

that seems connected with the gift of wisdom. In no place have I found Crowe discussing explicitly the "invisible mission" of the Son.

16 Crowe, *The Doctrine of the Most Holy Trinity*, 192.

17 Ibid., 193.

18 Ibid.

19 Crowe refers us to Lonergan, *De Deo Trino*, II, 252–3 [*The Triune God: Systematics*, 676–81], and Thomas Aquinas, *Summa Contra Gentiles*, IV, 19. As a commentary on Aquinas, he refers us to Lonergan's argument in *Verbum*, 209–11.

20 Crowe, *The Doctrine of the Most Holy Trinity*, 149.

21 Crowe, "Neither Jew Nor Greek," in *Appropriating the Lonergan Idea*, 49.

22 Crowe, *The Doctrine of the Most Holy Trinity*, 150.

23 Ibid. Crowe's way of relating the Word to the Holy Spirit recalls Lonergan's own idea of the Father as Speaker being related to the Son and the Spirit by one real ordering. Cf. Lonergan, "Assertion VI," in *The Triune God: Systematics*, 250–3.

24 Crowe, *The Doctrine of the Most Holy Trinity*, 148.

25 Ibid.

26 Ibid.

27 Ibid., 148.

28 Ibid., 160; "intelliguntur secundum similitudinem emanationis intelligibilis verbi a dicente, et amoris ab utroque." Cf. Crowe, *The Doctrine of the Most Holy Trinity*, 144ff. In terms of the inner word, Crowe writes:

> I have said understanding expresses itself in the concept, and this expression is the "emanatio intelligibilis." One way to approach this idea is by contrast with causality. Understanding and concept (the same applies to reflection and judgment) are related as cause and effect: the understanding *produces* its *verbum*. But the verbum is not merely the product, or effect, or *operatum* of the *intelligere*; it is also the rationally conscious expression of understanding. That is, when we define, not as parrots, but as intelligent men, we do so in virtue of understanding; when we judge not as bigots, but as rational men, we do so in virtue of reflection, and that "in virtue of" does not indicate causation in the ontological sense; it indicates that the *verbum* is not only *caused by* but also is *because of*, in the cognitional sense of proceeding from rationally conscious grounds. (*The Doctrine of the Most Holy Trinity*, 145–6; emphasis in the original)

In terms of love, Crowe writes: "This flow of love in the will from the *verbum* is also an *emanatio intelligibilis*; we do not love irrationally, at least love need not be irrational; we do not choose blindly; there is something of the rationality of intellect in the act of the will ... And this is the analogy for the procession of the Spirit in God" (146).

29 Ibid., 151.
30 Ibid.
31 Ibid.
32 Cf. ibid., 83ff.
33 Ibid., 151.
34 Ibid.
35 Ibid., 151–2
36 Ibid., 152.
37 Ibid.
38 Cf. Lonergan, "Assertion XI," in *The Triune God: Systematics*, 370, and "Assertion VI," in *The Triune God: Systematics*, 253.
39 Lonergan, "Assertion VI," in *The Triune God: Systematics*, 255.
40 Ibid., 253.
41 Ibid., 247.
42 Ibid., 251.
43 Ibid.
44 Crowe, *The Doctrine of the Most Holy Trinity*, 152.
45 Ibid. Crowe does not cite any of Scotus's works but is possibly referring to question 6 of Scotus's *Quaestiones Quodlibetales*. See John Duns Scotus, *Opera omnia*, ed. Luke Wadding, vol. 12 (Lyon: Durand, 1639), 142–68. For an English translation see Scotus, *God and Creatures: The Quodlibetal Questions*, ed. and trans. Felix Alluntis and Allan B. Wolter (Princeton, NJ: Princeton University Press, 1975), 130–58.
46 Crowe, *The Doctrine of the Most Holy Trinity*, 152.
47 Ibid.
48 Ibid.
49 Ibid., 191.
50 Ibid., 152.
51 Ibid., 155.
52 Ibid.
53 Ibid.
54 Ibid.
55 Ibid.
56 Ibid., 157.
57 Ibid.
58 Ibid., 158.
59 Ibid., 143.
60 Ibid., 162.
61 Ibid., 163.
62 Ibid.
63 Ibid., 165.
64 Ibid.,166. Cf. Maurice de la Taille, SJ, *The Hypostatic Union and Created Actuation by Uncreated Act* (West Baden Springs, IN: West Baden College, 1952).

65 Crowe, *The Doctrine of the Most Holy Trinity*, 166.

66 Ibid.

67 Ibid. Crowe is referring to Lonergan's work "*De Gratia Sanctificante: Supplementum* [*Supplementary Notes on Sanctifying Grace*]," in *Early Latin Theology* (Toronto: University of Toronto Press, 2011), 562–665. Lonergan discusses the ontological foundation for sanctifying grace, the habit of charity, the grace of union in the incarnate Son, and the light of glory. See "Theorem 2," in *Early Latin Theology*, 630–7.

68 Robert Doran, SJ, did not invent this phrase but made it popular. See Robert M. Doran, SJ, "Addressing Lonergan's Four-Point Hypothesis," *Theological Studies* 68 (2007): 674–82; and Jeremy D. Wilkins, "Grace in the Third Stage of Meaning Apropos Lonergan's 'Four-point Hypothesis,'" *Lonergan Workshop* 22 (2010): 443–67. Doran first heard the phrase from Philip McShane (private correspondence with the author).

69 Lonergan, *The Triune God: Systematics*, 471–3.

70 Ibid.

71 Crowe, *The Doctrine of the Most Holy Trinity*, 166 (emphasis mine).

72 Ibid., 170.

73 Ibid.

74 Ibid.

75 Lonergan, *The Triune God: Systematics*, 471. In *The Triune God: Systematics* Lonergan uses "secondary act of existence of the incarnation" in place of the phrase "grace of union" (472–3).

76 Crowe, *The Doctrine of the Most Holy Trinity*, 176.

77 Ibid., 172.

78 Ibid.

79 Ibid., 185 (emphasis mine). Cf. Lonergan, "Question 26," in *The Triune God: Systematics*, 470–1.

80 Crowe, *The Doctrine of the Most Holy Trinity*, 186.

81 Ibid., 185. The question of the meaningfulness of the entry of the Holy Spirit in the world will be discussed in my chapter 5.

82 Ibid., 173.

83 Thomas Aquinas, *Quaestiones disputatae de Veritate*, q. 8, art. 8, ad 1. Cf. Aquinas, *Expositio in librum beati Dionysii De divinis nominibus* (Rome: Marietti, 1950), c. 5, lec. 3.

84 Roy J. Deferrari, *A Lexicon of Saint Thomas Aquinas* (Fitzwilliam, NH: Loreto Publications, 2004), 391.

85 Crowe, *The Doctrine of the Most Holy Trinity*, 174.

86 Ibid.

87 Ibid.

88 Ibid., 188.

89 Ibid.

90 Ibid.

91 Ibid., 189.
92 Ibid.
93 Ibid.
94 Ibid., 190.
95 Ibid., 189. "A.U.C." refers to the foundation of the city of Rome, the urbs, and is short for *ab urbe condita* or *anno urbis conditae*. "Ab urbe condita" was the title of Livy's account of Roman history. See Livy, *History of Rome,* trans. B.O. Foster, 14 vols, Loeb Classical Library (Cambridge, MA: Harvard University Press, 1919–59).
96 Crowe, *The Doctrine of the Most Holy Trinity*, 190.
97 Ibid.
98 Ibid.
99 Ibid.
100 Ibid.
101 In *The Doctrine of the Most Holy Trinity*, unless otherwise noted, biblical translations of the New Testament are from *The New English Bible* (Oxford and Cambridge: Oxford University Press and Cambridge University Press, 1961) and of the Old Testament are from *The Bible: An American Translation* (Chicago: University of Chicago Press, 1935).
102 Ibid.
103 John 7:39. Cf. Crowe, *The Doctrine of the Most Holy Trinity*, 191. Crowe also refers us to John 16:7 and 20:22, and Acts 2:33.
104 Crowe, *The Doctrine of the Most Holy Trinity*, 190.
105 Ibid.
106 Ibid., 192.
107 Ibid.
108 Ibid.
109 Ibid. Crowe is referring to the Latin hymn "Veni, Creator Spiritus."
110 Crowe, *The Doctrine of the Most Holy Trinity*, 193.
111 Ibid.
112 Ibid., 194.
113 Ibid.
114 Ibid.
115 Ibid.
116 Ibid.
117 Ibid.
118 Ibid.
119 Ibid.
120 Ibid.
121 Ibid.
122 Frederick Crowe, "Development of Doctrine: Aid or Barrier to Christian Unity," *Catholic Theological Society of America Proceedings* 21 (1966): 1–20. Cf. Crowe, *Lonergan and the Level of Our Time*, 209.

202   Notes to pages 79–84

4 Who Provides the Context, the Son or the Spirit?

1   Crowe, *The Doctrine of the Most Holy Trinity*, 193.
2   Lonergan, "Question 28," in *The Triune God: Systematics*, 479.
3   Ibid.
4   Ibid.
5   Lonergan, "Question 25," in *The Triune God: Systematics*, 467.
6   Ibid.
7   Lonergan, "Question 27," in *The Triune God: Systematics*, 475.
8   Thomas Aquinas, *Summa Theologiae*, I-II, q. 110, art. 1.
9   Ibid.
10 Ibid.
11 Thomas Aquinas, *Summa Theologiae*, I-II, q. 110, art. 2 and art. 4.
12 Thomas Aquinas, *Summa Theologiae*, I-II, q. 110, art. 3, sed contra.
13 Thomas Aquinas, *Summa Theologiae*, I, q. 38, art. 2, ad 1.
14 Thomas Aquinas, *Summa Theologiae*, I, q. 37, art. 2.
15 Thomas Aquinas, *Summa Theologiae*, I, q. 38, art. 1, ad 4.
16 Thomas Aquinas, *Summa Theologiae*, I, q. 38, art. 2. For a longer discussion of grace and the Holy Spirit, see Jeremy Wilkins, "Trinitarian Missions and the Order of Grace according to Thomas Aquinas," in *Philosophy and Theology in the Long Middle Ages: Essays in Honor of Professor Stephen Brown*, ed. K. Emery, R. Friedman, and A. Speer (Leiden: E.J. Brill, 2011), 689–708.
17 Lonergan, "Question 28," in *The Triune God: Systematics*, 481.
18 Ibid.
19 Ibid., 483. Cf. Lonergan, "Mystical Body of Christ," in *Shorter Papers*, ed. Robert C. Croken, Robert M. Doran, and H. Daniel Monsour, vol. 20 of *CWL*, 106–11.
20 Lonergan, "Question 29," in *The Triune God: Systematics*, 491.
21 Ibid.
22 Lonergan, "Question 28," in *The Triune God: Systematics*, 487. For a more detailed study of Lonergan's thought, see Jeremy Wilkins, "Why Two Divine Missions? Development in Augustine, Aquinas, and Lonergan," *Irish Theological Quarterly* 77, no. 1 (2012): 1–30.
23 Lonergan, "Question 30," in *The Triune God: Systematics*, 491.
24 Cf. Thomas Aquinas, *Summa Theologiae*, I, q. 43, art. 5–7.
25 Lonergan, "Question 31," in *The Triune God: Systematics*, 499.
26 Ibid.
27 Crowe, *The Doctrine of the Most Holy Trinity*, 187.
28 Ibid., 189–90 (emphasis in the original).
29 Ibid., 190.
30 Crowe, *The Doctrine of the Most Holy Trinity*, 190. Although normally Crowe links the presence of the Holy Spirit with charity, here he says that

grace is the consequence of the gift of the Holy Spirit. As we saw in the previous chapter, Lonergan distinguished between passive and active spiration. Sanctifying grace gives us a participation in active spiration. Charity gives us a participation in passive spiration. But Crowe moves away from participation in four real relations to focusing on the three divine persons as the exemplars for created effects that indicate their presence. This may be partly why the distinction between grace and charity in Crowe becomes harder to find.

31 Ibid. Crowe is probably drawing this distinction from Aquinas's discussion of the order of the theological virtues. For example, Aquinas writes: "In the order of generation ... faith precedes hope, and hope precedes charity, according to their acts (for the habits are simultaneously infused). For an appetitive motion is not able to tend to something either by hoping for it or loving it, unless that thing is apprehended by the senses or intellect. Now through faith, the intellect apprehends those things which the appetite hopes for and loves" (*Summa Theologiae*, I-II, q. 62, art. 4).

32 Crowe, *The Doctrine of the Most Holy Trinity*, 191. But the Holy Spirit's presence, Crowe says, was not fully manifest until Pentecost (190).

33 Lonergan, "Horizons," in vol. 17 of *CWL*, 19. See also "Faith," in Lonergan, *Method in Theology*, ed. Doran and Dadosky, 111 [115].

34 Lonergan, "Horizons," in vol. 17 of *CWL*, 25.

35 On 14 September 1964, for example, Lonergan was already speaking of having fallen in love: "It is one thing to be in love, and another to discover that what has happened to you is that you have fallen in love. Being oneself is prior to knowing oneself. St. Ignatius said that love shows itself more in deeds than in words; but being in love is neither deeds nor words; it is the prior conscious reality that words and, more securely, deeds reveal." "*Existenz* and *Aggiornamento*," in *Collection*, vol. 4 of *CWL* (Toronto: University of Toronto Press, 1988), 229. This 1964 reference to having "fallen in love" can apply both to human love and to our love for God. Towards the end of that same talk Lonergan writes: "For the love of God, being in love with God, can be as full and as dominant, as overwhelming and as lasting an experience as human love" ("*Existenz* and *Aggiornamento*," 231).

36 Lonergan, "Theology and Man's Future," in *A Second Collection*, vol. 13 of *CWL*, 123 [145]. "Theology and Man's Future" was delivered at a conference in St Louis in October 1968 and first published in *Cross Currents* 19 (1969): 452–61.

37 See "The Future of Christianity," in *A Second Collection*, vol. 13 of *CWL*, 138 [161].

38 Crowe, "Pull of the Future and Link with the Past: On the Need for Theological Method," *Continuum* 7 (1969): 49.

39 Ibid., 45.

40 Ibid. For the background of what Crowe is saying about love and the Holy Spirit, see Aquinas's teaching in *Summa Theologiae*, I, q. 37, art. 2, ad 3; I, q. 38, art. 1, ad 4; I-II, q. 110, art. 1; I-II, q. 106, art. 1.

41 Crowe, "Pull of the Future and Link with the Past," 45.

42 Without adverting to it, Crowe is implicitly pointing towards a new kind of psychological analogy. He has the rudiments of an analogy from the level of love, to the level of judgment, to the level of understanding. He will make this move in his next stage of development, but here he does not make it thematic.

43 Crowe, "Pull of the Future and Link with the Past," 44.

44 Lonergan, "The Response of the Jesuit as Priest and Apostle in the Modern World," in *A Second Collection*, 140–58 [165–87]. His paper was first published in September 1970 in *Studies in the Spirituality of Jesuits* 2, no. 3.

45 Lonergan, "The Response of the Jesuit," in *A Second Collection*, 147 [173].

46 Ibid.

47 Ibid.

48 Ibid.

49 Ibid., 147–8 [174].

50 Ibid., 148 [174].

51 Ibid.

52 Ibid.

53 For God's love of his people see Deuteronomy 4:37, 7:8, 10:15; Isaiah 43:1–7; Hosea 2. For God's love compared to a parent's love and to a spouse's love see Hosea 11; Isaiah 49:14–15, 62:4–5; Ezekiel 16.

54 Crowe's tendency, as we will see later, is not to emphasize the declarations of love made *through the prophets*. He will emphasize the declaration of love made in the Son's incarnation.

55 Lonergan, *Method in Theology*, ed. Doran and Dadosky, 108 [112].

56 Ibid. This use of *inner word* differs greatly from the inner word about which Lonergan spoke in his earlier Trinitarian writings. In his *Verbum: Word and Idea in Aquinas*, inner word referred to the procession of a definition or a judgment from an act of understanding.

57 Lonergan, *Method in Theology*, ed. Doran and Dadosky, 108 [112]; cf. 272 [290–1].

58 Ibid., 108 [112].

59 Ibid., 109 [112–13].

60 Ibid., 109 [113].

61 Ibid.

62 Ibid.

63 Ibid., 115 [119].

64 Ibid. Cf. Crowe, *Theology of the Christian Word*, 141.

65 Lonergan, *Method in Theology*, ed. Doran and Dadosky, 270 [289].

66 Crowe, "The Relevance of Newman to Contemporary Theology," in *Developing the Lonergan Legacy*, 219.

67 Lonergan, *Method in Theology*, ed. Doran and Dadosky, 271 [289].

68 Ibid., 270 [289].

69 Cf. Lonergan, *Insight*, ed. Crowe and Doran, 358.

70 See "A Technical Note," in *Method in Theology*, ed. Doran and Dadosky, 116–17 [120–1].

71 *Method in Theology*, ed. Doran and Dadosky, 265 [282–3].

72 Crowe, "Eschaton and Worldly Mission in the Mind and Heart of Jesus," in *Appropriating the Lonergan Idea*, 223n44. This long lecture originally appeared in *Eschaton: A Community of Love*, ed. Joseph Papin, vol. 5 of *Theology Institute Villanova* (Villanova, PA: Villanova University Press, c. 1971). The lecture was translated into Italian and published as a book: Frederick E. Crowe and Giovanni B. Sala, *Escatologia e missione terrena in Gesù di Nazareth* (Catania, Sicily: Edizioni Paoline, 1976).

73 Crowe, "Eschaton and Worldly Mission," in *Appropriating the Lonergan Idea*, 223. Crowe cites *Method in Theology*, 92, 98, 105, 115, 118, and is also drawing the quotations from a paper that Lonergan gave at Villanova in 1971. See Bernard Lonergan, "Religious Commitment," in *The Pilgrim People: A Vision of Hope*, ed. Joseph Papin, vol. 4 of *Theology Institute Villanova* (Villanova, PA: Villanova University Press, 1970), 45–69.

74 Crowe, "Eschaton and Worldly Mission," in *Appropriating the Lonergan Idea*, 223n44.

75 Ibid.

76 Ibid.

77 Ibid. Crowe puts all of this in a footnote, "not wishing to clutter up this paper with questions that may be of greater interest to me than to my audience" (223n44).

78 Ibid.

79 Crowe, *The Doctrine of the Most Holy Trinity*, 190.

80 Ibid.

81 Crowe, "Lonergan's New Notion of Value," in *Appropriating the Lonergan Idea*, 56.

82 Crowe, "Pull of the Future and Link with the Past," 42n27. Cf. Crowe, "Dogma versus the Self-Correcting Process of Learning," in *Level of Our Time*, 261n18.

83 David Stanley, SJ (1914–1996), entered the Jesuit novitiate in Guelph, Ontario, in 1933. Ordained a few years before Crowe, he taught for many years at Regis College. Pope Paul VI appointed him a member of the Pontifical Biblical Commission.

84 H. Martin Rumscheidt, ed., *Footnotes to a Theology: The Karl Barth Colloquium of 1972* (Waterloo, ON: Corporation for the Publication of

Academic Studies in Religion in Canada, SR/CSR Office, Wilfred Laurier University, 1974), v. Cf. Crowe, "The Power of the Scriptures: An Attempt at an Analysis," in *Level of Our Time*, 293.

85 Crowe, "The Power of the Scriptures," in *Level of Our Time*, 280.

86 Ibid., 287.

87 Ibid., 279.

88 Ibid., 282.

89 Lonergan, *Method in Theology*, ed. Doran and Dadosky, 29 [28]. Cf. Crowe, "The Power of the Scriptures," in *Level of Our Time*, 284.

90 Crowe, "The Power of the Scriptures," in *Level of Our Time*, 291.

91 Lonergan, *Method in Theology*, ed. Doran and Dadosky, 108 [112]. Quoted by Crowe in his "Power of the Scriptures," 291.

92 Crowe, "Power of the Scriptures," in *Level of Our Time*, 291.

93 Ibid.

94 Ibid.

95 Lonergan, "Mission and Spirit," in *A Third Collection*, ed. Robert M. Doran and John D. Dadosky, 32 [32]. This paper by Lonergan was written in 1974 and published in 1976. Crowe may have known about it before he wrote his essay in honour of David Stanley, SJ.

96 Lonergan, *Method in Theology*, ed. Doran and Dadosky, 109 [112–13]. Quoted in Crowe, "The Power of the Scriptures," in *Level of Our Time*, 292. Note that Lonergan uses the word *context*.

97 Crowe, "The Power of the Scriptures," in *Level of Our Time*, 292.

98 Ibid.

99 Ibid.

100 Crowe, *Theology of the Christian Word*, 126.

101 Ibid., 142.

102 Ibid. See Eugene Webb's comparison of Crowe's approach with Byzantine approaches: "The Pneumatology of Bernard Lonergan: A Byzantine Comparison," *Religious Studies and Theology*, 5, no. 2 (May 1985): 13–23.

103 Crowe, *Theology of the Christian Word*, 142.

104 Ibid.

105 In fact, a couple of years after the publication of *Method in Theology*, Lonergan gave a talk at the University of Chicago, on 8 November 1974, entitled "Aquinas Today: Tradition and Innovation." At the end he spoke of a threefold giving that was part of God's giving of himself in love: "Finally, as Aquinas, so we too can place the meaning and significance of the visible universe as bringing to birth the elect – the recipients to whom God gives himself in love, in the threefold giving that is the gift of the Holy Spirit to those that love (Rom. 5:5), the gift of the divine Word made flesh and dwelling amongst us (John 1:14), the final gift of union with

the Father who is originating love (1 John 4:8, 16)." Lonergan, "Aquinas Today: Tradition and Innovation," in *A Third Collection*, ed. Doran and Dadosky, 51 (53).

106 Crowe, *Theology of the Christian Word*, 140. Cf. Lonergan, *Method in Theology*, ed. Doran and Dadosky, 109 [113].

107 Crowe, *Theology of the Christian Word*, 135.

108 Ibid.

109 Ibid., 127.

110 Ibid., 144.

111 Ibid., 145 (emphasis mine).

112 Ibid. In terms of Luther and Calvin, Crowe wrote: "Luther's stress on the passive side of faith led him to rely more on the inner feelings than on outer works for his assurance of salvation, just as faith itself was more a trust in God than an adherence to objective dogmas. Calvin followed this direction, and took up and wrestled with the problem Luther himself had, of giving some critical value to this internal witness" (*Theology of the Christian Word*, 136). On Calvin's notion of the Holy Spirit as internal witness see Veli-Matti Kärkkäinen, ed., *Holy Spirit and Salvation: Sources of Christian Theology* (Louisville, KY: Westminster John Knox Press, 2010), 170–1. Calvin writes, "God works in his elect in two ways: inwardly by his Spirit; outwardly, by his Word" (*Institutes of the Christian Religion*, trans. Henry Beveridge, vol. 1 [Grand Rapids, MI: Eerdmanns, 1975], 277). For a concise summary of Luther's, Calvin's, and Zwingli's pneumatologies see Veli-Matti Kärkkäinen, *The Holy Spirit: A Guide to Christian Theology* (Louisville, KY: Westminster John Knox Press, 2012), 46–53.

113 Crowe, "The Task of Interpreting Lonergan," in *Appropriating the Lonergan Idea*, 155.

114 Ibid. In his footnote Crowe tells us where to look for Trinitarian clues. The citation by Crowe has a slight mistake. His reference to the pagination from *A Third Collection* should read "pp. 93–5."

115 Crowe, "The Task of Interpreting Lonergan," in *Appropriating the Lonergan Idea*, 155n23.

116 Crowe, *Theology of the Christian Word*, 142.

117 Cf. Lonergan, *Method in Theology*, ed. Doran and Dadosky, 109 [112–13].

118 Crowe, "Son and Spirit: Tension in the Divine Missions?" in *Appropriating the Lonergan Idea*, 307.

119 Lonergan, "The Response of the Jesuit," in *A Second Collection*, 147 [174].

120 Ibid., 148 [174].

121 Cf. Crowe, *The Doctrine of the Most Holy Trinity*, 187.

122 See Crowe, "Son and Spirit: Tension in the Divine Missions?" (308), and "Son of God, Holy Spirit, and World Religions" (330), in *Appropriating the Lonergan Idea*.

123 Crowe, "Son and Spirit: Tension in the Divine Missions?" in *Appropriating the Lonergan Idea*, 308.
124 Ibid., 309.
125 Ibid.
126 Ibid.
127 Ibid., 309n23.
128 Ibid., 325.
129 Crowe, "Son of God, Holy Spirit, and World Religions," in *Appropriating the Lonergan Idea*, 325. This lecture was first published (along with Crowe's homily at the funeral of Bernard Lonergan) as *Son of God, Holy Spirit, and World Religions: The Contribution of Bernard Lonergan to the Wider Ecumenism* (Toronto: Regis College Press, 1985).
130 Crowe, "Son of God, Holy Spirit, and World Religions," 324.
131 Brian L. Hebblethwaite, *The Problems of Theology* (Cambridge: Cambridge University Press, 1980), 19. Cf. Crowe, "Son of God, Holy Spirit, and World Religions," in *Appropriating the Lonergan Idea*, 324–5.
132 Crowe, "Son of God, Holy Spirit, and World Religions," 325.
133 According to several contemporary Jesuits, Crowe and Lonergan were in regular contact between 1975 and 1983.
134 Crowe, "Son of God, Holy Spirit, and World Religions," in *Appropriating the Lonergan Idea*, 324.
135 Ibid., 325.
136 Ibid., 335.
137 Ibid.
138 Ibid., 338–9.
139 Ibid., 339.
140 Ibid.
141 Ibid., 329.
142 Crowe points us to Karl Rahner and Herbert Vorgrimler's article "Salvific Will of God," in *Dictionary of Theology* (New York: Crossroad, 1981), 459, for "an overview of the Roman Catholic position" (Crowe, *Appropriating the Lonergan Idea*, 324). Various statements by the Magisterium can be used to support this interpretation of 1 Timothy 2:1–6: DS, 2305; DS, 2430. Cf. DS, 2479; DS, 2865–7; DS, 3866–73; and *Lumen Gentium*, 14–16 (DS, 4136–40).
143 Crowe, "Son of God, Holy Spirit, and World Religions," in *Appropriating the Lonergan Idea*, 329.
144 Ibid., 330.
145 Ibid.
146 Ibid.
147 Ibid.
148 Ibid., 326.

149 Letter to Garth B. Wilson, 22 December 1971, Crowe Archive, A-3-1-2. See also Crowe, *Theology of the Christian Word*, 112–23.

150 Cf. Crowe, *Theology of the Christian Word*, 144.

151 Letter to Garth B. Wilson, 22 December 1971, Crowe Archive, A-3-1-2. Some effort would have to be made to distinguish God's more general word in history from his historical dealings with the people of Israel. In a unique way, the Law given to Moses anticipated Christ's incarnation.

152 See book 2.10 and book 4.29 in Augustine, *De Trinitate*, PL 42, 851, 908. See also Thomas Aquinas, *Summa Theologiae*, I, q. 43, art. 6, ad 1. Cf. *Catechism of the Catholic Church* (Vatican City: Libreria Editrice Vaticana, 1994), 731.

153 Crowe, "Son of God, Holy Spirit, and World Religions," in *Appropriating the Lonergan Idea*, 333n13.

154 Ibid.

155 Ibid.

156 Ibid.

157 Ibid.

158 Ibid.

159 Ibid., 332–3.

160 In 1989 Crowe admitted in a footnote: "there is a new specificity and fullness in that mission [of the Spirit] that is contingent upon the Son being faithful to his mission even to the cross" ("Rethinking God-with-Us," in *Level of Our Time*, 340n19).

161 St Luke's Lutheran Church is on Bayview Avenue in North York, Ontario, near Toronto, and not far from the old Regis College.

162 Crowe, "Son and Spirit in the Church," in *Grace and Friendship: Theological Essays in Honor of Fred Lawrence from His Grateful Students*, ed. M. Shawn Copeland and Jeremy D. Wilkins (Milwaukee, WI: Marquette University Press, 2016), 17–22.

163 Ibid., 20 (emphasis mine).

164 Crowe, "Son of God, Holy Spirit, and World Religions," in *Appropriating the Lonergan Idea*, 328.

5 Arguing with Church Authorities

1 Paul VI, *Humanae vitae*, encyclical letter of 25 July 1968, *Acta Apostolicae Sedis* 60 (1968): 481–503; translated as *On Human Life: Humanae vitae*, by Marc A. Calegari, SJ (San Francisco, CA: Ignatius Press, 2014).

2 Sacred Congregation for the Doctrine of the Faith, *Declaration on the Question of the Admission of Women to the Ministerial Priesthood* (Vatican City: Vatican Polyglot Press, 1976).

3 "Charismatic" is broader than the "charismatic movement" and refers to the Holy Spirit's role as "the source of life-giving movement in the church as a whole." Crowe, "Son and Spirit in the Church," in *Grace and Friendship*, 20. Nevertheless, Crowe was very interested in the charismatic movement (Cf. Crowe, *Old Things and New*, 141, and *The Lonergan Enterprise*, 96).

4 Crowe, "Son and Spirit in the Church," 17–22.

5 For a discussion of how the teachings on contraception of the Catholic Church's ordinary magisterium can meet the requirements for infallibility, see John C. Ford, SJ, and Germain Grisez, "Contraception and the Infallibility of the Ordinary Magisterium," *Theological Studies* 39 (1978): 258–312, esp. 259–61. For a defence of the Catholic Church's teaching prior to *Humanae vitae*, together with an analysis of its misunderstanding in North America, see Paul Quay, SJ, "Contraception and Conjugal Love," *Theological Studies* 22, no. 1 (1961): 18–40. For a recent review of the personalism debates before *Humanae vitae*, see Thomas Petri, OP, *Aquinas and the Theology of the Body: The Thomistic Foundations of John Paul II's Anthropology* (Washington, DC: Catholic University of America Press, 2016), 45ff.

6 Crowe, "Responsibility of the Theologian, and the Learning Church," in *Appropriating the Lonergan Idea*, 175.

7 Ibid.

8 Crowe, "The Christian University," in *Appropriating the Lonergan Idea*, 170. Crowe gave this address at the graduation ceremony, St Mary's University, Halifax, in May 1971. He was trying to offer a history of the Church in ten minutes.

9 Ibid., 169.

10 Ibid.

11 Ibid.

12 Ibid.

13 Ibid.

14 Ibid.

15 Ibid.

16 Ibid.

17 Ibid., 170.

18 Ibid., 169.

19 Ibid.

20 Ibid.

21 Ibid.

22 Ibid., 170.

23 Ibid.

24 Crowe, "Responsibility of the Theologian, and the Learning Church," in *Appropriating the Lonergan Idea*, 187.

25 Ibid.

26 Ibid.
27 Ibid., 188.
28 Ibid.
29 Ibid.
30 Ibid., 175.
31 "Students of Lonergan are supposed to be generalists" (Crowe, "The Future: Charting the Unknown with Lonergan," in *Developing the Lonergan Legacy*, 347. For the meaning of a *generalist* see Crowe, "The Genus 'Lonergan and …' and Feminism," in *Developing the Lonergan Legacy*, 143. For Lonergan's own 1977 words on being a generalist see Bernard Lonergan, *Philosophical and Theological Papers, 1965–1980*, 382–3.
32 Sacred Congregation for the Doctrine of the Faith, *Declaration on the Question of the Admission of Women to the Ministerial Priesthood* (Vatican City: Vatican Polyglot Press, 1976), 5.
33 Frederick Crowe, SJ, Sara Butler, MSBT, Anne Carr, BVM, Margaret Farley, RSM, and Edward Kilmartin SJ, *A Report on the Status of Women in Church and Society: Considered in Light of the Question of Women's Ordination* (New York: Catholic Theological Society of America, 1978), 1. Crowe wrote the prolegomena for the fourth part of the document (ibid., 19–21). He also co-authored the section "Arguments from the Praxis of Jesus, the Apostles, and the Church" (ibid., 21–5). All the other sections of the document, except the introduction and the summary and conclusions, are attributed to another member of the CTSA's task force. The introduction and the conclusion seem to me, however, to indicate the influence of Crowe.
34 Crowe et al., *A Report on the Status of Women*, 19.
35 Ibid., 20.
36 Ibid., 24. This section was also co-authored by Sara Butler and Elizabeth Fiorenza.
37 Ibid., 25. This section was also co-authored by Sara Butler and Elizabeth Fiorenza.
38 Ibid., 20.
39 Ibid., 21.
40 Ibid.
41 Ibid.
42 Ibid.
43 Ibid.
44 Sacred Congregation for the Doctrine of the Faith, *Declaration on the Question*, 16. Part of this quotation is found in Crowe et al., *A Report on the Status of Women*, 34.
45 For why theology needs the human sciences see Lonergan, *Method in Theology*, ed. Doran and Dadosky, 335 [364].

46 With the rise of questions of transgenderism and the fiftieth anniversary of *Humanae vitae* in 2018, it seems an opportune time for new studies of both artificial birth control and the role of women in the Church. What data is there for the sociological and psychological effects of artificial birth control? What data can the human sciences provide regarding the practice of the Catholic Church to restrict ordination to men?

47 Crowe, "Eschaton and Worldly Mission," in *Appropriating the Lonergan Idea*, 196.

48 Crowe et al., *A Report on the Status of Women*, 22.

49 Crowe, "Lonergan's Early Use of Analogy," in *Level of Our Time*, 57.

50 Crowe, "Son and Spirit: Tension in the Divine Missions?" in *Appropriating the Lonergan Idea*, 307.

51 Ibid.

52 Ibid.

53 Ibid., 308.

54 On this distinction between dimensions of the Church see also *Catechism of the Catholic Church*, 773.

55 Crowe, "Son and Spirit: Tension in the Divine Missions?" in *Appropriating the Lonergan Idea*, 298.

56 Ibid., 308.

57 Ibid., 304.

58 Ibid.

59 Kilian McDonnell, "A Trinitarian Theology of the Holy Spirit?," *Theological Studies* 46, no. 2 (June 1985): 215.

60 Crowe's article first appeared in *Science et Esprit* 35 (1983): 153–69. The paper was delivered earlier that same year in June at the Lonergan Workshop in Boston.

61 McDonnell, "A Trinitarian Theology?," 210.

62 Ibid.

63 Ibid., 226.

64 Ibid., 227.

65 Kilian McDonnell, *The Other Hand of God: The Holy Spirit as the Universal Touch and Goal* (Collegeville, PA: Liturgical Press, 2003), 199–200.

66 *The New Encyclopedia Britannica*, vol. 4, 15th ed. (Chicago: University of Chicago Press, 1989), s.v. "ellipse," 459.

67 Lonergan, *Insight*, ed. Crowe and Doran, 31 [7]. See the whole discussion, *Insight*, 31–7 [7–13].

68 Crowe, "Son and Spirit: Tension in the Divine Missions?," in *Appropriating the Lonergan Idea*, 304.

69 Ibid.

70 Ibid.

71 Ibid.

72 Ibid.

73 Ibid.
74 For an excellent treatment of transposition see Matthew Lamb, "Lonergan's Transposition of Augustine and Aquinas: Exploratory Suggestions," in *The Importance of Insight: Essays in Honour of Michael Vertin*, ed. John J. Liptay Jr and David S. Liptay (Toronto: University of Toronto Press, 2007), 3–21.
75 Crowe, "Son and Spirit: Tension in the Divine Missions?," 305.
76 DS, 1331; "The Father, Son, and Holy Spirit are not three principles of creation, but one principle."
77 Crowe, "Son and Spirit: Tension in the Divine Missions?" in *Appropriating the Lonergan Idea*, 305.
78 Cf. Crowe, "Theological Background for an Ecumenical Program," in *Level of Our Time*, 252.
79 Lonergan, *Method in Theology*, ed. Doran and Dadosky, 70 [73]. Cf. Lonergan, "Time and Meaning," in *Philosophical and Theological Papers*, 101–2, 105.
80 Lonergan, *Method in Theology*, ed. Doran and Dadosky, 70 [73].
81 Ibid.
82 Crowe, "Son and Spirit: Tension in the Divine Missions?" in *Appropriating the Lonergan Idea*, 305.
83 Ibid.
84 Ibid. Cf. Lonergan, *Method in Theology*, ed. Doran and Dadosky, 76 [78].
85 Crowe, "'The Spirit and I' at Prayer," in *Developing the Lonergan Legacy*, 298.
86 Anscar Vonier, "The Coming of the Spirit," in *The Collected Works of Abbot Vonier*, vol. 2 (London: Burns Oates, 1952), 8.
87 Ibid. (emphasis mine).
88 Crowe, *The Doctrine of the Most Holy Trinity*, 24–5.
89 Vonier, "The Coming of the Spirit," 12.
90 Ibid.
91 Ibid., 13–14.
92 Paul VI, *Divinae consortium naturae*, in *Documents on the Liturgy, 1963–79: Conciliar, Papal, and Curial Texts* (Collegeville, MN: Liturgical Press, 1982), 767. For the original Latin, see *Acta Apostolicae Sedis* 63 (1971): 659.
93 See *Catechism of the Catholic Church*, 686, 731. Cf. Acts 2:33–6.
94 Crowe, "Son and Spirit: Tension in the Divine Missions?," in *Appropriating the Lonergan Idea*, 308.
95 Ibid.
96 Ibid., 305.
97 Ibid., 310.
98 Ibid.
99 Ibid., 311.
100 Ibid.
101 Ibid. (emphasis in the original).
102 Ibid.

103 Ibid.

104 Ibid.

105 Ibid.

106 Ibid.

107 Ibid.

108 Ibid., 312.

109 Ibid.

110 Ibid.

111 Ibid.

112 Ibid., 313.

113 Ibid. St Ignatius of Loyola (1491–1556) first published the *Spiritual Exercises* in 1548. For a contemporary commentary on St Ignatius's *Spiritual Exercises* see Michael Ivens, SJ, *Understanding the Spiritual Exercises: Text and Commentary; A Handbook for Retreat Directors* (Leominster, UK: Gracewing, 2008; first published 1998).

114 Crowe, "Son and Spirit: Tension in the Divine Missions?," in *Appropriating the Lonergan Idea*, 313.

115 Ibid.

116 Crowe, "The Church as Learner: Two Crises, One *Kairos*," in *Appropriating the Lonergan Idea*, 372.

117 Ibid.

118 Ibid., 374.

119 Crowe, "Son and Spirit: Tension in the Divine Missions?" in *Appropriating the Lonergan Idea*, 309n23.

120 Ibid., 325.

121 Ibid. (emphasis mine).

122 For a text that implies the distinction between what is first for us and first in itself, Crowe refers us to Aquinas's commentary on a passage from book 2 of Aristotle's *Metaphysics*. See Aquinas, *Expositio metaphysicorum Aristotelis* (Turin: Marietti, 1950), lect. 1, no. 278. He also cites Lonergan's article "Theology and Understanding," in *Collection*, ed. Crowe and Doran, 127–30.

123 Crowe, "Son of God, Holy Spirit, and World Religions," in *Appropriating the Lonergan Idea*, 333.

124 Ibid., 334.

125 Ibid.

126 Ibid.

127 Ibid. Cf. Thomas Aquinas, *Summa Theologiae*, I, q. 38, art. 2.

128 Crowe, "Son of God, Holy Spirit, and World Religions," in *Appropriating the Lonergan Idea*, 335. Crowe points us to these pages in Lonergan, *Method in Theology*, 81–5, 105–9, 273, 277–8.

129 Crowe, "Son of God, Holy Spirit, and World Religions," in *Appropriating the Lonergan Idea*, 335. Cf. Lonergan, *Method in Theology*, ed. Doran and Dadosky, 109 [112–13], 265 [282–3].

130 Crowe, "Son of God, Holy Spirit, and World Religions," in *Appropriating the Lonergan Idea*, 335.
131 Ibid., 331. Cf. Levering's brief discussion of Larry Hurtado's idea that the devotional practice of the early Church was "binitarian," in *Engaging the Doctrine of the Holy Spirit*, 3n6.
132 Crowe, "Son of God, Holy Spirit, and World Religions," in *Appropriating the Lonergan Idea*, 331. In using the word *behaviorists*, Crowe emphasizes the tendency to focus exclusively on external stimuli that can be measured and sensed. Cf. *Encyclopedia Britannica*, s.v. "behaviourism," https://www.britannica.com/topic/behaviourism-psychology, accessed 22 April 2017.
133 Crowe, "Son of God, Holy Spirit, and World Religions," in *Appropriating the Lonergan Idea*, 331.
134 Ibid.
135 Ibid., 339n26.
136 Ibid., 335.
137 For a rich discussion of the Holy Spirit's role in the liturgy and the sacraments see Jean Corbon, *The Wellspring of Worship*, trans. Matthew J. O'Connell (Eugene, OR: Wipf & Stock Publishers, 2001), 65–74. See also *Catechism of the Catholic Church*, 1091–112. Cf. St John of Damascus, *De fide orthodoxa*, *Patrologiae Cursus Completus*, Series Graeca 94, ed. Jacques-Paul Migne, 1145a (Paris, 1857–66) (hereafter cited as PG), vol. 94, col. 94, sec. 1145a.
138 See Webb, "The Pneumatology of Bernard Lonergan," 3–4. In the light of some of Crowe's remarks (cf. *Theology of the Christian Word*, 142), Webb stresses the need to think more about the way the Holy Spirit works within the humanity of the incarnate Son.
139 Crowe, *The Most Holy Trinity* (Toronto: Loyola Institute of Sacred Studies, 1973), 8. This booklet began in 1962 as notes for a course on the Trinity for members of various Catholic religious orders looking for further education.
140 In a couple of essays after 1984, Crowe takes up questions of how the Church learns before she teaches. See Crowe, "The Magisterium as Pupil: The Learning Teacher," in *Developing the Lonergan Legacy*, 283–92; and Crowe, "Law and Insight," in *Developing the Lonergan Legacy*, 267–82.

6 Intentionality Analysis

 1 Crowe, "Son of God, Holy Spirit, and World Religions," in *Appropriating the Lonergan Idea*, 333n13.
 2 Lonergan, "Doctrinal Pluralism," in vol. 17 of *CWL*, 85. Cf. Lonergan, *Method in Theology*, ed. Doran and Dadosky, 314–15 [340]. For a recent defence of Lonergan's use of intentionality analysis see Jeremy D. Wilkins, "What 'Will' Won't Do: Faculty Psychology, Intentionality Analysis, and the Metaphysics of Interiority," *Heythrop Journal* 57, no. 3 (2016): 473–91.

3 Cf. Lonergan, *Insight*, ed. Crowe and Doran, 28 [4]. This description corresponds to what Lonergan calls "the essential dynamism of human intelligence" (*Insight*, 57 [33]). He speaks of this intellectual eros as an operator of development: "on the intellectual level the operator is the concretely detached and disinterested desire to know" (*Insight*, 555 [532]).

4 Crowe, "Rethinking God-with-Us: Categories from Lonergan," in *Level of Our Time*, 350.

5 Crowe, *Theology of the Christian Word*, 49.

6 Cf. Lonergan, *Insight*, ed. Crowe and Doran, 300 [274–5].

7 Crowe, *The Doctrine of the Most Holy Trinity*, 145.

8 Ibid., 144–5.

9 Notice how Crowe in 1965 has integrated Aquinas's notion of two kinds of inner words (concept and judgment) with Lonergan's notion of levels of consciousness. I think that Crowe was right to connect Aquinas and Lonergan in this way. I also think that Crowe had good reasons for using the idea of a *procession within a level* for his analogy of an intelligible emanation of an inner word.

10 Lonergan's 1947–9 *Verbum* articles imply that the movements within the second and third levels are analogies for the Son's procession. I do not think that Crowe first came to this point in 1965, but he explicitly stated it in his 1965–6 notes, possibly in response to questions from his students.

11 In *Insight* there are at least two places where Lonergan seems to indicate that the "will" belongs to another level beyond "experience, understanding, and judgement." See *Insight*, ed. Crowe and Doran, 594, 653 [571, 630]. For a helpful discussion of these texts, see Jeremy W. Blackwood, *"And Hope Does Not Disappoint": Love, Grace, and Subjectivity in the Word of Bernard J.F. Lonergan, S.J.* (Milwaukee, WI: Marquette University Press, 2017), 32–4.

12 Crowe, "Complacency and Concern in the Thought of St Thomas," *Three Thomist Studies*, 88n33. For a similar figure see Crowe, *The Doctrine of the Most Holy Trinity*, 147.

13 Cf. Lonergan, "Question 4," in *The Triune God: Systematics*, 218ff. Lonergan claims that Aquinas never retracted what he taught in *Quaestiones disputatae de veritate*, q. 4, art. 2, ad 7. For a lengthy discussion of these issues in Aquinas, see Jeremy Wilkins's forthcoming article, "The Spiration of Love in God according to Aquinas and His Interpreters."

14 Lonergan, *Insight*, ed. Crowe and Doran, 619 [596].

15 Crowe, "Lonergan's New Notion of Value," in *Appropriating the Lonergan Idea*, 54.

16 Crowe, "Neither Jew Nor Greek, but One Human Nature and Operation in All," in *Appropriating the Lonergan Idea*, 37 (emphasis mine). For the four levels, as opposed to just three levels, Crowe appeals to Lonergan's 1964 article "Cognitional Structure," in *Collection*, 205–21.

17 Crowe, "Pull of the Future and Link with the Past," 49.

18 Ibid., 45. It must be kept in mind that the act of faith spoken about here is a judgment or assent made on the basis of love and is prior to an understanding of what is believed.

19 In the light of extensive documentation made by Jeremy Blackwood of Lonergan's references to a fifth level, it appears that Crowe was assimilating Lonergan's notion of a fourth level of consciousness when Lonergan was beginning to speak of a fifth level. Was Crowe aware that on 9 December 1972 Lonergan used the phrase *the fifth level*? (Lonergan, "The Functional Specialty 'Systematics,'" in *Philosophical and Theological Papers, 1965–1980*, 193). Crowe was aware that Lonergan had begun to speak about a fifth level in addition to the four levels of consciousness (Cf. Crowe, "Lonergan's New Notion of Value," in *Appropriating the Lonergan Idea*, 57). Crowe refers readers to the fact that Lonergan had spoken in a similar way in a May 1973 CBC radio interview that was broadcast on 24 October 1973 (Cf. Crowe, "Lonergan's New Notion of Value," 57n32). Crowe recognized the question of a fourth versus a fifth level; he also was alive to the vast implications of there being a fourth level and even a fifth level. But this particular issue of a fifth level of consciousness was not a focus of his writings. As we will see, Crowe treats the fourth level as both the level of moral responsibility and the level of God's love being poured into our hearts in religious experience. Crowe's own position on the fourth level of consciousness very much corresponds, it seems, with a remark made by Lonergan in the third question-and-answer session at the 1982 Boston College Lonergan Workshop on Wednesday, June 16. In answer to a question about the fifth level of consciousness, Lonergan said: "There are sensitive consciousness, intellectual consciousness, rational consciousness, moral consciousness, and religious consciousness. But if you have religious consciousness as well as moral, it takes over the moral; it's a perfection added to the moral, with a broader horizon. So we're back to four. However, it's a different four for different people. Religious consciousness has a fuller horizon than a purely moral consciousness, and the two are joined inasmuch as grace perfects nature, the supernatural perfects the natural" (https://www.bernardlonergan.com/pdf/9993ADTE080.pdf, accessed 10 March 2019). This passage (transcribed by Robert Doran) can also be found in Jeremy Blackwood, *And Hope Does Not Disappoint*, 140. According to Blackwood, this passage from Lonergan complicates but does not rule out the possibility that Lonergan held a distinct fifth level (*And Hope Does Not Disappoint*, 140). In terms of Crowe's own thought, however, this passage expresses the actual way in which Crowe discusses the fourth level of consciousness. He tends to treat religious love as a kind of expansion of the fourth level.

20 Crowe, "The Task of Interpreting Lonergan," in *Appropriating the Lonergan Idea*, 158.

21 Lonergan, "Natural Right and Historical Mindedness," in *A Third Collection*, ed. Doran and Dadosky, 174–5 [180–1], a lecture given at the fifty-first annual meeting of the American Catholic Philosophical Association, Detroit, 16 April 1977. In *The Lonergan Enterprise* Crowe provides a list of the other instances after 1974 in which Lonergan referred to these two paths (115n37).

22 Crowe, *Old Things and New*, 14.

23 Crowe, "An Expansion of Lonergan's Notion of Value," in *Appropriating the Lonergan Idea*, 347.

24 Crowe, *Old Things and New*, 96.

25 Ibid., 17.

26 Ibid., 96.

27 Crowe, "An Expansion of Lonergan's Notion of Value," in *Appropriating the Lonergan Idea*, 346.

28 Crowe, *Old Things and New*, 96.

29 Crowe, "An Expansion of Lonergan's Notion of Value," in *Appropriating the Lonergan Idea*, 346.

30 Ibid., 350.

31 Lonergan, *Method in Theology*, ed. Doran and Dadosky, 56 [57].

32 Crowe, "An Expansion of Lonergan's Notion of Value," in *Appropriating the Lonergan Idea*, 350n24. Cf. Lonergan, *Method in Theology*, ed. Doran and Dadosky, 56–7 [57–9].

33 Crowe, "An Expansion of Lonergan's Notion of Value," in *Appropriating the Lonergan Idea*, 350.

34 Ibid. For the line "Stern Daughter of the Voice of God" see the poem "Ode to Duty" by William Wordsworth.

35 Crowe, "An Expansion of Lonergan's Notion of Value," in *Appropriating the Lonergan Idea*, 350. Cf. Lonergan, *Verbum*, 29.

36 Jacques Dupuis, letter to Crowe, 10 November 1985, Crowe Archive, A-2-1-2.

37 Crowe, letter to Fr Francis Clooney, SJ, 9 December 1986, Crowe Archive, A-2-1-2. For Clooney's biography see the following interview: http:// groups.creighton.edu/sjdialogue/documents/articles/clooney_frontline .html. For a review of Clooney's accomplishments, see Gavin D'Costa's review of *St Francis De Sales and Sri Vedanta Desika on Loving Surrender to God*, by Francis X. Clooney," *Reviews in Religion & Theology* 17, no. 3 (July 2010): 297–9.

38 This article has five main sections. In the final section Crowe suggests three or four implications of his theology, including rethinking aspects of the liturgical year to bring more focus on the Holy Spirit. "I am sure," he

writes, "that many besides myself have felt like a sheer physical pain the cutting back of the liturgy of the Holy Spirit: where we once had at least an octave, we now have only one day" ("Rethinking God-with-Us," in *Level of Our Time*, 351).

39 In the next chapter I will argue that this question becomes thematized and the focus of Crowe's attention in his 1995 article "Rethinking the Trinity: Taking Seriously the *Homoousios*."

40 Crowe, "Rethinking God-with-Us," in *Level of Our Time*, 343.

41 Ibid.

42 Ibid.

43 Ibid.

44 Ibid., 341.

45 Ibid., 345.

46 Ibid. Crowe dedicated *Lonergan and the Level of Our Time* to the memory of his five siblings.

47 Crowe, "Rethinking God-with-Us," in *Level of Our Time*, 345.

48 Ibid.

49 Ibid.

50 Lonergan, *Method in Theology*, ed. Doran and Dadosky, 315 [341]. Cf. Crowe, "Rethinking God-with-Us," in *Level of Our Time*, 345.

51 This shift to the name of Mystery, rather than Father, corresponds with Crowe's growing desire in the third stage of his development to use inclusive language. In 1989 he wrote in the preface to *Appropriating the Lonergan Idea*: "Let me end with a word of thanks and one of apology: ... of apology to the female half of our race – it was only around 1984 that I abandoned the pretence that God and the whole human race were male, so only a few of these essays reflect the change that decision necessitated in my writing style" (xiv).

52 Crowe, "Rethinking God-with-Us," in *Level of Our Time*, 346–7.

53 Ibid., 347.

54 Ibid. Cf. Bernard Lonergan, "Christology Today: Methodical Reflections," in *A Third Collection*, ed. Robert M. Doran and John D. Dadosky, 92 [94].

55 Lonergan, "Christology Today," in *A Third Collection*, ed. Doran and Dadosky, 91 [93]. Cf. Crowe, "Rethinking God-with-Us," in *Level of Our Time*, 347. For Lonergan's account of judgments of value and their distinction from judgments of fact, see *Method in Theology*, ed. Doran and Dadosky, 37–41 [36–41], and "Christology Today," 91 [93]).

56 Lonergan, "Christology Today," in *A Third Collection*, ed. Doran and Dadosky, 92 [94].

57 Crowe, "Interpreting Lonergan," in *Appropriating the Lonergan Idea*, 158.

58 Crowe, "Rethinking God-with-Us," in *Level of Our Time*, 348.

59 Ibid.

60 Ibid.

61 This is not the first time that Crowe has put a judgment of value on the third level. See his *Doctrine of the Most Holy Trinity*, 160. See also Crowe, "An Expansion of Lonergan's Notion of Value," in *Appropriating the Lonergan Idea*, 350.

62 Crowe, "Rethinking God-with-Us," in *Level of Our Time*, 348.

63 Lonergan, "Christology Today: Methodical Reflections," in *A Third Collection*, ed. Doran and Dadosky, 91 [93].

64 Ibid.

65 Lonergan, *Method in Theology*, ed. Doran and Dadosky, 38 [37].

66 On the fourth level as the level of values see Lonergan, *Method in Theology*, ed. Doran and Dadosky, 117 [121], 230–2 [245–7].

67 Crowe, *The Doctrine of the Most Holy Trinity*, 144.

68 Crowe, "Rethinking God-with-Us," in *Level of Our Time*, 348.

69 In short, I find no evidence that Crowe is still thinking of the Father as a reflective act of understanding that speaks a word within the third level.

70 Crowe, "Rethinking God-with-Us," in *Level of Our Time*, 348.

71 Ibid.

72 Ibid.

73 Thomas Aquinas, *Summa Theologiae*, I, q. 43, art. 5, ad 2.

74 Crowe, "Eschaton and Worldly Mission," in *Appropriating the Lonergan Idea*, 223.

75 Ibid. (emphasis mine).

76 For a restating of this same position see Crowe, "Son and Spirit?" in *Appropriating the Lonergan Idea*, 306–7.

77 Crowe, "Eschaton and Worldly Mission," in *Appropriating the Lonergan Idea*, 223n44.

78 For example, Crowe added this note, when his June 1974 lecture "Lonergan's New Notion of Value" was reprinted in 1989: "At the time of this lecture, 1974, I did not know of Lonergan's two ways of development" (*Appropriating the Lonergan Idea*, 56n30).

79 Crowe, "Rethinking God-with-Us," in *Level of Our Time*, 348.

80 Ibid., 358.

81 Ibid., 349.

7 Hiding His Goal

1 Robert Doran's *Missions and Processions*, vol. 1 of *Trinity in History: A Theology of the Divine Missions* (Toronto: University of Toronto Press, 2012) can be seen as beginning to take up this challenge.

2 Conversation with Gilles Mongeau, SJ, after my thesis proposal examination, 1 October 2015.

3 Crowe Archive, A-3-4-1. Crowe had to reapply to the Toronto School of Theology for status to teach an advanced degree course. He was glad, in the end, that he did the course, but he told Gilles Mongeau, "That was a lot of work. I will not do that again." Conversation with Gilles Mongeau, SJ, during my thesis proposal examination, 1 October 2015. Another graduate student, Gerard Whelan, SJ, also sat in on the course.

4 Frederick Crowe, "Rethinking the Trinity: Taking Seriously the *Homoousios*," *Science et Esprit* 47, no. 1 (1995): 13–31. See also "Rethinking the Trinity: Taking Seriously the *Homoousios*," in *Lonergan and the Level of Our Time*, 394–415.

5 For the Council of Nicaea's doctrine of the Father and Son as consubstantial or *homoousioi*, see DS, 125. Crowe also commonly refers to Lonergan's explanation of *consubstantial* according to Athanasius: "that the same things are said of the Son as are said of the Father, with the exception of Fatherhood" ("Rethinking the Trinity," in *Level of Our Time*, 394). Cf. Lonergan, *The Triune God: Doctrines*, 175–7, 195–7. Lonergan refers us to Athanasius, *Oratio 3 contra Arianos*, 4 (PG 26: 329b).

6 Cf. George L. Prestige, *God in Patristic Thought* (London: SPCK, 1952), 213.

7 Thomas Aquinas says: "it is necessary for there to be an order according to origin but without priority (*Unde oportet ibi esse ordinem secundum originem, absque prioritate*)" (*Summa Theologiae*, I, q. 42, art. 3).

8 Crowe, "Rethinking the Trinity," in *Level of Our Time*, 414.

9 Ibid., 407. Lonergan defined relation as "ordo unius ad aliud (the order of one to another)" (*The Triune God: Systematics*, 246–7; cf. 687n1). A relation is real when it *"non tantum concipitur sed etiam vere est* (is not only conceived but also truly is)" (ibid., 246–7). Cf. Thomas Aquinas, *Summa Theologiae*, I, q. 28, art. 1.

10 Crowe, "Rethinking the Trinity," in *Level of Our Time*, 407.

11 Ibid., 411.

12 This essay was originally published in *Method: Journal of Lonergan Studies* 19, no. 2 (2001): 173–80. See also "'Stare at a Triangle …': How to Get an Insight and How Not To," in *Level of Our Time*, 126–32.

13 Crowe, "Stare at a Triangle …," 131.

14 See Lonergan's account of phantasms, insights, and teachers in his *Verbum: Word and Idea in Aquinas*, 42. Cf. Lonergan, *Insight*, ed. Crowe and Doran, 299.

15 Crowe, "Rethinking the Trinity," in *Level of Our Time*, 396.

16 Ibid., 398.

17 Ibid., 414.

18 Ibid.

19 Ibid., 405.

20 Ibid., 411.

21 Ibid., 406, 406n22.
22 Ibid., 406. In referring to our return to the Father, Crowe clearly, therefore, does not think that emphasizing the equality of all three persons rules out relations of origin in the Trinity. The Son of God is God, for example, precisely as receiving the divine nature from the Father. By the gift of the Holy Spirit we return to the Father by sharing in the Son's unique relationship with the Father.
23 Basil of Caesarea, *De Spiritu Sancto*, PG 32: 153b. Crowe's translation comes from *The Later Christian Fathers: A Selection from the Writings of the Fathers from St Cyril of Jerusalem to St Leo the Great*, ed. and trans. Henry Bettenson (London: Oxford University Press, 1970), 84.
24 Basil of Caesarea, *The Later Christian Fathers*, 84. Cf. Basil of Caesarea, *De Spiritu Sancto*, PG 32: 153c. See Crowe, "Rethinking the Trinity," in *Level of Our Time*, 406n24.
25 Crowe, "Rethinking the Trinity," in *Level of Our Time*, 406.
26 Ibid., 396.
27 Ibid., 406.
28 Ibid.
29 In the September 1994 issue of the *Lonergan Studies Newsletter* (15, no. 3) Crowe wrote: "Fr Francois Bourassa died Christmas day in Montreal. A pupil of Lonergan at the College of the Immaculate Conception in the 1940s, and later his colleague for a year at the Gregorian University in the 1960s, he was especially devoted to the theology of the Trinity, and wrote extensively on that topic. René Latourelle has an article in the current issue of *Science et Esprit* (46:1: 5–11), "François Bourassa, S.J.: Un grand théologien." Of special interest is a paragraph on how Père Bourassa succeeded Lonergan in teaching the Trinity at the Gregorian University, and won the at first reluctant respect of students who had been greatly attached to Lonergan." Cf. http://www.lonerganresearch.org/site/assets/files/1184/lsn_set_3_-_90-94.pdf. The *Lonergan Studies Newsletter* was started in 1980 as a quarterly publication. Crowe took over as editor of the eight-to-ten-page publication in 1988 (cf. *Lonergan Studies Newsletter* 15, no. 28).
30 Crowe, "Rethinking the Trinity," in *Level of Our Time*, 406n25.
31 Crowe, *The Doctrine of the Most Holy Trinity*, 124.
32 See Aquinas's way of explaining the term in *Summa Theologiae*, I, q. 37, art. 2, ad 1; and II-II, q. 1, art. 8, ad 3.
33 Crowe, "Rethinking the Trinity," in *Level of Our Time*, 406n25.
34 Ibid., 407.
35 Ibid., 406n25.
36 Ibid., 407.
37 Ibid.

38 Crowe, *The Doctrine of the Most Holy Trinity*, 97.

39 Ibid.

40 Cf. Ibid., 165.

41 "Ordo unius ad aliud"; ibid., 99.

42 Sometimes Crowe speaks of the Father as a relation, the Son as a relation, and the Holy Spirit as a relation (cf. *The Doctrine of the Most Holy Trinity*, 152). At other times, however, he seems to be thinking of the relation as something between them. He seems to be imagining the relation, for example, as the road between Athens and Thebes (cf. *The Doctrine of the Most Holy Trinity*, 154). The same road can be taken in two directions. We can see an example of his thinking of the relation as between the persons on page 107 in the same text.

43 Crowe, "Rethinking the Trinity," in *Level of Our Time*, 407.

44 In his *Doctrine of the Most Holy Trinity* Crowe does not discuss, as far as I can tell, the Spirit's role in the human life of the Son. One wonders how his theology of the missions would have changed if he had reflected more on the working of the Holy Spirit in the humanity of Christ.

45 Crowe, "Rethinking the Trinity," in *Level of Our Time*, 407.

46 Ibid., 409.

47 Crowe, *The Doctrine of the Most Holy Trinity*, 118.

48 Crowe, "Rethinking the Trinity," in *Level of Our Time*, 395.

49 Ibid., 410.

50 Ibid.

51 Ibid.

52 Ibid., 409.

53 Ibid., 410.

54 Lonergan, "Philosophy of God, and Theology, Lecture 3," in *Philosophical and Theological Papers, 1965–1980*, 218.

55 Lonergan, "Philosophy of God, and Theology, Lecture 1," in *Philosophical and Theological Papers, 1965–1980*, 178.

56 Lonergan, "Philosophy of God, and Theology, Lecture 3," in *Philosophical and Theological Papers, 1965–1980*, 204.

57 Crowe, "Rethinking the Trinity," in *Level of Our Time*, 410.

58 Ibid.

59 Ibid.

60 Ibid.

61 Cf. Aquinas's words in the beginning of *Summa Theologiae*, I, q. 3: "Sed quia de Deo scire non possumus quid sit, sed quid non sit, non possumus considerare de Deo quomodo sit, sed potius quomodo non sit." (Since we are not able to know what God is, but what he is not, we are not able to consider how God is, but rather how he is not.)

62 Crowe, "Rethinking the Trinity," in *Level of Our Time*, 410.

63 Ibid. It might seem that Crowe is saying that the Word and the Father (Mystery) have their origin in the Spirit, but this is not true. He says that the Word is the "expression" (407) of the Father, the "One uttering the Word" (410); the Word's origin is from another.

64 Crowe, "Rethinking the Trinity," in *Level of Our Time*, 410.

65 Ibid.

66 Ibid.

67 Ibid.

68 Ibid., 411.

69 Cf. Lonergan, "Natural Right and Historical Mindedness," in *A Third Collection*, ed. Doran and Dadosky, 174–5 [180–1].

70 The levels are related to one another through operators, and those operators are questions. What do the operators correspond to in God? I do not really think there can be an answer to these questions.

71 Crowe, general editors' preface to *The Triune God: Systematics*, by Lonergan, xx.

72 Crowe, "Rethinking the Trinity," in *Level of Our Time*, 403.

73 Crowe, general editors' preface to *The Triune God: Systematics*, by Lonergan, xx.

74 Ibid.

75 Crowe, "Rethinking the Trinity," in *Level of Our Time*, 403.

76 Ibid.

77 Ibid.

78 Ibid., 404.

79 Ibid.

80 Ibid., 403.

81 Ibid., 411.

82 After he wrote *The Doctrine of the Most Holy Trinity*, Crowe made hardly any references to the addition of the Filioque to the Nicene-Constantinopolitan Creed. In those notes, however, he made a vigorous defence of the doctrine of the Spirit's procession from the Father and the Son (or through the Son). Cf. Crowe, *The Doctrine of the Most Holy Trinity*, 106–13.

83 Crowe, "Rethinking the Trinity," in *Level of Our Time*, 410.

84 "If in the Trinitarian order the Holy Spirit is consecutive to the relation between the Father and the Son, since he takes his origin from the Father as Father of the only Son, it is in the Spirit that this relationship between the Father and the Son itself attains its Trinitarian perfection. Just as the Father is characterized as Father by the Son he generates, so does the Spirit, by taking his origin from the Father, characterize the Father in the manner of the Trinity in relation to the Son and characterizes the Son in the manner of the Trinity in his relation to the Father: in the fullness of the Trinitarian mystery they are Father and Son in the Holy Spirit."

Pontifical Council for Promoting Christian Unity, "The Greek and Latin Traditions Regarding the Procession of the Holy Spirit," *L'Osservatore Romano* (weekly edition in English), 20 September 1995, 3. For a longer discussion of this statement see Levering, *Engaging the Doctrine of the Holy Spirit*, 22n53, 117–20, 165–6.

85 Pontifical Council for Promoting Christian Unity, "The Greek and Latin Traditions," 3.

86 Michael Vertin to Crowe, 22 December 1994, Crowe Archive, A-2-2-1. The letter was in response to Vertin's having received a copy of Crowe's article "Rethinking the Trinity."

87 Crowe, general editors' preface to *The Triune God: Systematics*, by Lonergan, xx.

8 Conclusion

1 In his 1943 article, "Finality, Love, and Marriage," Lonergan refers to *complacentia* as the first of the four aspects of love (see Lonergan, "Finality, Love, and Marriage," in Collection, vol. 4 of *CWL* [Toronto: University of Toronto Press, 1988], 23). In 1955 Lonergan also mentions complacency in his Trinity course ("Appendix 2B: From the Image to the Eternal Exemplar," in *The Triune God: Systematics*, 674–5).

2 Crowe, *The Doctrine of the Most Holy Trinity*, 123, 127–31. The area, therefore, in which one must engage Crowe's pneumatology is in the adequacy of his theory of love. Professor Michael Vertin, for example, stressed in the classes that I took with him (2012–14) how people's theories of knowing influence their philosophy and theology. The editors of a volume of essays in Vertin's honour called this epistemological issue "the focus of Vertin's teaching and scholarly career, the central theme and preoccupation that he has called attention to in all his publications; for Vertin is convinced that at the heart of empirical disputes over a broad range of disciplines and issues is the philosophical problem of articulating an adequate theory of knowledge." John J. Liptay Jr and David S. Liptay, eds, *The Importance of Insight: Essays in Honour of Michael Vertin* (Toronto: University of Toronto Press, 2007), x. This kind of cognitional analysis is certainly relevant in engaging Crowe's thought in terms of pneumatology, but, possibly more importantly, one must evaluate Crowe's theory of love.

3 Charles Hefling, private correspondence with author, 27 October 2018.

4 Neil Ormerod, private correspondence with author, 28 October 2018.

5 Ibid.

6 See Mark Sheridan, ed., *Ancient Christian Commentary on Scripture: Old Testament II; Genesis 12–50* (Downers Grove, IL: InterVarsity Press, 2002), 60–8.

7 Cf. Sherwin, *By Knowledge and by Love*, 78n67.

8 Crowe, *Three Thomist Studies*, 134. See figure 3, "Diagram for Under-standing the Act of Complacent Love," in chapter 2 and my subsequent discussion.

9 David Burrell, CSC, "Indwelling: Presence and Dialogue," *Theological Studies* 22, no. 1 (1961): 4n5.

10 Philip McShane, "The Hypothesis of Intelligible Emanations in God," *Theological Studies* 23, no. 4 (1962): 548n5.

11 Fred Lawrence, ed., *The Structure and Rhythms of Love: In Honor of Frederick E. Crowe, SJ*, vol. 13 of *Lonergan Workshop*. (Boston: Boston College, 1997), iii.

12 Ibid.

13 Robert Doran, SJ, "'Complacency and Concern' and a Basic Thesis on Grace," in Lawrence, *The Structure and Rhythms of Love*, 57. For Jeremy Blackwood's helpful discussion of the distinctiveness of Doran's notion of *complacentia boni*, see *And Hope Does Not Disappoint*, 193–6, 222.

14 Vertin, "The Two Modes of Human Love," 31–45.

15 Ibid., 43.

16 Crowe, "Complacency and Concern in the Risen Life," in Fred Lawrence, ed., *The Structure and Rhythms of Love*, 17–32, esp. 29–30.

17 Crowe, *Three Thomist Studies*, 77, 179. Cf. De Caussade, *Self-Abandonment to Divine Providence*. Jean Pierre de Caussade, SJ (1675–1751) "lived as an obscure Jesuit. Little more is known of him than the dates of main events of his life." Mark Gibbard, "Jean Pierre de Caussade," in Jones, Wain-wright, and Yarnold, SJ, *The Study of Spirituality*, 416.

18 Crowe, *Three Thomist Studies*, 85n28.

19 Cf. de Sales, *Treatise on the Love of God*, book 6, chap. 1, 231.

20 Crowe, "Complacency and Concern," in *Three Thomist Studies*, 85n28.

21 Ibid.

22 Elizabeth Stopp, "François de Sales," in Jones, Wainwright, and Yarnold SJ, *The Study of Spirituality*, 381.

23 Cf. Clooney, *Beyond Compare*, 15–16, 216n38. For an overview of St Francis de Sales's anthropology see Alexander T. Pocetto, OSFS, "An Introduc-tion to Salesian Anthropology," *Salesian Studies* 6, no. 3 (July 1969): 36–62. For the complete French works of St Francis de Sales see *Oeuvres de Saint François de Sales: Évêque de Genève et Docteur de l'Église*, 27 vols. (Annecy, France: Imprimerie J. Niérat, 1892–1964). Volume 3 of the complete works is the *Introduction to the Devout Life*. The *Treatise on the Love of God* is found in volumes 4 and 5 and is available online in French and English: http://www.franz-von-sales.de/icss_en/index.html.

24 De Sales uses the word *complaisance* or *complaysance* over 180 times in his *Treatise*. For some of the crucial references see *Treatise on the Love of God*, book 1, chaps. 4, 7, 16; book 2, chaps. 13–15; book 5, chaps 1–5, 9–10; book 6, chap. 1; book 8, introduction; book 9, chap. 6; book 12, chap. 1.

25 Cheslyn, Wainwright, and Yarnold, SJ, *The Study of Spirituality*, 417. As
   an Oratorian, I have a personal interest in Francis de Sales, who established an Oratory of St Philip Neri in Thonon in the 1590s, before he was
   named a bishop. Neri, the founder in Rome of the Oratorians, wrote
   hardly anything and has been nicknamed the "Roman Socrates." Louis
   Bouyer de L'Oratoire, *The Roman Socrates: A Portrait of St Philip Neri*, trans.
   Michael Day, Cong. Orat. (Westminster, MD: Newman Press, 1958), 13.
   According to Jerome Bertram, "we find in the writings of St. Francis de
   Sales the spiritual and moral teaching that St. Philip himself never wrote
   down." Bertram, *Philip Neri: The Light of Holy Joy* (London: Catholic Truth
   Society, 2002), 21.
26 Marcel Viller, SJ, *Dictionnaire de Spiritualité*, vol. 1 (Paris: Gabriel Beauchesne, 1937), s.v. "abandon," 25a. Cf. Clooney's connection of his term *loving surrender* with St Francis's *abandon* in *Beyond Compare*, 218n47.
27 Doran, *Missions and Processions*, xi. According to Doran, if there is a
   universal mission of the Spirit to all peoples, there may be data in other
   religions that need to be incorporated into a new systematic theology. It
   seems that Crowe never went this far.
28 Robert M. Doran, SJ, *Trinitarian Elements in a Theology of Religion: A Tribute
   to Frederick E. Crowe*, vol. 42 of *Essays in Systematic Theology: An E-Book*
   (2011), 2. See https://www.lonerganresource.com/book.php?1, accessed
   27 October 2018.
29 Robert M. Doran, SJ, *"The Trinity in History: First Steps Beyond Volume 1,"*
   vol. 52 of *Essays in Systematic Theology* (2014), 4. See https://www
   .lonerganresource.com/book.php?1, accessed 27 October 2018.
30 Ibid., 5. Cf. Crowe, "Son of God, Holy Spirit, and World Religions," in
   Appropriating the Lonergan Idea, 325.
31 Doran, "Trinitarian Elements," 23.
32 Crowe, *Theology of the Christian Word*, 112.
33 Ibid., 144.
34 How one explains these claims and relates them to the eternal processions is another question, a question that Crowe did not fully answer.
35 Jean-Marc Laporte, SJ, *God One and Triune: Retrievals and Explorations*
   (Halifax, NS: Jesuits of Halifax, 2014), 166n.7. Laporte was Crowe's
   student and then succeeded him as professor for the Trinity course at
   Regis College, Toronto. In the preface to *God One and Triune* he explains
   the influence of Crowe's 1965–6 course notes on his own teaching:
   "I began teaching using materials already at hand, especially the text of
   my esteemed teacher Frederick Crowe, whose mimeographed *Doctrine of
   the Most Holy Trinity* gave me an excellent foundation and acquainted me
   with the perspective of Bernard Lonergan" (iii).
36 Ibid.

37 D. Juvenal Merriell, *To the Image of the Trinity: A Study in the Development of Aquinas' Teaching* (Toronto: Pontifical Institute of Medieval Studies, 1990), 18–35. For a list of others who have considered the centrality of the Holy Spirit in Augustine's work, see Merriell, *To the Image of the Trinity*, 19–20n19. Merriell, for example, writes, "It is better to see books 5 to 7 as a stage in the movement of the *De Trinitate,* a stage in which Augustine begins to shift his attention from the first problem of the equality of the three Persons to the second problem about the procession of the Holy Spirit" (22).

38 After speaking of the problem of how the Three work inseparably, but only one of the divine persons is said to do certain things, Augustine writes: "Another puzzle is in what manner the Holy Spirit is in the three, being begotten neither by the Father nor Son nor both of them, while being the Spirit of the Father and the Son" (*The Trinity*, ed. Hill, 70; PL 42: 824).

39 Crowe, "Rethinking the Trinity," in *Level of Our Time*, 408.

40 Crowe was not alone in trying to think about how the Father and the Son were eternally characterized by the Holy Spirit or even "depended" on the Holy Spirit. We saw in chapter 7 that a similar question arose at the end of "The Greek and Latin Traditions Regarding the Procession of the Holy Spirit," the 1995 clarification by the Pontifical Council for Promoting Christian Unity. Cf. Neil Ormerod, *The Trinity: Retrieving the Western Tradition* (Marquette, WI: Marquette University Press, 2005), 26–7. Ormerod gives a brief review of four other Catholic theologians who had written on the same issue: David Coffey, Thomas Weinandy, Leonardo Boff, and Gavin D'Costa.

41 Lonergan, *Verbum*, 215–16.

42 See Lonergan, "Theology and Understanding," in *Collection*, 133. Cf. Lonergan, *Verbum*, 219.

43 Lonergan, *Verbum*, 218. Cf. Thomas Aquinas, *Summa Theologiae*, I, q. 32, art. 1, ad 2. But in "Assertion 1" of *The Triune God: Systematics* Lonergan argues "that there does not seem to be another analogy for forming a systematic conception of a divine procession" (144ff).

44 Crowe, *The Doctrine of the Most Holy Trinity*, 142 (emphasis in the original).

45 Cf. Pocetto, "An Introduction to Salesian Anthropology," 36.

46 Cf. Neil Ormerod, *The Trinity: Retrieving the Western Tradition*, 18–20, 84–7, 96. For Hans Urs von Balthasar's preference for analogies other than the psychological analogy, see Anne Hunt, *Trinity* (Maryknoll, NY: Orbis Books, 2005), 48–51, 216–17, and "The Trinity through Paschal Eyes," 472–89. For a concise response to Hunt and von Balthasar, see Levering, *Engaging the Doctrine of the Holy Spirit*, 6–9, especially 7n19.

47 Karl Rahner, *The Trinity* (New York: Crossroad, 1997), 118. For a detailed discussion of Rahner's critique and of problems with the English

translation of Rahner's *The Trinity*, see Wilkins, *Before Truth*, 298–314. See also Wilkins, "Method, Order, and Analogy in Trinitarian Theology: Karl Rahner's Critique of the 'Psychological' Approach," *The Thomist* 74 no. 3 (2010): 563–92.

48 Ibid., 117.

49 The three divine persons are looking down upon a large stone sculpture of the earth. Cf. Ignatius of Loyola, *The Spiritual Exercises of St Ignatius*, trans. Louis J. Puhl, SJ, preface by Avery Dulles, SJ (New York: Vintage Books, 2000), 41–3.

50 Louis Ponnelle and Louis Bordet, *St Philip Neri and the Roman Society of His Times (1515–1595)*, trans. Ralph Francis Kerr (London: Sheed & Ward, 1932), 99–103. St Philip sent the first Italians to the Society of Jesus.

51 One of St Philip's greatest disciples, the Church historian Cesare Baronius, was one of the closest friends of St Robert Bellarmine, SJ, and was intimately connected with the work of the Jesuits. James Broderick, SJ, *Robert Bellarmine: Saint and Scholar* (Westminster, MD: Newman Press, 1961), 177–80, 417.

52 Cf. *Nova Vulgata* (Rome: Libreria Editrice Vaticana, 1986), 1950.

53 On praying to the Holy Spirit, see *Catechism of the Catholic Church*, 2670–2.

54 Crowe, *The Doctrine of the Most Holy Trinity*, 172 (emphasis in the original).

55 Gilles Emery, OP, *The Trinity: An Introduction to Catholic Doctrine on the Triune God*, trans. Matthew Levering (Washington, DC: Catholic University of America Press, 2011), 139.

56 Brian Daley, SJ, "Revisiting the 'Filioque': Part One, Roots and Branches of an Old Debate," *Pro Ecclesia* 10, no. 1 (2001): 62.

57 "Veni Creator Spiritus," in *Liturgia Horarum*, Pentecost, Vespers I. Cf. *The Adoremus Hymnal* (San Francisco, CA: Ignatius Press, 1997), 441, 443.

Bibliography

PRIMARY SOURCES

Frederick E. Crowe's Writings

Crowe Archive. Lonergan Research Institute, Toronto.
Crowe, Frederick E., SJ. *Appropriating the Lonergan Idea*. Edited by Michael
  Vertin. Toronto: University of Toronto Press, 2006.
– *Christ and History: The Christology of Bernard Lonergan from 1935 to 1982*.
  Toronto: University of Toronto Press, 2015. First published 2005.
– "Complacency and Concern." *Cross and Crown* 11 (1959): 180–90.
– "Complacency and Concern in the Thought of St Thomas." *Theological
  Studies* 20 (1959): 1–39, 198–230, 343–95.
– *Developing the Lonergan Legacy: Historical, Theoretical, and Existential Themes*.
  Edited by Michael Vertin. Toronto: University of Toronto Press, 2004.
– "Development of Doctrine: Aid or Barrier to Christian Unity." *Catholic
  Theological Society of America Proceedings* 21 (1966): 1–20.
– *De Verbo Dei cum hominibus communicato*. Toronto: Regis College, 1963.
– *The Doctrine of the Most Holy Trinity*. Willowdale, ON: Regis College, 1970.
  First published 1965.
– "Doctrines and Historicity in the Context of Lonergan's *Method in Theology*:
  A Review Article." *Theological Studies* 38 (1977): 115–44.
– "Early Jottings on Bernard Lonergan's *Method in Theology*." *Science et Esprit*
  25 (1973): 121–38.
– *Escatologia e missione terrena in Gesù di Nazareth*. Catania, Sicily: Edizioni
  Paoline, 1976.
– "Eschaton and Worldly Mission in the Mind and Heart of Jesus." In *Eschaton:
  A Community of Love*, edited by Joseph Papin, 105–44. Vol. 5 of *Theology
  Institute Villanova*. Villanova, PA: Villanova University Press, c. 1971.

– "For Inserting a New Question (26A) into the *Pars Prima.*" *The Thomist* 64 (2000): 565–80.

– *Lonergan.* London: Geoffrey Chapman; Collegeville, MN: Liturgical Press, 1992.

– *Lonergan and the Level of Our Time.* Edited by Michael Vertin. Toronto: University of Toronto Press, 2010.

– "The Lonergan Center." *Jesuit Bulletin,* 1975.

– *The Lonergan Enterprise.* Cambridge, MA: Cowley Press, 1980.

– *The Most Holy Trinity.* Toronto: Loyola Institute of Sacred Studies, 1973.

– *Old Things and New: A Strategy for Education.* Supplementary Issue of the *Lonergan Workshop,* vol. 5. Atlanta, GA: Scholars Press, 1985.

– "On the Method of Theology." *Theological Studies* 23, no. 4 (1962): 637–42.

– "The Origin and Scope of Bernard Lonergan's *Insight.*" *Sciences ecclésiastiques* 9 (1957): 203–95.

– "Pull of the Future and Link with the Past: On the Need for Theological Method." *Continuum* 7 (1969): 30–49.

– "Rethinking the Trinity: Taking Seriously the *Homoousios.*" *Science et Esprit* 47, no. 1 (1995): 13–31.

– Review of *Bible et tradition chez Newman: Aux origins de la théorie du développement,* by Jean Stern. *Theological Studies* 29, no. 4 (1968): 777–9.

– "Son and Spirit in the Church." In *Grace and Friendship: Theological Essays in Honor of Fred Lawrence from His Grateful Students,* edited by M. Shawn Copeland and Jeremy D. Wilkins, 17–22. Milwaukee, WI: Marquette University Press, 2016.

– *Son of God, Holy Spirit, and World Religions: The Contribution of Bernard Lonergan to the Wider Ecumenism.* Toronto: Regis College Press, 1985.

–, ed. *Spirit as Inquiry: Studies in Honor of Bernard Lonergan, S.J.* Chicago: Continuum, 1964.

– "St Thomas and the Isomorphism of Human Knowing and Its Proper Object." *Sciences ecclésiastiques* 13 (1961): 167–90.

– *Theology of the Christian Word: A Study in History.* New York: Paulist Press, 1978.

– *Three Thomist Studies.* Edited by Michael Vertin. Supplementary issue of *Lonergan Workshop,* vol. 16, edited by Fred Lawrence. Boston: Boston College, 2000.

– *A Time of Change: Guidelines for the Perplexed Catholic.* Milwaukee, WI: Bruce Publishing, 1968.

– "Universal Norms and the Concrete *Operabile* in St Thomas Aquinas." *Sciences ecclésiastiques* (1955): 115–49, 257–91.

Crowe, Frederick, SJ, Sara Butler, MSBT, Anne Carr, BVM, Margaret Farley, RSM, and Edward Kilmartin, SJ. *A Report on the Status of Women in Church and Society: Considered in Light of the Question of Women's Ordination.* New York: Catholic Theological Society of America, 1978.

Bernard Lonergan's Writings

Lonergan, Bernard J.F. *Collection*. Edited by Frederick E. Crowe, SJ, and Robert
   M. Doran. Vol. 4 of *Collected Works of Bernard Lonergan*. Toronto: University
   of Toronto Press, 1988.
– *De Deo Trino: Pars analytica*. Rome: Pontificia Universitas Gregoriana, 1961.
– *Divinarum Personarum conceptionem analogicam evolvit Bernardus Lonergan, S.I.*
   Rome: Gregorian University Press, 1957.
– *Early Latin Theology*. Translated by Michael G. Shields, edited by Robert
   M. Doran and H. Daniel Monsour. Vol. 19 of *Collected Works of Bernard
   Lonergan*. Toronto: University of Toronto Press, 2011.
– "The Future of Christianity." *Holy Cross Quarterly* 2, no. 2 (1969): 5–10.
– *Grace and Freedom*. Edited by J. Patout Burns, SJ, with an introduction by
   Frederick E. Crowe, SJ. London: Darton, Longman, & Todd, 1971.
– *Grace and Freedom: Operative Grace in the Thought of St Thomas Aquinas*. Edited
   by Frederick E. Crowe and Robert M. Doran. Vol. 1 of *Collected Works of
   Bernard Lonergan*. Toronto: University of Toronto Press, 2000.
– *Insight: A Study of Human Understanding*. New York: Philosophical Library,
   1970.
– *Insight: A Study of Human Understanding*. Edited by Frederick E. Crowe and
   Robert M. Doran. Vol. 3 of *Collected Works of Bernard Lonergan*. Toronto:
   University of Toronto Press, 1992.
– *Method in Theology*. Toronto: University of Toronto Press, 1990. First
   published 1972.
– *Method in Theology*. Edited by Robert M. Doran and John D. Dadosky. Vol. 14
   of *Collected Works of Bernard Lonergan*. Toronto: University of Toronto Press,
   2017.
– *Philosophical and Theological Papers, 1965–1980*. Edited by Robert C. Croken
   and Robert M. Doran. Vol. 17 of *Collected Works of Bernard Lonergan*. Toronto:
   University of Toronto Press, 2004.
– *Philosophy of God and Theology*. Philadelphia, PA: Westminster Press, 1974.
– "Religious Commitment." In *The Pilgrim People: A Vision of Hope*, edited by
   Joseph Papin, 45–69. Vol. 4 of *Theology Institute Villanova*. Villanova, PA:
   Villanova University Press, 1970.
– *A Second Collection*. Edited by William F.J. Ryan and Bernard J. Tyrrell.
   Philadelphia, PA: Westminster Press, 1974.
– *A Second Collection*. Edited by Robert M. Doran and John D. Dadosky. Vol. 13 of
   Collected Works of Bernard Lonergan. Toronto: University of Toronto Press, 2016.
– *Shorter Papers*. Edited by Robert C. Croken, Robert M. Doran, and H. Daniel
   Monsour. Vol. 20 of *Collected Works of Bernard Lonergan*. Toronto: University
   of Toronto Press, 2007.
– "St Thomas' Thought on *Gratia Operans*." *Theological Studies* 2 (1941): 289–324;
   3 (1942): 69–88, 375–402, 533–78.

– "Theology and Man's Future." *Cross Currents* 19 (1969): 452–61.
– *A Third Collection.* Edited by Frederick E. Crowe. New York: Paulist Press, 1985.
– *A Third Collection.* Edited by Robert M. Doran and John D. Dadosky. Vol. 16 of *Collected Works of Bernard Lonergan.* Toronto: University of Toronto Press, 2017.
– *The Triune God: Doctrines.* Translated from *De Deo Trino: Pars dogmatica* (1964) by Michael G. Shields, edited by Robert M. Doran and H. Daniel Monsour. Vol. 11 of *Collected Works of Bernard Lonergan.* Toronto: Published for Lonergan Research Institute of Regis College, Toronto, by University of Toronto Press, 2009.
– *The Triune God: Systematics.* Translated from *De Deo Trino: Pars systematica* (1964) by Michael G. Shields, edited by Robert M. Doran and H. Daniel Monsour. Vol. 12 of *Collected Works of Bernard Lonergan.* Toronto: Published for Lonergan Research Institute of Regis College, Toronto, by University of Toronto Press, 2007.
– *Verbum: Word and Idea in Aquinas.* Edited by David Burrell. Notre Dame, IN: University of Notre Dame Press, 1967.
– *Verbum: Word and Idea in Aquinas.* Edited by Frederick E. Crowe and Robert Doran. Vol. 2 of *Collected Works of Bernard Lonergan.* Toronto: University of Toronto Press, 1997.

SECONDARY SOURCES

Agnelli, Francesco Antonio. *The Excellences of the Congregation of the Oratory of St Philip Neri.* Translated from the Italian and abridged by Frederick Ignatius Antrobus of the Congregation of London. Oxford: Oxford Oratory, 2012.
Augustine. *De Trinitate.* In *Patrologiae Cursus Completus*, Series Latina 42, edited by J.P. Migne et al., 820–1097. Paris, 1886.
– *The Trinity.* Translated by Edmund Hill. Hyde Park, NY: New City Press, 2012.
Ayres, Lewis. *Augustine and the Trinity.* Cambridge: Cambridge University Press, 2012.
Bacci, Pietro Giacomo. *The Life of St Philip Neri, Apostle of Rome.* Vol. 2. London: Thomas Richardson & Sons, 1847.
Basil the Great. *Against Eunomius.* Translated by Mark Del Cogliano and Andrew Radde-Gallwitz. Washington, DC: Catholic University of America Press, 2011.
– *De Spiritu Sancto.* In *Patrologiae Cursus Completus*, Series Graeca 32, edited by J.P. Migne et al., 67–218. Paris, 1886.
– "Epistola 236." In *Patrologiae Cursus Completus. Series Graeca* 32. Edited by J.P. Migne et al., 875–86. Paris, 1886.
– *On the Holy Spirit.* Translated by Stephen Hildebrand. Crestwood, NY: St Vladimir's Seminary Press, 2011.

Bettenson, Henry, ed. and trans. *The Later Christian Fathers: A Selection from the Writings of the Fathers from St Cyril of Jerusalem to St Leo the Great*. London: Oxford University Press, 1970.

Bertram, Jerome. *Philip Neri: The Light of Holy Joy*. London: Catholic Truth Society, 2002.

Billot, Ludovicus. *De Deo Uno et Trino*. Rome: Gregorian University Press, 1910.

Blackwood, Jeremy W. *"And Hope Does Not Disappoint": Love, Grace, and Subjectivity in the Word of Bernard J.F. Lonergan, S.J.* Milwaukee, WI: Marquette University Press, 2017.

Blanche, F.A. Review of *Autour de la solution thomiste du problème de l'amour*, by H.D. Simonin. *Bulletin Thomiste* 3 (1930–3): 523–8.

Bouyer de L'Oratoire, Louis. *The Roman Socrates: A Portrait of St Philip Neri*. Translated by Michael Day, Cong. Orat. Westminster, MD: Newman Press, 1958.

Broderick, James, SJ. *Robert Bellarmine: Saint and Scholar*. Westminster, MD: Newman Press, 1961.

Browning, Robert. "Weiss's Doctrine of Concern." *Review of Metaphysics* 9 (1955–6): 334.

Burrell, David, CSC. "Indwelling: Presence and Dialogue." *Theological Studies* 22, no. 1 (1961): 1–17.

Calvin, John. *Institutes of the Christian Religion*. Translated by Henry Beveridge. Vol. 1. Grand Rapids, MI: Eerdmanns, 1975.

Catechism of the Catholic Church. Vatican City: Libreria Editrice Vaticana, 1994.

Cates, Diana Fritz. *Aquinas on the Emotions: A Religious-Ethical Inquiry*. Washington, DC: Georgetown University Press, 2009.

– *Choosing to Feel: Virtue, Friendship, and Compassion for Friends*. Notre Dame, IN: University of Notre Dame Press, 1997.

Chambat, Lucien, OSB. *Presence et union: Les missions des personnes de la Trinité selon Saint Thomas Aquinas*. Abbaye Saint-Wandrille, France: Fontenelle, 1945.

Clooney, Francis X, SJ. *Beyond Compare: St Francis de Sales and Sri Vedanta Desika on Loving Surrender to God*. Washington, DC: Georgetown University Press, 2005.

Coffey, David. *Deus Trinitas: The Doctrine of the Triune God*. Oxford: Oxford University Press, 1999.

Congar, Yves. *I Believe in the Holy Spirit*. Translated by David Smith. New York: Crossroad, 2013.

Connolly, John R., and Brian W. Hughes, ed. *Newman and Life in the Spirit*. Minneapolis, MN: Fortress Publishers, 2014.

Copeland, M. Shawn, and Jeremy D. Wilkins, ed. *Grace and Friendship: Theological Essays in Honor of Fred Lawrence from His Grateful Students*. Milwaukee, WI: Marquette University Press, 2016.

Corbon, Jean. *The Wellspring of Worship*. Translated by Matthew J. O'Connell. Eugene, OR: Wipf & Stock Publishers, 2001.

Cunningham, Francis, OP. *The Indwelling of the Trinity: A Historical Study of the Theory of St Thomas Aquinas*. Dubuque, IA: Priory Press, 1955.

Daley, Brian, SJ. "Revisiting the 'Filioque': Part One, Roots and Branches of an Old Debate." *Pro Ecclesia* 10, no. 1 (2001): 31–62.

D'Costa, Gavin. Review of *St Francis De Sales and Sri Vedanta Desika on Loving Surrender to God*, by Francis X. Clooney. *Reviews in Religion & Theology* 17, no. 3 (July 2010): 297–9.

De Caussade, Jean-Pierre. *Self-Abandonment to Divine Providence*. Translated by Algar Thorold. London: Burns & Oates, 1933; Rockford, IL: TAN Books, 1987.

De la Taille, Maurice. *The Hypostatic Union and Created Actuation by Uncreated Act*. West Baden Springs, IN: West Baden College, 1952.

Denzinger, Heinrich Joseph Dominicus, ed. *Enchiridion symbolorum*. Barcelona: Herder, 1976.

De Sales, Francis. *Treatise on the Love of God*. Translated by Henry Benedict Mackey, OSB. Rockford, IL: Tan Books, 1997.

De Sales, François. *Oeuvres de Saint François de Sales: Évêque de Genève et Docteur de l'Église*. 27 vols. Annecy, France: Imprimerie J. Niérat, 1892–1964.

Dictionary of Jesuit Biography: Ministry to English Canada, 1842–1987. Toronto: Canadian Institute of Jesuit Studies, 1991.

Doorley, Mark J. "Resting Reality: Reflections on Crowe's 'Complacency and Concern.'" *Lonergan Workshop* 13 (1997): 33–56.

Doran, Robert M., SJ. "Addressing Lonergan's Four-Point Hypothesis." *Theological Studies* 68 (2007): 674–82.

– "'Complacency and Concern' and a Basic Thesis on Grace." *Lonergan Workshop* 13 (1997): 57–78.

– *Missions and Processions*. Vol 1 of *The Trinity in History: A Theology of the Divine Missions*. Toronto: University of Toronto Press, 2012.

– *Trinitarian Elements in a Theology of Religion: A Tribute to Frederick E. Crowe*. Vol. 42 of *Essays in Systematic Theology: An E-Book*. Marquette, 2010–16. https://www.lonerganresource.com/book.php?1

– "*The Trinity in History*: First Steps beyond Volume 1." Vol. 52 of *Essays in Systematic Theology: An E-Book*. Marquette, 2010–16.

Dunne, Thomas A., and Jean-Marc Laporte, eds. *Trinification of the World*. Toronto: Regis College Press, 1978.

Emery, Gilles, OP. *Trinitarian Theology of Saint Thomas Aquinas*. Translated by Francesca Aran Murphy. Oxford: Oxford University Press, 2011.

– *The Trinity: An Introduction to Catholic Doctrine on the Triune God*. Translated by Matthew Levering. Washington, DC: Catholic University of America Press, 2011.

Fletcher, Christine. *The Artist and the Trinity: Dorothy Sayers' Theology of Work.* Eugene, OR: Pickwick, 2013.

Ford, John C., SJ, and Germain Grisez. "Contraception and the Infallibility of the Ordinary Magisterium." *Theological Studies* 39 (1978): 258–312.

Gallonio, Antonio. *The Life of St Philip Neri.* Translated from the Latin by Jerome Bertram of the Oratory. San Francisco: Ignatius Press, 2005.

– *La Vita di San Filippo Neri.* Rome: Presidenza del Consiglio dei Ministri, 1995. First published 1601.

Gilley, Sheridan. *Newman and His Age.* London: Darton, Longman, & Todd, 1990.

Gioia, Luigi. *The Theological Epistemology of Augustine's "De Trinitate."* Oxford: Oxford University Press, 2008.

Hebblethwaite, Brian L. *The Problems of Theology.* Cambridge: Cambridge University Press, 1980.

Hendry, G.S. *The Holy Spirit in Christian Theology.* Philadelphia: Westminster Press, 1965.

Hildebrand, Stephen M. *The Trinitarian Theology of Basil of Caesarea: A Synthesis of Greek Thought and Biblical Truth.* Washington, DC: Catholic University of America Press, 2007.

Hunt, Anne. *Trinity.* Maryknoll, NY: Orbis Books, 2005.

– "The Trinity through Paschal Eyes." In *Rethinking Trinitarian Theology: Disputed Questions and Contemporary Issues in Trinitarian Theology,* edited by Robert J. Wozniak and Giulio Maspero, 472–89. London: T&T Clark, 2012.

Ignatius of Loyola. *The Spiritual Exercises of St Ignatius.* Translated by Louis J. Puhl, SJ, with preface by Avery Dulles, SJ. New York: Vintage Books, 2000.

Ivens, Michael, SJ. *Understanding the Spiritual Exercises: Text and Commentary; A Handbook for Retreat Directors.* Leominster, UK: Gracewing, 2008. First published 1998.

Jeffries, Cecil. *Early Schools of Kings County, New Brunswick.* Published by Kings County Retired Teachers' Association. Sussex, NB: Royal Printing, 1985.

John of Damascus. *De fide orthodoxa.* In *Patrologiae Cursus Completus,* Series Graeca 94, edited by J.P. Migne, 789–1227. Paris, 1864.

John of St Thomas. *Cursus theologicus.* Vol. 4 of Solesmes edition. Paris: Desclés, 1953.

Jones, Cheslyn, Geoffrey Wainwright, and Edward Yarnold, SJ, eds. *The Study of Spirituality.* New York: Oxford University Press, 1986.

Kärkkäinen, Veli-Matti. *The Holy Spirit: A Guide to Christian Theology.* Louisville, KY: Westminster John Knox Press, 2012.

–, ed. *Holy Spirit and Salvation: Sources of Christian Theology.* Louisville, KY: Westminster John Knox Press, 2010.

Lamb, Matthew L. "Fr. Giovanni Sala, S.J., Philosopher and Theologian." *Nova et Vetera* (English edition) 15, no. 1 (2017): 75–88.

– "Lonergan's Transposition of Augustine and Aquinas: Exploratory Suggestions." In *The Importance of Insight: Essays in Honour of Michael Vertin*, edited by John J. Liptay Jr and David S. Liptay, 3–21. Toronto: University of Toronto Press, 2007.

Laporte, Jean-Marc, SJ. *God One and Triune: Retrievals and Explorations*. Halifax, NS: Jesuits of Halifax, 2014.

Lawrence, Fred, ed. *The Structure and Rhythms of Love: In Honor of Frederick E. Crowe, SJ*. Vol. 13 of *Lonergan Workshop*. Boston: Boston College, 1997.

Leo XIII, Pope. *Aeterni Patris*. Encyclical Letter on the Restoration of Christian Philosophy. Boston, MA: St Paul Books and Media, 1985.

Levering, Matthew. *Engaging the Doctrine of the Holy Spirit: Love and Gift in the Trinity and the Church*. Grand Rapids, MI: Baker Academic, 2016.

– *Scripture and Metaphysics: Aquinas and the Renewal of Trinitarian Theology*. Malden, MA: Blackwell, 2004.

Liptay, John L., Jr, and David S. Liptay, eds. *The Importance of Insight: Essays in Honour of Michael Vertin*. Toronto: University of Toronto Press, 2007.

Livy. *History of Rome*. Translated by B.O. Foster. 14 vols. Loeb Classical Library. Cambridge, MA: Harvard University Press, 1919–59.

Loyer, Kenneth M. *God's Love through the Spirit: The Holy Spirit in Thomas Aquinas and John Wesley*. Washington, DC: Catholic University of America Press, 2014.

Marshall, Bruce D. "The Deep Things of God: Trinitarian Pneumatology." In *The Oxford Handbook of the Trinity*, edited by Gilles Emery, OP, and Matthew Levering, 400–12. Oxford: Oxford University Press, 2011.

Mathews, William A. *Lonergan's Quest: A Study of Desire in the Authoring of "Insight."* Toronto: University of Toronto Press, 2005.

Mauriac, François. *The Frontenac Mystery*. Translated by Gerard Hopkins. London: Eyre and Spottiswoode, 1971.

McDonnell, Kilian, OSB. *The Other Hand of God: The Holy Spirit as the Universal Touch and Goal*. Collegeville, PA: Liturgical Press, 2003.

– "A Trinitarian Theology of the Holy Spirit?" *Theological Studies* 46, no. 2 (June 1985): 191–227.

McDonough, William. "Etty Hillesum's Learning to Live and Preparing to Die: *Complacentia boni* as the Beginning of Acquired and Infused Virtue." *Journal of the Society of Christian Ethics* 25, no. 2, (2005): 183–7.

McShane, Philip, SJ. "The Hypothesis of Intelligible Emanations in God." *Theological Studies* 23, no. 4 (1962): 545–68.

Merriell, D. Juvenal. *To the Image of the Trinity: A Study in the Development of Aquinas' Teaching*. Toronto: Pontifical Institute of Medieval Studies, 1990.

Morelli, Eric James. "Insight and the Subject." *International Philosophical Quarterly* 51, no. 2 (2011): 137–48.

Neri, Philip. *The Maxims and Counsels of St Philip Neri: Arranged for Each Day of the Year*. Toronto: Toronto Oratory, 2011.

Newman, John Henry. *An Essay in Aid of a Grammar of Assent*. Notre Dame, IN: University of Notre Dame Press, 2008.

– *Idea of a University*. Oxford: Oxford University Press, 1976.

– *Letters and Diaries of John Henry Newman*. Vol. 25. Edited at the Birmingham Oratory with notes and an introduction by Charles Stephen Dessain of the same Oratory and Thomas Gornall, SJ. Oxford: Clarendon Press, 1973.

– "Fragment of a Life of St Philip." In *Newman the Oratorian*. Edited by Placid Murray, OSB. Leominster, UK: Fowler Wright Books, 1980.

– *Parochial and Plain Sermons*. Vol. 2, sermon 19. London: Longmans, Green, 1902.

– *Prayers, Verses, and Devotions*. San Francisco: Ignatius Press, 2000.

Nova Vulgata. Rome: Libreria Editrice Vaticana, 1986.

Nygren, Anders. *Agape and Eros*. Translated by P.S. Watson. London: SPCK, 1953.

Ormerod, Neil. *The Trinity: Retrieving the Western Tradition*. Milwaukee, WI: Marquette University Press, 2005.

Pambrun, James R. "Revelation and Interiority: The Contribution of Frederick Crowe, S.J." *Theological Studies* 67, no. 2 (2006): 320–44.

Paul VI. *Divinae consortium naturae. Acta Apostolicae Sedis* 63 (1971): 657–64.

– *Divinae consortium naturae*. In *Documents on the Liturgy, 1963–79: Conciliar, Papal, and Curial Texts*. Collegeville, MN: Liturgical Press, 1982.

– "Humanae vitae." *Acta Apostolicae Sedis* 60 (1968): 481–503.

– *On Human Life: Humanae Vitae*. Translated by Marc A. Calegari, SJ. San Francisco: Ignatius Press, 2014.

Penido, M. "Gloses sur la procession d'amour dans la Trinité. " *Ephemerides Theologicae Lovanienses* 14 (1937): 33–68.

Petri, Thomas, OP. *Aquinas and the Theology of the Body: The Thomistic Foundations of John Paul II's Anthropology*. Washington, DC: Catholic University America Press, 2016.

Pocetto, Alexander T., OSFS. "An Introduction to Salesian Anthropology." *Salesian Studies* 6, no. 3 (July 1969): 36–62.

Ponnelle, Louis, and Louis Bordet. *St Philip Neri and the Roman Society of His Times (1515–1595)*. Translated by Ralph Francis Kerr. London: Sheed & Ward, 1932.

Pontifical Council for Promoting Christian Unity. "The Greek and Latin Traditions Regarding the Procession of the Holy Spirit." *L'Osservatore Romano* (weekly edition in English), 20 September 1995.

Prestige, George L. *God in Patristic Thought*. London: SPCK, 1952.

Quay, Paul, SJ. "Contraception and Conjugal Love." *Theological Studies* 22, no. 1 (1961): 18–40.

Rahner, Karl. *The Trinity*. New York: Crossroad, 1997.

240   Bibliography

Rahner, Karl, and Herbert Vorgrimler. "Salvific Will of God." In *Dictionary of Theology*. New York: Crossroad, 1981.

Robinson, Jonathan. *In No Strange Land: The Embodied Mysticism of St Philip Neri*. Kettering, OH: Angelico Press, 2015.

Rousselot, Pierre. *The Problem of Love in the Middle Ages: A Historical Contribution*. Marquette Studies in Philosophy 24. Milwaukee, WI: Marquette University Press, 2002.

Roy, Louis, OP. *Engaging the Thought of Bernard Lonergan*. Montreal and Kingston: McGill-Queen's University Press, 2016.

Rumscheidt, H. Martin, ed. *Footnotes to a Theology: The Karl Barth Colloquium of 1972*. Waterloo, ON: Corporation for the Publication of Academic Studies in Religion in Canada, SR/CSR Office, Wilfred Laurier University, 1974.

Sacred Congregation for the Doctrine of the Faith. *Declaration on the Question of the Admission of Women to the Ministerial Priesthood*. Vatican City: Vatican Polyglot Press, 1976.

Scotus, John Duns. *God and Creatures: The Quodlibetal Questions*. Edited and translated by Felix Alluntis and Allan B. Wolter. Princeton, NJ: Princeton University Press, 1975.

– *Opera omnia*. Edited by Luke Wadding. Vol. 12. Lyon: Durand, 1639.

Sheridan, Mark, ed. *Ancient Christian Commentary on Scripture: Old Testament II; Genesis 12–50*. Downers Grove, IL: InterVarsity Press, 2002.

Sherwin, Michael S., OP. *By Knowledge and by Love: Charity and Knowledge in the Moral Theology of St Thomas Aquinas*. Washington, DC: Catholic University of America Press, 2005.

Simonin, Henri-Dominique. "Autour de la solution thomiste du problème de l'amour." *Archives d'histoire doctrinale et littéraire du moyen-âge* 6 (1931): 174–276.

S.M.C. *Brother Petroc's Return*. Boston: Little, Brown, 1937.

Swan, Michael. "Jesuits, 1611–2011: 400 Years of Giving." *The Catholic Register*, 15 September 2011.

Thomas Aquinas, Saint. *Expositio in librum beati Dionysii De divinis nominibus*. Rome: Marietti, 1950.

– *Expositio metaphysicorum Aristotelis*. Turin: Marietti, 1950.

– *Quaestiones disputatae de veritate*. Turin: Marietti, 1964.

– *Summa contra gentiles*. Turin: Marietti, 1961.

– *Summa Theologiae*. Turin: Edizioni San Paulo, 1988.

Vertin, Michael. "*The Two Modes of Human Love*: Thomas Aquinas Interpreted by Frederick Crowe." *Irish Theological Quarterly* 69 (2004): 31–45.

Viller, Marcel, SJ, ed. *Dictionnaire de Spiritualité*. Vol. 1. Paris: Gabriel Beauchesne, 1937.

Vonier, Anscar, OSB. "The Coming of the Spirit." In *The Collected Works of Abbot Vonier*, vol. 2. London: Burns Oates, 1952.

Walshe, Sebastian, OP. "*Beata Trinitas*: The Beatitude of God as Prelude to the Trinitarian Processions." *The Thomist* 76 (2012): 189–209.

Webb, Eugene. "The Pneumatology of Bernard Lonergan: A Byzantine Comparison." *Religious Studies and Theology* 5, no. 2 (May 1985): 13–23.

Weiss, Paul. *Nature and Man*. New York: Holt, 1947.

Wilhelmsen, Frederick D. "The Priority of Judgment over Question: Reflections on Transcendental Thomism." *International Philosophical Quarterly* 14, no. 4 (1974): 475–93.

Wilkins, Jeremy D. *Before Truth: Lonergan, Aquinas, and the Problem of Wisdom*. Washington, DC: Catholic University of America, 2018.

– "Grace and Growth: Aquinas, Lonergan, and the Problematic of Habitual Grace." *Theological Studies* 72, no. 4 (2011): 723–49.

– "Grace in the Third Stage of Meaning apropos Lonergan's 'Four-Point Hypothesis.'" *Lonergan Workshop* 22 (2010): 443–67.

– "Method, Order, and Analogy in Trinitarian Theology: Karl Rahner's Critique of the 'Psychological' Approach." *The Thomist* 74 no. 3 (2010): 563–92.

– "Trinitarian Missions and the Order of Grace According to Thomas Aquinas." In *Philosophy and Theology in the Long Middle Ages: Essays in Honor of Professor Stephen Brown*, ed. K. Emery, R. Friedman, and A. Speer, 689–708. Leiden: E.J. Brill, 2011.

– "What 'Will' Won't Do: Faculty Psychology, Intentionality Analysis, and the Metaphysics of Interiority." *Heythrop Journal* 57, no. 3 (2016): 473–91.

– "Why Two Divine Missions? Development in Augustine, Aquinas, and Lonergan." *Irish Theological Quarterly* 77, no. 1 (2012): 1–30.

Williams, Rowan. *On Augustine*. London: Bloomsbury, 2016.

Index

132, 138, 153–6, 162, 170, 172,
174; at Pentecost, 66, 72–3,
102–3, 119, 120, 124, 169, 203n32;
presence of, 67–72, 73–5, 84,
119–20, 122; as proceeding Love,
4, 49–53, 59–60, 61–4, 74–5, 81,
118–19, 154; sanctifying grace
as gift of, 67–8, 80–3, 87, 89–90,
125, 202–3n30. *See also* Father,
God the; Filioque; inner word;
Jesus Christ; missions, divine;
processions; relations, divine;
Trinitarian order
homoousios, 147–8, 149, 221n5
human autonomy, 107–8
Humanae vitae (Paul VI), 6, 105, 106,
210n1, 210n5, 212n46
Hunt, Anne, 9, 10, 229n46

Ignatius of Loyola, St, 123, 173–4,
203n35
imperialism, theological, 107–10
impression of love, 49–50
incarnate meaning, 117–20
The Incarnate Word (Lonergan), 13
inclinatio, as term, 46–7, 52, 195–6n74
inner word: as analogous to Son's
processions, 11, 23–4, 28, 30,
50–1, 53, 86, 133–4, 157–8, 172,
198n28, 204n56, 216n9; as gift
of God's love, 88–90, 93, 96–7,
118, 169, 207n112. *See also* Holy
Spirit; Jesus Christ
Insight (Lonergan), 20, 23, 29–37, 91,
132–5, 137, 163, 216n11
institution vs charismatic
dimensions of the Church, 58,
105, 123, 126, 210n3
intellect: role in bringing forth
complacentia, 24, 44, 46, 47; as
distinct faculty from will, 48,
134, 187n75, 194n39. *See also*

consciousness; intentionality
analysis
intelligible emanation, 23–5, 27–8, 61,
132–4, 158–9, 172, 198n28, 216n9
intentio, as term, 43, 49
intentionality analysis, as term, 91–2,
165, 215n2; distinct from using
faculty psychology, 131, 134,
145. *See also* consciousness
intersubjective love, 132, 137–8, 145,
153–6, 162, 165, 170, 172, 174
invisible mission, 82–3, 93–4, 116,
197–8n15
isomorphism, 32

Jane Frances de Chantal, St, 193n26
Jesuits. *See* Society of Jesus
Jesus Christ: and Christocentric
focus, 114, 121–2, 126; and
contemporary Scripture
scholarship, 92–3, 112–13, 120;
declares God's love, 87, 98, 101,
124, 143, 154; filiation/sonship,
61–2, 68–9, 72; historicity
of, 112–13, 120, 122; and the
Holy Spirit's mission, xii, 5,
72–5, 80–104, 110, 119, 121–2,
123–7, 140, 148–150, 152, 161,
169; human need for, 72–6;
incarnate meaning of, 117–18,
120; incarnation, 12, 54, 66–7,
70–4, 83, 93, 105, 118–19, 168–9;
mediates the Father to us, xii,
82, 95; paschal mystery of, 9–10,
21, 74, 103, 123, 169; possessing
beatific vision on earth, 84;
presence of, 67–72, 73–5;
primary to us, 21, 169; as Son
eternally, 7–14, 23, 59–65, 68–72,
131–2, 149, 152–9, 172–4; as
spirating the Holy Spirit, 7, 36,
51–3, 59–62, 118, 142–5, 172, 174;

Schopenhauer, Arthur, 192n13

sciences, 3–4, 22–3, 30–1, 64, 107, 112–13, 126, 211n45, 212n46

Scotus, John Duns, 63, 65, 199n45

Second Vatican Council, 14, 75–6, 100, 106, 108, 127

self-abandonment, 45–6, 166–7

self-knowledge, 29–30, 32

Sherwin, Michael, 41, 47, 48, 191n3, 196n78

Simonin, Henri-Dominique, 46–7

simplicity, divine, 58–9

Society of Jesus: connection to St Philip Neri, 172, 229n50; Crowe's entrance and studies, 17–18, 182n18; Crowe's later life in, 21, 184n47, 187n82

Son. *See* Jesus Christ

"Son of God, Holy Spirit, and World Religions" (Crowe), 124–6, 139, 168

spiration: active and passive, 7, 61–3, 68–9, 202–3n30; of complacency, 47, 53; in psychological analogy, 61–4

Spirit. *See* Holy Spirit; processions

"St Thomas and the Isomorphism of Knowing and Its Proper Object" (Crowe), 32

"St Thomas' Thought on *Gratia Operans*" (Lonergan), 19

Stanley, David, 92, 205n83, 206n95

structure of consciousness. *See* consciousness

Summa Theologiae (Aquinas), 7, 9, 25–7, 44–5, 49–52, 64, 155, 191n12

teaching vs learning Church, 106, 108, 123–4

tendency, love as, 42, 43, 44–7, 50, 52, 196n78

Tertullian, 11, 12, 64

theological imperialism, 107–10

theology, methodical, 33–6, 89–90

Theology of the Christian Word: A Study in History (Crowe), 4–5, 13, 95–7, 184n48

Theophilus of Antioch, 11

Three Thomist Studies (Crowe), 13. *See also* "Complacency and Concern in the Thought of St Thomas"

Tillich, Paul, 192n13

A Time of Change: Guidelines for the Perplexed Catholic (Crowe), 13, 105, 177n10

Tracy, David, 22, 165

Treatise on the Love of God (St Francis de Sales), 45, 166–7

Trinification, xii, 56, 66–7, 72–6, 95, 114, 173, 177n5

Trinitarian order: evaluating Crowe's approach to, 8, 169–73; intersubjective love in, 132, 137–8, 145, 153–6; and ordering of human consciousness, 29–32, 34–6, 86, 132–8, 146, 156–8, 216n3, 217n19; and psychological analogy, 86, 139–46, 157–8, 160–1; reasons for rethinking, 8, 148–53. *See also* relations, divine

Trinity: and creation, 51, 53; as *homoousios*, 147–8, 149, 221n5; human need for, 72–6; 140; presence of, 67–72, 73–5, 141–2; psychological analogy as method for understanding, 7–12, 58–61. *See also* Father, God the; God; Holy Spirit; Jesus Christ; missions, divine; processions; relations, divine